D0327337

THE
SINGING
DETECTIVE

THE
SINGING
DETECTIVE

DENNIS POTTER

VINTAGE BOOKS
A Division of Random House
NEW YORK

The Singing Detective was first broadcast on BBC Television in November and December 1986.

The cast was as follows:

P. E. MARLOW	Michael Gambon
PHILIP (Aged 9)	Lyndon Davies
NICOLA	Janet Suzman
MARK BINNEY/FINNEY/RAYMOND	Patrick Malahide
NURSE MILLS	Joanne Whalley
DR GIBBON	Bill Paterson
MRS MARLOW	Alison Steadman
MR HALL	David Ryall
NURSE WHITE	Imelda Staunton
REGINALD	Gerard Horan
1ST MYSTERIOUS MAN	Ron Cook
2ND MYSTERIOUS MAN	George Rossi
HOSPITAL PORTER	Geff Francis
NIGHT NURSE	Sharon D. Clarke
SISTER MALONE	Mary McLeod
SONIA	Kate McKenzie
AMANDA	Charon Bourke
DR FINLAY	Simon Chandler
ALI	Badi Uzzaman
MR TOMKEY/NODDY	Leslie French
GEORGE ADAMS	Charles Simon
SCHOOLTEACHER/SCARECROW	Janet Henfrey
GRANCHER	Richard Butler
GRAN	Maggie Holland
CLOTH CAP/BARMAN	Trevor Cooper
SOLDIER	Niven Boyd
GRANDAD BAXTER	Wally Thomas
AUNT EMILY	Jo Cameron Brown
UNCLE JOHN	Ken Stott
MARY	Angela Curran
DRUMMER	John Sheraton
GIRL EVANGELIST/NURSE GODFREY	Heather Tobias
BUSKER	Nigel Pegram

POLICEMAN	Malcolm Storey
CONSULTANT	Richard Pescud
REGISTRAR	Thomas Wheatley
HOUSEMAN	Paul Lacoux
VISITING DOCTOR	John Matshikiza
MRS ADAMS	Joan White
MORTUARY ATTENDANT 1	Errol Shaker
MORTUARY ATTENDANT 2	Astley Harvey
HOSTESS 1	Emma Myant
HOSTESS 2	Susie Ann Watkins
PHYSIOTHERAPIST	Tricia George
MARK (Aged 9)	William Speakman
RITA	Claire Phelps
BRIAN	Neil Pittaway
HAROLD	Martin Camm
GEORGE	Darren Williams
BARBARA	Samantha Bryant
2ND SOLDIER	David Thewlis
Costume designer	Hazel Pethig
Make-up designer	Frances Hannon
Designer	Jim Clay
Photography	Ken Westbury
Executive producers	Kenith Trodd
	Rick McCallum
Producer	John Harris
Director	Jon Amiel

1

A misty, moody, highly atmospheric 'thrillerish', winter's evening in London, 1945. Cold and forlorn, near a lamp-post which dimly shows wisps of mist, a pathetic old busker is playing an achingly melancholy 'Peg o' My Heart' on a mouth-organ. This seems odd: there is no one about. The music takes us along the empty street.

A railed flight of stone steps twists down from the pavement to a wide basement. A neon sign above the door says SKINSCAPE'S. A hard-faced doorman is just coming out to stand in front of the door, at the bottom of the steps. He is buttoning his uniform, putting on his cap, strangely out of breath. He notices the back of his hand as he does this. It has a nasty smear of something on it. He pulls out a handkerchief, and rubs at it. A voice explains, side-of-the-mouth style.

MARLOW: (*Voice over*) The doorman of a nightclub can always pretend that it's lipstick and not blood on his hands. But how'd it get there? Let's be economical. Nothing fancy. If he smacked some dame across her shiny mouth, then he's got both answers in one.

The sad busker continues playing, alone, and seemingly for no one. Then suddenly into view comes a well-dressed man in a good overcoat, Mark Binney. He stops. His eyes narrow. He is looking a length of darkish and misty paving stones at the busker, with an alert caution. The busker soon picks up on Binney. His face amazingly transforms. His eyes swivel, and his expression instantly switches from near-cretinous vacancy to sharp intelligence. Without once stopping playing, he inserts into 'Peg o' My Heart' distinctly recognizable bars from 'Deutschland über Alles'. Binney nods, passes, and as though it were an afterthought drops a coin into the busker's otherwise empty hat. The busker now stops playing in order to dive at the hat, like a starving man seizing a crust, calling out – in an idiot croak –

BUSKER: Gawdblessya Guv Gawdblessya – Cockles of me – Guv! Warm the – Gawdblessya real gentch'are!

Binney takes no notice, going on towards the basement steps, as
the busker scrambles away in the opposite direction in a curious,
lurching, chuckling, frog-like hop, the coin clutched in his
fingerless mitten. Close on the busker as, at the turn of the
street, he stops, looks about, looks at the coin, and we see that it
is wrapped in silver paper, a message inside.

(*Whisper*) Thank you, sir. Jolly well done, old sport.

A slightly odd perspective as Binney's head seems level with the
pavement, and then, bob-bob, disappears from view as he
continues on down the steps into Skinscape's club.

The neon glow of SKINSCAPE'S, above pavement level, and
with a recalcitrant flicker on the 'c', gradually fills the screen,
as –

MARLOW: (*Voice over*) And so the man went down the hole, like
Alice. But there were no bunny rabbits down there. It
wasn't that sort of hole. It was a rat-hole.

An empty bed in a daytime hospital ward, the present day.
Rumpled, the sheets pulled back, the pillows askew, a pyjama
jacket tangled. At first sight, like the small arena of previous and
energetic sexual activity. 'I've Got You Under My Skin' swells
from SKINSCAPE'S neon to the bed, in sugary syncopation. The
chart at the foot of the head of the bed reveals the absent patient
to be one, Mr P. E. Marlow.

(*Voice over*) Into the rat-hole. Down, down, down. And the
one thing you don't do when you find yourself in one of
those is to underestimate the rats in residence –

There is a mix of cardiac and skin patients in an old ward in a
big London hospital. It is teatime, and busy. Bread and butter,
a blob of jam, and a cake for each patient, are dispensed from a
rodently squeaking trolley. There is no break in Marlow's voice
over –

(*Voice over*) – No, sir. The way those creatures nibble and
gnaw at your soft underbelly can do a lot of damage to your
nerves.

The patients at the top end of the ward are, indeed, nibbling
and gnawing in ways that have some affinity with the words.
The tea trolley is under the command of starchily formidable
Staff Nurse White, who now deals with a patient – a very old

man, Mr Tomkey, too ill or too weak to take or to want his tea. But Nurse White tries to make him hold his cup, in a bullying hearty manner.

STAFF NURSE WHITE: Your tea, Mr Tomkey! Teatime! Come along now, Mr Tomkey! Tea! No more nodding off now!

Which is not nice, because Tomkey, from now on called Noddy, has a perpetual, pronounced, near ga-ga (apparently) nod-nod-nod of his old head.

You can't expect to sleep at night if you do so in the middle of the afternoon, can you? Mmm? Mr Tomkey! Come along!

At the other end of the big ward, on the far side of the opened double doors, a seemingly irascible (but essentially ingratiating) small shopkeeper, Mr Hall, cardiac patient, glares across at the distant tea trolley.

MR HALL: Will you kindly take a look at that trolley! Just look at it, Reginald. Stopped again. It's worse than a number 11 bus. And what has it stopped for? Why has it stopped? So that ga-ga old bugger up there can spill his tea down his pyjamas! The tea, Reginald, will be cold, my boy. Won't it? *Won't it?*

He looks fiercely at the young man in the next bed down, who is reading a dog-eared, folded-over, obviously cheap paperback with such slow concentration that his lips are discernibly forming the words. This is Reginald, who does not look up.

REGINALD: What's that, Mr 'All?

MR HALL: (*Snarl*) The tea!

REGINALD: It'll be cold.

Coming along the drab, long corridor into the main ward is the absent patient, Philip Marlow, being wheeled back to his bed by a very tall black porter, who has an illicit Sony Walkman at his ears, and a face and a lithe body movement that shows the (silent) music. Marlow is glowering morosely, crumpled into himself, and his face badly disfigured with a ragingly acute psoriasis, which looks as though boiling oil has been thrown over him. He is wearing a fully sleeved white X-ray smock. Very close, so that we know or hear his thoughts – and recognize the voice.

MARLOW: (*Voice over*) No, sir. The way those creatures gnaw

3

and nibble can do a lot of damage to your nerves full stop
new paragraph But there's one thing you've got to admit
full stop A rat always knows where its tail is . . .
Thoughts which take us back to Skinscape's, and 1945 –

Binney, now appearing to be a nervous and hesitant
businessman not certain that he is going to have a good time, or
even that he should, approaches the bar through a discreetly
underlit, almost crypt-like series of arches, low at the ceiling.
Clearly, once the enormous cellars of what was a considerable
house.
   His feet sound on the floor, oddly echo-like. The barman,
cleaning glasses with a cloth, stops his arm movements as he sees
Binney half-hesitantly approaching. No one else can be seen,
which makes it a little creepy, and although the barman quickly
masks it, his first expression is one of hatred.
   (*Voice over*) A rat always knows where its tail is. But when
Mark Binney went down into Skinscape's he might just as
well never have learned the difference between *his* tail and
his elbow.

Back to reality, and the hospital, as Marlow, in his wheelchair,
'composes' the story.
BARMAN: (*Voice over*) G'evening, sir. What is your poison?
   What'll it be, sir? *Ouch–h–!*
Marlow, jolted by a bump on the chair as it trundles along the
corridor, winces with pain.
MARLOW: (*To himself, hiss*) Concentrate. Concentrate.
BARMAN: (*Voice over*) G'evening, sir. What is your poison – ?

The bar at Skinscape's reasserts its occupation of the screen.
   What'll it be, sir?
Binney looks from side to side, along empty stools, and empty
spaces which fade off into arches of near darkness.
BINNEY: Well. Company for a start.
BARMAN: It's early yet, sir. But you're the first and you'll get
   the pick, won't you?
BINNEY: But of what?
BARMAN: The apples on the bough, sir. What you drink, sir?

BINNEY: Scotch and soda.
BARMAN: Just the stuff, eh? And for the young lady?
BINNEY: What – ?
Suddenly, it seems, there is a girl at the next but one stool along
the bar, who has obviously slipped in from one of the arched,
ill-lit alcoves. Binney's face changes. She is young, and shapely,
garbed in black stockings, a semblance of a skirt, a sailor's hat
which says HMS AMANDA. She is Amanda, a 'hostess'.
AMANDA: Hello, sugar.
BINNEY: Hello yourself. Sugar. Would you like a –
AMANDA: Champagne, toots.
BINNEY: Yes. Ah. Of course. Toots.

Completing the wheeling of Marlow along the drab corridor to
his bed in the ward.
MARLOW: (*Just aloud*) Sugar.
The porter can only hear his own music, but a walking patient,
passing, looks at Marlow.
    (*Just aloud*) Toots.
The disfigured Marlow comes through the wide-open double
doors into the big ward, where the teatime activity is
continuing.
PORTER: (*Indifferent*) Hey. Back in time for the tea party.
    Bed 7. Little way from heaven. Here we is. Stand up, eh?
MARLOW: Can't.
The porter looks at him, lifts off one of his little ear-pads.
PORTER: Bed 7. You home now.
MARLOW: I can't. Can't get up.
Marlow, sunk down into his scabbed and scaled self, looks
utterly miserable and uncommunicative.
PORTER: O-*Kay*. Let's be locking them wheels, low-roller.
He does so. Then, very easily, and tenderly, lifts Marlow up
on to the bed, so that he is in a sort of slumped, sitting
position. But Marlow clearly has to stifle wretched gasps of
pain during the movement, though his head remains rigid, as
with one who cannot turn his neck. The porter contemplates
him briefly, nods sympathetically, then starts to untie the
drawstrings at the back of Marlow's smock, with soft clicking
noises.

Tsk! Tsk! Oh, man.

MARLOW: (*Urgent hiss*) Draw the curtains!

PORTER: Aw, aw, now – We's all boys in here together –

MARLOW: Draw the curtains! Draw the bloody curtains – !

But the porter has already untied the strings. As the smock falls away, his face changes.

PORTER: Hooo, man. Jesus holy shit.

For Marlow is an example of extreme psoriasis at its worst. He is cracked, scabbed, scaled, swollen, scarlet and snowy white, and boiling with pain. Further down the ward, Mr Hall is disgusted.

MR HALL: It would be enough to put you off your bread and jam. If they bothered to give you any.

Reginald has actually looked up from his reading.

REGINALD: (*Matter of fact*) Poor sod.

MR HALL: We all suffer, Reginald. Some of us choose not to show it, that's all. That's why we're *penalized*.

The porter belatedly draws the curtains shut around Marlow's bed, completely shutting it off from the rest of the ward.

PORTER: OK? Want help in there? You OK?

No answer comes from behind the curtains. The porter shrugs, looks to see that Staff Nurse White is engaged, slyly replaces his Walkman pads, and races off with the wheelchair, like one escaping.

Helpless and marooned, in a kind of sitting position on the edge of the bed, within a space now like a tent because the curtains are closed, Marlow gasps and struggles and sucks in his breath in pain and – more importantly for him – a terrible inner rage and sense of humiliation. The passion of it momentarily passes and he holds himself dead still. A beat. Then – weirdly, he imitates *exactly* what he mostly cannot possibly have heard. That is, he lip-synchronizes precisely to the real voices.

MARLOW: (*Lip-syncs in Mr Hall's voice*) 'It would be enough to put you off your bread and jam. If they bothered to give you any.' (*Tiny pause.*) Sugar. (*Then, in Reginald's voice*) 'Poor sod.' (*Tiny pause.*) Toots. (*Then in porter's voice*) 'Hooo, man. Jesus holy shit.'

Silence. He holds very still. And then his own voice cracks out, full of venom.

Bastards! I'll wipe you out! Don't you know who I am? I'm

the – (*gasp*) – I'm the Singing Detective –
He starts to laugh, bitterly, but this turns into another wince
and gasp of pain. Slowly, stiffly, with immense effort, he turns
his torso rather than his head to see the pyjama jacket on the
bed. He so desperately wants it that he tries to twist a little
more, and reach out with clubbed hands, but he cannot possibly
manage to gather up the jacket.

(*Between his teeth*) C'mon – c'mon – *c'mon* – !
But he topples sideways on the bed. He has no control over his
joints. He is stranded. Squeak of trolley, chink of cups, on the
far side of the curtains – the trolley has approached Marlow's
curtained-off bed space, and is now at the adjoining bed,
occupied by an Asian universally known in the ward as Ali, a
cardiac patient.

STAFF NURSE WHITE: Tea, Ali.

ALI: Tea. No bread. No cake. Tea.

She stares at him, with a face as starched as cuffs.

STAFF NURSE WHITE: Please.

ALI: Tea. No bread. No cake.

STAFF NURSE WHITE: Please.

Tiny pause. He looks at her, cautiously.

ALI: What?

STAFF NURSE WHITE: Say 'please', Ali. Not 'what'. I won't
    have 'what'. I'll have 'please', thank you very much.

ALI: Tea. Thank you very much.

STAFF NURSE WHITE: Tea *please*.

ALI: Tea. Please. Thank you very much.

STAFF NURSE WHITE: There's a good chap.

ALI: What?

A little thrown by the dangerously amused twinkle in his eyes,
she slaps the tea down on his bed trolley in a way that shows she
doesn't like him.

(*Amused*) Tea. No bloody bread. No bloody cake.
But she has moved starchily onward, to the curtained-off bed
space.

Staff Nurse White's severe face pokes through the curtains,
almost comically, like a head in a puppet show. Marlow, of
course, is still hopelessly stranded, side on to her.

STAFF NURSE WHITE: Mr Marlow! What *are* we trying to do?

She comes on into the curtained space.

MARLOW: (*Gasp*) Why – why is it –

STAFF NURSE WHITE: Now, we've got to *stop* doing this, haven't we?

MARLOW: – why is it – that – (*gasp*) when you lose your health, the entire medical profession takes it as axiomatic that you have also lost your *mind* – !

STAFF NURSE WHITE: Now, now, now. We'll have none of that.

A strong woman, she pulls him up, but in a way that hurts him a lot.

MARLOW: Oooch.

STAFF NURSE WHITE: What did you think you were trying to do? Rather silly-billy of us, wasn't it?

Her tone, his pain, infuriates him.

MARLOW: I was trying to get my pyjama top. (*Evenly*) My sodding, bloody, buggering, fu–

STAFF NURSE WHITE: *Mr Marlow!*

Silence. Then he sighs, and speaks like a chastened little boy, but with a dreadful jeer.

MARLOW: My ickle jacket pleeeese. I wants my closey-woseys.

Meanwhile, there is indignation down the ward about the delayed tea trolley.

MR HALL: Reginald. Are we going to do anything about it? Are we just going to accept it?

REGINALD: What – ?

He does not really look up from his lip-moving reading, which further irritates the older man.

MR HALL: Nine times out of ten they go up that side first. Nine times out of ten they turn *left* when they come through those doors. Breakfast. Lunch*eon*. Tea. Supper. Left, they go. Bloody Scargillites. I've counted. I'm telling you, I've counted!

REGINALD: (*Automatic*) Yeh.

He is clearly on an exciting bit. Hall glares at him ferociously, stoking himself up.

MR HALL: Cold tea never did anybody any harm. At least, I don't bloody well *suppose* so – But injustice. That's another matter. Injustice eats the insides out of you. *Why* do they

8

always go up that side first? Eh? Eh? Tell me that!
Reginald is excited by what he is reading.
REGINALD: (*Softly*) Cor – !
MR HALL: She should turn right every other time, that ugly nurse. God, she is ugly. Don't you think she's one of the ugliest and nastiest and meanest bitches ever to walk the earth? Eh?
REGINALD: (*Avidly reading*) What?
A venomous little pause.
MR HALL: Why don't you move your bed?
Reginald at last looks up.
REGINALD: Whafor?
MR HALL: Up to the other end. Move next to that bloody Paki or whatever he thinks he is. Go on.
REGINALD: No, fanks.
MR HALL: Well, you're no company, are you? No bloody company. Always got your snout buried in that book –
REGINALD: (*Severely*) Nose, Mr Hall. This is a *nose* I got.
MR HALL: Well, whatever it is, my boy –
REGINALD: It's a nose.
MR HALL: And it's always stuck in a book! *I* might as well be stuck in the middle of the desert. Three weeks, and hardly a word with a living soul! Living hell, that's what this is. A living –
But his expression instantly turns nervously ingratiating. The tea trolley is, at last, suddenly upon them.
STAFF NURSE WHITE: And how are we today, Mr Hall? Ready for our cup of tea?
MR HALL: (*Timidly*) That would be very nice, staff nurse. Thank you very much indeed.
REGINALD: He thinks you ought to turn right sometimes.
STAFF NURSE WHITE: What?
Hall virtually jerks with anxiety.
MR HALL: No, no, no – Just sharing a little *repartee* with my young friend here –
REGINALD: Mr Hall thinks something ought to be done about it –
MR HALL: (*Sidelong hiss*) Shut your mouth, Reginald.
REGINALD: – By the time *we* get it, the tea's either cold or

stewed to buggery –

STAFF NURSE WHITE: Language!

MR HALL: (*Quickly*) But very welcome it is, miss, in *this* bed.
Whichever way you turn.

And then a tiny moment of horrified silence from him, as he
takes the full measure of his hapless *double entendre*.

A River Police launch bobs gently on the river, which is oily
black as the night slowly yields to first light. Two River Police
are grappling with hooks and nets in the slow waters at
something which looks almost like a furry sort of creature in the
river. Absolute, eerie silence, the sky lightening over
Hammersmith Bridge, looking over the scene.

There is a strange row of people on the pedestrian walkway of
the bridge, dream-like, looking down into the dark water. We
see that the people staring down are mostly in pyjamas. They
include Mr Tomkey (Noddy), Ali, Mr Hall, Reginald, other
patients seen having their tea in the ward, Staff Nurse White,
yet to be seen nurses, the Sony-Walkman porter. Their faces are
intent, silent, accusing.

At first, the only sound is the slap-slap of the water against the
boat, which has its engine switched off. The other, natural
noises increase as the struggling, grunting policemen slowly pull
in and up on to the deck of the launch the naked, drowned body
of a beautiful young woman. During which –

AMANDA: (*Voice over*) Hello, sugar.

BINNEY: (*Voice over*) Oh. Hello yourself. Sugar. Would you like
a –

AMANDA: Champagne, toots.

They are covering the body with a blanket, on the slowly
bobbing deck. All the dream-like figures watching silently from
the ornate bridge have gone. There is but one person there now,
in a trilby, his coat collar turned up, distantly lonely like the
man in the old cigarette advertisement ('You're never alone with
a . . .') It is Marlow, 1945-style, without psoriasis or seized
joints. He is watching the recovery of the body with a burning
intensity of expression. Then – he looks straight at us, lip
curling.

MARLOW: Entertainment.

His face goes dead, except for the burning eyes.

In the hospital the psoriatic, arthritic Marlow also has eyes
burning. A moment. Then the tension seems to lift from him a
little. He sighs.

> (*Voice over*) Cigarette. I want a cigarette.

His eyes swivel to the cigarette packet on top of the locker at the
side of the bed. We see him register the fact that there is no way
he can turn his limbs enough to reach the cigarettes. He sighs
again, comically heavy.

> Cigarettes, sugar. Toots. (*Tiny pause.*) Faggy-waggy,
> nursey. (*Sighs again, then, out loud*) Ali.

But Ali, in the next bed, is contemplating nothingness.

MARLOW: Ali!

ALI: (*Surfacing*) What you want?

MARLOW: Ali. Get my cigarettes for me.

ALI: Please.

MARLOW: What – ?

ALI: Say 'please'. Not 'what'. I won't have 'what'. Thank you
very much.

MARLOW: Oh, for Christ's sake.

ALI: No cigarettes!

MARLOW: Please. All right, please. You bastard.

ALI: (*Smirk*) Doctor say if something wrong *here* (*slaps his chest*)
and you bloody smoking cigarette. There's something
wrong *here* (*slaps his forehead*) as well. No! No cigarette.

MARLOW: That's you cardiacs. You heart patients, nig-nog. I'm
skin, Ali. Skin! How many times!

ALI: (*Smirk*) I must stay in bed. He say – (*bellow*) – 'Stay in
bed, nig-nog!'

MARLOW: *What*? (*Indignant*) He said *that* – ? The *doctor* did – ?

Ali laughs infectiously so that Marlow knows that such words
were not used.

> Ach, you're padding up and down half the night, Ali, you
> sly old sod. I've seen you sneaking out of bed. Talking to
> Allah or somebody.

ALI: Oh, bloody God no.

MARLOW: Ali. Don't be a hypocrite. I'm *dying* for a cigarette.
Please, Ali. Please. Love your little brown chops.

ALI: OK, OK. Bloody dog, me.
There is obviously an affection between them. Ali gets out of bed, and gets the cigarettes for Marlow.
MARLOW: They keep putting them on my locker. It's what they call *tidying* my trolley. Like all morons with a mania for order, they put everything I really want exactly where I can't get it. Do you know how many O levels you have to fail to be a nurse? Oh, good man, Ali. Blessings on your head, old son.
This latter spurt of warmth because Ali has put a cigarette into his, Marlow's mouth, and standing at the bedside, is going click-click-click at the button on Marlow's so-called electronic lighter. Without getting a flame.
ALI: No bloody flame.
MARLOW: Conviction. Do it with conviction.
Click again, and the flame jumps up too high, almost singeing Ali.
ALI: Oh, my God.
MARLOW: Turn it down! Turn the wheel!
It is like a blow torch.
Ali – the little wheel – !
Ali finds how to reduce the flame.
ALI: Good. Yes?
MARLOW: I could see the deadlines. 'Another Asian Burnt to Death.'
Ali, grinning, lights Marlow's cigarette. Marlow sucks in smoke. No. That sort of thing doesn't make the headlines any more, does it? Not now the National Front are investing in tandoori ovens.
Ali watches with fascination as Marlow eagerly drags in too much smoke, coughs, hurts himself, but beams with pleasure.
ALI: Good?
MARLOW: Good? (*Cough, splutter.*) Bloody (*cough*) marvellous – (*Cough, splutter, wince.*) All my wants and desires and fondest aspirations have finally been reduced to their true dimensions, my old son.
And he coughs again.
ALI: Yes. Your lungs.
MARLOW: Look at that blue smoke, Ali. See – the way it coils

and drifts. (*Nasty cackle.*) Just like every human hope.

ALI: Yes, yes, very bloody wise.

MARLOW: I used to think I wanted the good opinion of honourable men and the ungrudging love of beautiful women.

He laughs, then realizes he meant it.

But now I know *for sure* that all I really want is a cigarette. Just one more cigarette, Ali.

He blows out a column of smoke.

ALI: Poison. It's poison.

MARLOW: One thing about this place, Ali – it strips away all the unimportant stuff – like skin – like work – love – loyalty – like passion and belief –

ALI: Oh!

With a soft moan of apparently inexplicable despair Ali suddenly darts back into his bed, and pulls the sheet right over his head like someone in fear for his very life. Marlow is comically astounded.

MARLOW: Oy! I know I'm boring – but surely not as much as that!

But an extremely earnest young houseman, Dr Finlay, is striding towards them.

DR FINLAY: (*Severely*) Were you out of bed? I said – Were you out of bed?

Ali is forced to lower the sheet at the firmly repeated question.

ALI: No, Doctor Finlay, sir. No, no.

DR FINLAY: Oh yes you jolly well were! And what have I told you? What is the point of my –

MARLOW: (*Interrupting*) It's my fault.

DR FINLAY: Oh?

MARLOW: I asked him to get me a cigarette –

DR FINLAY: Well, you shouldn't and he shouldn't. You're taking advantage of him. In any case, you shouldn't be smoking. Not if you had any sense.

MARLOW: You're not *my* doctor. Thank God.

DR FINLAY: Whether I am or not, I am telling you not to encourage this man to get out of his bed. You're being selfish –

MARLOW: Now, look –

DR FINLAY: – putting *his* health at risk for the sake of *your* vice –

MARLOW: Listen –

DR FINLAY: – if he has another heart attack, then you'll be responsible, won't you?

MARLOW: That'll be one less, then. Won't it?

Deadly little pause.

DR FINLAY: (*Cold*) What are you talking about?

MARLOW: Immigrants, sunshine.

The young doctor stares at Marlow, then turns abruptly to Ali.

DR FINLAY: Are you having trouble with this fellow?

ALI: (*Beam*) Oh yes, my God yes.

DR FINLAY: Has he been making offensive remarks about your origins?

ALI: (*Puzzled*) Origins?

DR FINLAY: Your – ah – race, or – ?

ALI: Race?

DR FINLAY: (*Irritated*) Yes. Your race!

MARLOW: Go on. Tell him. You brown bugger.

Ali gives a whoop of laughter. Dr Finlay, taken aback, goes to say something but – *bleep-bleep-bleep!* goes his bleeper, and he turns on his heels to stride away, angrily flustered.

Jumped up little snot. You get out of bed when you want, Ali, old pal.

ALI: No, no, no.

MARLOW: Well – why not? What's the point? What are we waiting for? Why endure one moment more than you have to? Go on! Get out of bed, Ali! Jump up and down! And then hold a pillow down over my face! Come on!

He stops abruptly, like one suddenly aware of the true extremity of his feelings, and the depths of his bitterness or despair. Very close on Marlow. A beat. Then –

(*Whisper*) At first comma the only sound is the slap hyphen slap of the water against the boat comma which has its engine switched off double space The other comma natural noises increase as the –

On the cold river, at dawn, the struggling, grunting policemen slowly pull in and up on to the deck of the launch the naked, drowned body of a beautiful young woman.

On the screen of a word processor, a bright glow of letters softly blip-blips across the monitor –
> The other, natural noises increase as the struggling, grunting policemen slowly pull up on to the deck of the launch the naked, drowned body of a beautif–

In the hospital ward, an attractive young nurse, Nurse Mills, is suddenly, on the uncompleted word 'beautiful', standing at the foot of Marlow's bed. Marlow, jolted out of reverie, stares at her.

MARLOW: The naked, drowned body of a beautiful woman.

NURSE MILLS: What are you talking about, Mr Marlow?

Marlow recovers. He studies her, with a half-amused glint.

MARLOW: I had on my best pyjamas, the ones with red stripes and blue forget-me-nots. I was all dressed up and talcumed under the armpits. A million dollars was about to call. I was ready for it.

NURSE MILLS: High temperature again, have we?

MARLOW: When she moved her lips like that I felt like a tulip in the dry season when the first raindrop smacked into it. I decided to open up. Boy, was I green. Or do I mean, wet?

NURSE MILLS: Oh, I see.

MARLOW: Your eyes are not for seeing, Nurse Mills. They are for being looked at.

NURSE MILLS: We're in a *good mood*, are we? We're actually *talking* today, are we, Mr Marlow?

Marlow's Chandleresquerie switches off, instantly.

MARLOW: What you mean?

NURSE MILLS: According to Report you didn't speak one word yesterday. Not to anybody. And that's not the first time you've done that, is it?

MARLOW: Me?

NURSE MILLS: Yes. You.

She stoops down to open the door of his locker.

MARLOW: (*Alarmed*) You mean they put that sort of thing on Report?

NURSE MILLS: Oh, yes. Everything.

She is taking a large tub of grease, and some polythene gloves
from the locker, and putting them on to his bed-trolley, ready
for use.

MARLOW: Is that why they – ?

But he stops, biting off the question.

NURSE MILLS: Go on. Ask it.

MARLOW: Is that why they think I'm a bit touched? Loopy?

NURSE MILLS: No!

MARLOW: What then?

NURSE MILLS: Depressed.

MARLOW: Tranquillizers – no worse – those antidepressants.
The head-mashers. Brain-drainers. Is that why they try to
make me swallow them?

NURSE MILLS: Well, if they help people –

MARLOW: (*Quickly interrupting*) I'm not taking those things! I've
got work to do. Got a lot of thinking to do. If I don't *think*
I'll never get out of here. I'll – (*Abruptly*) Are you going to
grease me?

NURSE MILLS: If you're ready.

MARLOW: As ready as a back-axle.

She starts to draw shut the curtains around the bed, but before
they are completely closed, shutting Marlow off from the rest of
the ward, a plaintive and oddly furtive call from Mr Hall at the
other end of the ward –

MR HALL: Nurse. Nurse.

She calls across the ward to him, as though used to such a call.

NURSE MILLS: What is it, Mr Hall?

MR HALL: (*Furtive*) Could you spare a little moment, nurse?
Over here – ?

NURSE MILLS: No. Tell me!

MR HALL: Please, nurse. Please can you come here a
mom–Please, miss – !

Rolling her eyes a little, the beautiful nurse, watched by all the
eyes that are open, leaving the curtains incompletely drawn,
crosses the ward –

NURSE MILLS: You're going to wear us all out, Mr Hall. You
know that, don't you – Now what is it?

As she arrives he puts the side of his hand to his mouth, like a
pantomime conspirator.

MR HALL: (*Sotto voce*) Beg pardon my dear – I need the – ah – you know – very badly – sorry – the – ah – the contraption – sorry –

NURSE MILLS: Contraption? What contraption?

MR HALL: (*Sotto voce*) Tuppence. Want to spend tuppence. You know.

NURSE MILLS: (*Brisk*) Reginald. Would you *please* go and get a bedpan for Mr Hall and close his curtains.

Reginald sighs and reluctantly puts down his paperback. Hall crunches up inside. Nurse Mills is already on her way back to Marlow.

REGINALD: Got the shits have you, Pop?

MR HALL: Shhh! Shhh!

REGINALD: You want to stop eating them bleed'n grapes. Whatchoodo? Swallow the pips, or what?

MR HALL: Please, my boy! Please!

Marlow's curtained-off bed space is a private world in its feeling, a tent separate from everything else. Marlow has a gleam as he looks at the attractive nurse, as she begins to pull on polythene gloves. The polythene tightens and clings against her fingers. It looks unexpectedly erotic. She speaks brightly as she does this.

NURSE MILLS: Bit like being in a tent in here, isn't it? With the curtains shut like this –

MARLOW: Yeh. And the desert all around.

NURSE MILLS: Shall we do the top or the bottom half first?

MARLOW: I – I don't mind –

The anxiety is a shade too obvious.

NURSE MILLS: You still can't get your own pyjamas off, can you?

MARLOW: No.

She pulls back the bed clothes, decisively.

NURSE MILLS: All right. I'll start down below first. Let's get these trousers off. Can you hold on to me – I'll try not to hurt –

She has to lift him a little to start getting his trousers down. He gasps.

MARLOW: Th–thanks –

NURSE MILLS: All right. Relax. We can start now.

Marlow's face fills the screen, showing comical anxiety and

17

sexual disturbance. Swoop in soaring violins, Mantovani style –
then stop them dead, as –

MARLOW: (*Voice over, whispered intensity*) *Oh cock do not crow,
Poor cock do not stir*

– and swoop the violins back in again, exactly where they had
been interrupted. Polythene fingers dip into soft and slippery
ointment as the violins quiver.

NURSE MILLS: I'll be as gentle as I can.

Marlow's face again fills the screen, intense concentration,
comical strain, and a whispered urgency in the voice over –

MARLOW: (*Voice over*) Think of something boring – For Christ's
sake think of something very very boring – Speech a speech
by Ted Heath a sentence long sentence from Bernard Levin
a quiz by Christopher Booker a – oh think think think – !
Really boring! A Welsh male-voice choir – Everything in
Punch – Oh! Oh! –

Nurse Mills rhythmically works in the grease, her shapely body
bending to the bed, the tip of her tongue showing in
concentration, and, as he gasps, she makes a sympathetic lip-
purse of a noise –

NURSE MILLS: Ooh – I'm sorry – Oh you poor thing –

She does not seem to realize how incredibly erotic this makes
her look and sound. Marlow closes his eyes a moment, as though
submitting to his sense of sexual excitement, and then visibly
forces such thoughts away, in a desperate, voice-over gabble –

MARLOW: (*Voice over*) Wage rates in Peru James Burke
Finnegans Wake all the bloody Irish the dog in *Blue Peter*
blue Brian Clough and especially James Henry and Clive
and Australian barmen ecologists semiologists think think
the *Guardian* Women's Page oh dear Christ yes the Bible
and oh God *Reader's Digest* Special Prize Draw no the Bible
think Bible Psalms Song of Solomon thy breasts are like –
no no! – oh – oooh! –

NURSE MILLS: Oh, I'm sorry. Is it too hard?

MARLOW: (*Little suppressed yelp*) Too hard – ! Yes!

NURSE MILLS: I'm being as gentle as I can. But it's worst of all
here, inside your thighs –

MARLOW: (*Gasp*) It's – oof – it's like iodine in a cut or – No.
It's not your fault. No, no –

NURSE MILLS: (*Matter of fact*) Sorry. But I shall have to lift
     your penis now to grease around it.
Marlow's face is suddenly a cinema poster, so to speak, for *The
Agony and the Ecstasy*. Very briefly held, then crash in music –

At Skinscape's, the singer by the small bandstand is Nurse Mills
and 'The Blues in the Night' is the song she lip-syncs. She is
1945-glamorous, and sings with her hip and her hands in full
play. The glamorously metamorphosed 'Nurse Mills' is
performing before two- or three-seater banquette dining
lay-outs, where now a few score men, mostly middle-aged and
business-suited or uniformed, are dining with the fairly scantily
clad and yet 'sophisticated' (1945) 'hostesses', each of whom
wears a sailor hat and a HMS-plus-her-name motif.
     Picking out Binney and Amanda. Amanda's speech is full of
wrong notes, pseudo-American with an undertow of cockney
and occasional diversions into Mayfair-idiot-upper-class, a 1940s
nightclub mix.
AMANDA: She's a corker, ain't she? Carlotta. I mean –
     genuweenly artistic.
BINNEY: Top hole.
AMANDA: (*Picking up on the song's words*) It's right, too. What a
     girl should be told.
BINNEY: Sorry?
AMANDA: I mean – a guy can get very excited, can't he?
BINNEY: You're telling me.
AMANDA: It's all fizz – and he'll say anything – promise the
     earth – and then –
BINNEY: (*Interrupting*) You're not eating, Amanda.
But all the time his eyes are flicking about. He is either very
distracted, or looking for something.
AMANDA: No. One can only consume so much, you know.
BINNEY: Where do they get this meat? It's real steak. I haven't
seen meat like this since before the war. Six long years of Spam.
AMANDA: Ask no questions, I'll tell no lies.
BINNEY: Still, and all – is it legal? Or is it horse?
He pokes at his steak with his fork, frowns, stands.
AMANDA: What's up, sugar?
BINNEY: I need the gents.

AMANDA: What? Now? When Carlotta's singing?
BINNEY: She's nearly done. I've heard the song.
AMANDA: Know where it is, sugar?
BINNEY: I'll find it. Toots.
This comes out tight-faced, almost threatening. She shrugs as he
goes, and then looks at her nails, horribly bored. Binney moves
through the dining area, all shadows, as 'Nurse Mills' finishes
the song.
   Two mysterious men, later to feature regularly, spaced widely
apart, look at each other and nod as he passes, menacingly.
   Nurse Mills, or 'Carlotta', finishes 'Blues in the Night' with
an erotic little pout. Applause. She smiles. Then –
NURSE MILLS: (As 'Carlotta') Sorry. But I shall have to lift your
      penis now to grease around it.
Every paunchy, middle-aged, tipsy man in Skinscape's dining
area rises. They all cheer and bang their palms together in
raucous delight, whistling and whooping and stamping their
feet.

The excess male applause continues over Marlow's curtained-off
bed space. Then total silence. Then – comically – in strained
embarrassment –
MARLOW: (Off) I'm – ah – nurse. I'm very sorry. It – that's the
      one part of me that still sort of functions. I do beg your
      pardon.
Within the curtained-off bed space, Marlow's lower limbs are
now covered with the sheet, and Nurse Mills is greasing his
chest. Normally cool, even clinical, she now looks flustered, her
eyes swivelling away.
NURSE MILLS: It's all right – I – I understand.
MARLOW: It seems to have a will of its own –
NURSE MILLS: We don't need to talk about it, do we?
MARLOW: No.
Silence. Her fingers gently applying the greasy ointment on his
disfigured flesh. Then – in a different tone –
NURSE MILLS: How long have you had this?
MARLOW: (Abrupt) Twenty, thirty years.
NURSE MILLS: As bad as this?
MARLOW: No. It's at its peak now, almost. I'm starting to lose

control of my body temperature. I keep going over the top.

NURSE MILLS: Yes!

He accepts the rebuke. Then winces as she accidentally hurts him too much.

MARLOW: It makes me – I think I sort of hallucinate, a bit –

NURSE MILLS: That happens.

MARLOW: I thought there was a cat in the bed this morning. *In* it. Not on it. Systematically and meticulously chewing off my toes, one by one.

He winces again.

NURSE MILLS: I'm trying not to hurt you.

MARLOW: (*In pain*) Sometimes – sometimes these – hallucinations – they're better than the real thing. People can sing in them or dance or – I don't mind. I don't mind. I like pictures. I don't care.

But there is a terror in his voice, which she cannot fail to notice. Still working away with polythened fingers, systematically covering every square inch of his afflicted torso, she changes the subject, in a way.

NURSE MILLS: You write detective stories. Don't you?

MARLOW: (*Almost hostile*) Who told you that?

NURSE MILLS: Oh, a little bird.

MARLOW: Well, the little bird is wrong. I used to write them. Used to. Used to.

His voice is threatening to go out of control.

NURSE MILLS: (*Gently*) Hey.

Silence. She has nearly finished. But his eyes show the same distress.

MARLOW: (*Eventually*) Got to work.

NURSE MILLS: Sorry – ?

MARLOW: Got to work. I've got to work. Somehow, I've got to work.

And then, greatly to his own embarrassment, an only half-suppressed sob of distress hurtles up his throat.

NURSE MILLS: Hey, now –

MARLOW: (*Choke*) Christ. Sorry – !

NURSE MILLS: That's all right –

He fights for self-control.

MARLOW: You'd think – phoo! – You'd think my mother would

have had more sense than to call me Philip, wouldn't you! I mean, with a name like Marlow. Philip Marlowe. I haven't got an 'e' on the end, but it sounds the same.

NURSE MILLS: Same as what?

MARLOW: (*Indignant*) Philip Marlowe! You've heard of him surely? Christ Almighty. What else could I have done except write detective stories? She should have called me Christopher.

They are dancing back at Skinscape's, but beyond the dining tables, through the crypt-like arches, Binney moves, supposedly in search of the lavatories.

(*Voice over, from Marlowe, C.*)
'Hell hath no limits nor is circumscrib'd
In one self place, where we are is Hell,
And where Hell is, there must we ever be – '

Binney looks about, alert, then darts off into a small passage, thinking no one can see him. But the two mysterious men have slid along the walls to get into observing positions.

The band, off, is playing 'On the Sunny Side of the Street', and the elongated shadows of the dancers make an ominous chiaroscuro of oddly moving shapes on the walls where the two mysterious men watch and wait. Cautious Binney opens a door to a tall wardrobe-like cupboard that seems distinctly out of place.

Inside the cupboard, skewered to the wood at the back, is the busker, murdered, his eyes staring glassily back at Binney. Binney looks steadily at the dead man. Then – without any emotion –

BINNEY: (*Whisper*) Goodbye, old fruit.

And he closes the Busker's eyes, then closes the cupboard door. The band still plays.

It is night in the hospital ward. At first, no sounds except the grunts and snores of the sleeping patients in very dim light, like the foraging noises of unknown beasts. Then Marlow's Marlowe comes again, over –

MARLOW: (*Voice over*)
'And where Hell is, there must we ever be.

And to be short, when all the world dissolves
And every creature shall be purified,
And places shall be Hell that are not heaven.'
At the top of the ward, the night nurse dozes, half slumped at
the table. The quotation takes in her, the sleeping patients, the
dark shapes, and as it ends – close in on Marlow, eyes gleaming
in the half-dark, stiffly propped up against his pillows, wide
awake. A moment. Then –

> (*Soft croak*) Baking. Burning. I'm burning up. Burning. On
> the – On the Sunny Side. On the Sunny Side of the Street.

At Skinscape's, no or little time has elapsed because the small
band is still playing the same number. The businessmen cling to
their girls on the tiny dancing space in front of the tables.
Binney is starting to sweat as he moves back to Amanda. A
quick darting glance before he sits reveals to him the two
mysterious men. And he is suddenly very scared.

AMANDA: Find it all right?

BINNEY: (*Grimly*) I found it all right.

AMANDA: What's the matter, sugar?

BINNEY: I – it's hot down here. Baking. I feel I'm burning up.

AMANDA: Gawd. You're *dripping*. That shows a passionate
nature, sugar.

BINNEY: And what about you? You look very cool to me.

AMANDA: Only when I'm upright.

BINNEY: (*Distracted*) Oh no. Not *another* bottle.

For a sad-eyed, beautiful girl with long black hair, not *decisively*
recognizable as the girl pulled naked out of the river, is upon
them, bearing a fresh champagne bottle on a silver tray.

AMANDA: Oh, you got to keep coughing up here. If you want
my company. Sorry, toots. Ain't I worth it? No need to
drink it, though.

BINNEY: What? At two pounds ten a bottle!

He gets a huge white £5 note from a fold of them in his wallet.
Amanda, seeing the cash he has, greedily glints, and crosses
glances with the new girl, Sonia.

AMANDA: Mark – it *is* Mark, isn't it – ?

BINNEY: As in the second gospel.

AMANDA: Whatchewmean?

BINNEY: Never mind.

AMANDA: Mark. This is my best friend Sonia.

SONIA: (*Accented*) Hello.

And she stares too hard at him. He puts the big white note on the tray.

AMANDA: Sonia likes a tip, Mark.

BINNEY: Well – let's hope I get something back for all this.

SONIA: (*Accented*) Sank you.

AMANDA: (*Coy*) That all depends, don't it, sugar?

BINNEY: On what?

AMANDA: On what you mean.

Binney is sweating profusely. Sonia stares at him, oddly, wide-eyed.

BINNEY: Hot. Why is it so hot? Why am I so hot?

It is morning in the hospital ward, and the place is busy again. Crash in 'The Entry of the Queen of Sheba', startlingly, as in a highly stylized balletic prance, a consultant, his registrar, his houseman, a visiting doctor, sister (Malone) and Staff Nurse White come swirling through the double doors into the ward.

To the music, and choreographed, they prance and strut straight to Marlow's bed and take up positions on either side of it, with the imperious consultant aloof at the front.

Marlow is wearing only a tiny loincloth – normal practice when seeing a dermatology consultant – exposing his hideously disfigured skin to clinical gaze.

He is helplessly flat on his back, laid out like a corpse, on top of the bed clothes, on a paper sheet already soaked with grease. The music cuts out, abruptly, and the medical team looms in a tilted, odd, disturbing perspective around Marlow, from his point of view. He is struggling on the very edge of hallucination. Overlay an echo-like, troubled voice, his own.

MARLOW: (*Voice over, strange resonance*) *Hot. Why is it so hot? Why am I so hot?*

Sonia is in the middle of the medical team, staring down wide-eyed at him, with a bottle of champagne on a silver tray. Then back to 'normal' around the bed, and –

CONSULTANT: (*Boom*) Good morning to you! Let me see. You are – Mr – ah –

MARLOW: Mar—

SISTER MALONE: Marlow, sir.

CONSULTANT: Of course, of course. And how are you feeling this morning?

MARLOW: Well. I —

REGISTRAR: Very inflamed. Extensive lesions.

HOUSEMAN: Temperature too high.

VISITING DOCTOR: Marked arthrosis.

REGISTRAR: Difficult. Difficult.

VISITING DOCTOR: How long have you had this psoriatic arthropathy — ?

MARLOW: Twen—

REGISTRAR: Twenty-five years.

CONSULTANT: How much movement in the joints?

MARLOW: Not v—

HOUSEMAN: (*Instant interruption*) Hydrocortisone injections all major joints. Including the toes.

VISITING DOCTOR: (*Unexpectedly*) Tootsie-wootsies.

REGISTRAR: Prednisone and then Prednisolone in short bursts, orally, then for longer periods. But with Betnovate and then Dermovate topical application under total occlusive dressings — (*Shrugs.*) Well. You can see the damage. Latterly, with such relentless occlusions, one might almost with reluctance have to describe it as —

VISITING DOCTOR: Iatrogenic.

CONSULTANT: Mmmmmmmmmm.

Pause. They wait for the consultant to pronounce. Then, from Marlow's feverish point of view, as the consultant and medical team menacingly contemplate him, hard-eyed, looming, rather elongated. And in the middle of them, Sonia, with tears on her cheeks. Then back to 'normal', and —

History?

HOUSEMAN: Prior to this, pretty usual sequence.

CONSULTANT: Precise. Be precise!

HOUSEMAN: Initially, coal tar. Then gold injections. Butazolodin. Indomethocine, not successful. The short courses Prednisone, Prednisolone, lengthening. Then Methotrexate, after positive liver biopsies.

REGISTRAR: Vomiting?

HOUSEMAN: Vomiting.

REGISTRAR: Finally withdrawn.

HOUSEMAN: Ten years of occlusive dressings, corticosteroid unguents. Each night. Twelve hours. Then –

REGISTRAR: Razoxane. Also cytotoxic.

HOUSEMAN: Induced neutrophenia. Wart-like lesions. Odd cell shapes. Removed. Withdrawn.

CONSULTANT: (*Long, low*) Mmmmmmmmmmm.

Pause. The four doctors fondle their jaws contemplatively. The two nurses wait. Marlow sweats.

VISITING DOCTOR: I've seen one or two cases as bad as this in Baltimore. Not many. What are you going to do? One of the retinoids?

CONSULTANT: Mmmmmmmm. Ye–e–e–es.

REGISTRAR: I would have said so.

VISITING DOCTOR: Worth a try.

CONSULTANT: Mmmmmmmm.

Marlow desperately wants to speak.

MARLOW: Excuse m–

CONSULTANT: (*Abruptly*) This hyperventilation. Any odd thoughts in the brain box, eh, old chap?

He taps his head as though Marlow is a child.

MARLOW: (*Gasp*) I th–

HOUSEMAN: (*Cutting in*) On Tuesday he insisted there was a cat in the bed chewing at his feet. Isn't that so, staff nurse?

STAFF NURSE WHITE: Yes. A cat. Attacking his toes.

VISITING DOCTOR: (*Amused*) Tootsie-wootsie, eh?

SISTER MALONE: We don't allow cats in the ward. No animals.

They look at her. She has a strong Irish accent. They are embarrassed.

CONSULTANT: Quite so. Quite so. (*Looks hard at* MARLOW.) Well, now. There's another drug which might help you. Mr – ah – How do you feel about trying one of the new retinoids, mmm?

Absolute silence. Marlow does not attempt to speak, not this time. The pause lengthens, comically. They all look at each other. The consultant leans in to speak again, as though to a retarded child.

Do–you–understand–the–question?

MARLOW: No. I don't think so.

26

CONSULTANT: I am asking if you'd –

MARLOW: (*Cutting in*) I don't understand because I seem to have
regressed into the helpless and pathetic condition of total
dependency. Of the kind normally associated with infancy.

Astonishment. The consultant, who was leaning in, straightens
like a shot.

VISITING DOCTOR: (*Astounded*) What's he say?

But Marlow, who can scarcely lift his head, and who is burning
up, gives them the full blast, and not at all calm.

MARLOW: The last time I experienced anything remotely like
this was in my bloody pram! Being drooled over by
slobbering cretins –

SISTER MALONE: Mr Marlow – !

MARLOW: – who turned out to be escapees from the local loony
bin. They thought they were doctors and nurses.

Tiny, shocked silence. Then suddenly, as abrupt as a yelp from
a surprised dog, the consultant throws back his head and lets out
a single explosion of a laugh. Given their signal, so to speak, the
others dutifully chuckle and snicker.

CONSULTANT: What do you *do*, Mr–ah–Marlow? Forgive me,
what used you to do? By way of earning a crust?

MARLOW: I'm an author.

CONSULTANT: Oh. I didn't realize –

MARLOW: Detective stories.

CONSULTANT: (*Disappointed*) Oh. How interesting.

MARLOW: (*Desperate*) Listen. Please listen to me. Will you
please – please – listen to me?

The consultant feels in danger of breaking precedent.

CONSULTANT: Well. What is it?

MARLOW: I can't talk to you lying flat out like this. I need help
to sit up. Please.

The consultant nods at the nurses, reluctantly.

CONSULTANT: We haven't got all day, you know.

Sister Malone and Staff Nurse White pull him up, prop the back
rest and settle him back on it. It looks like the raising of
Lazarus.

MARLOW: (*Gasp*) Thank you –

CONSULTANT: What is it you wish to say?

Marlow, hurt by the movement, has to gather up strength and

concentration. He sounds out of breath. Almost on the verge of panting.

MARLOW: The thing is – the thing – I – listen! – I can't – I've reached the end –

CONSULTANT: Oh. Of what?

MARLOW: My tether.

SISTER MALONE: (*Shocked*) Oh, hush now.

MARLOW: I'd like – Christ, I'd – like to get out of it. I don't want – I can't – listen – I can *not* stand it really truly can not not stand this any more. I can't get on top of it or see clear of it or think straight or – or – tell what is from what isn't – and – (*Rising panic*) And if I don't tell someone, if I don't admit it – I'll never never never get out of it, never beat it off and neverneveernever –

He is laughing, half crying.

Tears even bloody useless tears, sorry about, shame of, even tears oozing bloody useless, hurt the – ooh, the skin on my face and – hee! hee! – laugh – ooh it hurts my jaw and God! Talk about the Book of – the Book of Job I'm a prisoner inside my oooh own skin and and and bones –

He suddenly stops, worn out, ashamed, stiff and still. A pause. They all look at each other.

CONSULTANT: Librium.

REGISTRAR: Valium.

VISITING DOCTOR: Antidepressants.

HOUSEMAN: And a barbiturate.

From Marlow's point of view, the medical team beams down at him, in a wholly unnatural, hallucinatory fashion. They repeat themselves, each with a click of the fingers.

CONSULTANT: Barbiturate!

REGISTRAR: Antidepressants!

VISITING DOCTOR: Valium!

REGISTRAR: And Librium!

As Fred Waring's Pennsylvanians' music crashes in, the lighting switches to vaudeville colours. Music: 'Dry Bones'.

The consultant and his team lip-sync to the zestful vocals, complete with clicking dry-bone sounds and bouncy music, whereas the rest of the ward (initially) carries on unaffected,

28

unconcerned.

Driving, crashing rhythm, bone sounds, and, then, up and down the ward, hands shaking from the wrist minstrel-style, exuberant, gleeful, the medical team move up a gear into the bone-by-bone enumeration of the song. Suddenly, and of course inexplicably, they have little reflex-testing hammers in their hands. And a chorus line of beautiful nurses, led by a diaphanous Nurse Mills, comes from between the rows of beds, dancing, allowing their shapely limbs to be 'tested'.

And then, as the pitch and tempo changes on the original Fred Waring recording –

We are suddenly in an English forest. Unexpectedly, the music continuing, coming in fast and dream-like over the tops of the billowing trees – finding, through initially protective foliage, high in a swaying old tree, preferably an oak, the peeping, pale, oddly withdrawn little face of a pensive 9-year-old boy, Philip.

He stares back at us, almost accusingly, as the music continues without any break.

Back, abruptly, in the ward, Marlow is troubled, even frightened, and drenched with his own sweat, light fading as the 'Dry Bones' song continues to bounce.

As the record repeats the chorus, faster, with Revivalist cries, the medical team begins to cluster back into their proper positions around Marlow's bed, their dancing steps becoming more normal, but –

CONSULTANT: *Oooh!*

REGISTRAR: *Aaay-men!*

MEDICAL TEAM: *Now hear the word of the Lord!*

And everything is suddenly as it was before the song.

CONSULTANT: Do you wish to see the Padre? Would that help at all?

Marlow does not answer. They look at him. Then –

REGISTRAR: (*Sotto voce*) Or a psychiatrist, perhaps.

VISITING DOCTOR: (*Sotto voce*) Looks like it to me.

CONSULTANT: Mmmmmm. (*Then, brisk*) Good morning to you. Keep your – ah – pecker up, old chap.

And he sweeps on with his entourage.

Marlow scarcely seems aware that they have gone. He is staring into nothing. Bereft. Creep in closer and closer to his dead eyes, his reverie. Faint, then growing, comes a man's voice, calling. It is the voice of someone later identified as Marlow's father, Mr Marlow.

MR MARLOW: (*Voice over*) Philip! Phil! Philip! Where bist? Phil–ip – Why doesn't thee answer?

The Forest forms itself out of Marlow's dead eyes. The small boy is in the treetop, high above the rolling lesser trees.

(*Off, calling*) Where bist, our Phil! Philip! Come th'on, o' butty!

ALI: (*Voice over*) Hey! Hey – !

In the Ward, Ali is eagerly trying to get Marlow's attention. Hey! Hey!

MARLOW: (*Surfacing*) Sorry – what – ?

ALI: He say when you *go*?

MARLOW: What?

ALI: Go! When you go out!

MARLOW: For Christ's sake, Ali –

ALI: Out! Out of this bloody place!

MARLOW: Where to, old mate? There's no place else to go – Besides, I *like* it here, Ali. I've made up my mind. I'm going to stay. I'm never going to leave.

Ali flaps his hand in disgust, and pulls on his radio headphones, from the wall attachment.

ALI: Shut up, shut up.

MARLOW: You've forgotten what it's like out there. Ali. In the real world. Listen, Ali. Listen to me. It's not safe out there.

But Ali taps on his headphones.

ALI: It's good!

MARLOW: They chew each other up out there. Ach! Ali? Give me one of my cigarettes. There's a pal.

But the (unheard) headphone music is now absorbing all of Ali's attention. He settles back on his pillows contentedly.

(*Again*) Ali!

No response. Pause.

(*Again, gloomily*) I could do with a cigarette. There is
nothing I can think of which I want more. (*Shout*) Ali!
(*Gloomily*) A smoke. A length of ash slowly building. Oh,
tube of delight. Blessed nicotine. (*Blows out air.*) Hot. Why
is it so hot in here? (*Mimics*) 'Gawd. You're *dripping*. That
shows a passionate nature, sugar.' (*Tiny pause.*) Her
glittering comma sidelong glance is –

Greenish letters blip-blip on the word processor's screen –
sidelong glance is very cold suddenly. He takes his hand off her
knee.

And at Skinscape's –
AMANDA: I'm not a tart. But a girl's got to live, ent she? Put a
    figure on it.
BINNEY: A round one?
He is sweating. He looks, sounds, anxious.
AMANDA: A round one what?
BINNEY: A nice round figure. Ten pounds.
AMANDA: Odd ones is better.
BINNEY: Sorry?
AMANDA: Fifteen, sugar.
BINNEY: This is a very expensive evening.
AMANDA: I'm not being greedy. It's not for little me.
BINNEY: Who's it for, then? Your sick mother?
AMANDA: I thought you was a nice guy. I thought you were
    going to be nice. I'm used to pigs at the trough, but I
    thought *this* was something else –
BINNEY: All right. Fifteen. I hope you're worth it.
AMANDA: (*Firmly*) I'm good. I'm very very wizard. It's about
    the only thing I *am* good at. Bed. (*Suddenly*) Mark. This is
    my friend Sonia.
Exactly as though she has not said this before. Sonia has
suddenly arrived, bearing more champagne on the silver tray.
SONIA: Hello.
She keeps her steady, sad gaze on Binney. He half groans, takes
out three pound notes this time.
BINNEY: I hope I'm – let's hope I get –
He stops. He has noticed something. It is one of the two

31

mysterious men, standing against the wall, arms folded, staring at him.

AMANDA: That you're going to get something back. That's what you were going to say.

Binney forces himself to attend.

BINNEY: Well. You know what I mean.

AMANDA: We're not allowed to leave with the customers. Are we, Sonia?

SONIA: No.

AMANDA: Sonia don't talk much, do she?

BINNEY: Why should she?

But he looks at her. She seems to nod to him, with meaning. He frowns.

AMANDA: She comes from Russia. She's only been here six or seven months.

BINNEY: (*Too intent*) Oh? Really? From where? Where in Russia, Sonia?

SONIA: Leningrad.

Binney is now looking hard at her. He speaks Russian, as though to test her out.

BINNEY: Nelzya v dooshe nye soglasitaya shto Lyeneengrad ochen prekrasnee gorod – da?

SONIA: Vui govoritye po rooski – ?

BINNEY: Mnye oocheelos rooskomoo yazikoo mnogo lyet tamoo-nazad

AMANDA: Here. What you jabbering?

But she seems to exchange a covert look with Sonia, and the tiniest of nods. Everything seems too full of significance, but puzzlingly so.

SONIA: (*To* BINNEY) Your Russian is – it is not bad. Not good.

BINNEY: Well, it's a long time since I had chance to use it.

SONIA: You *are* allowed to order champagne for Sonia too, you know. They let you do that.

BINNEY: (*Faint edge*) They?

SONIA: (*Heavy accent*) I get commission.

BINNEY: And what do I get?

Sonia leans in, and kisses Binney, erotically, lingeringly, then pulls back and looks at him.

SONIA: Guess.

32

Ronnie Ronalde (on record) begins whistling 'Bird Song at Eventide'.

In the ward, Ali is raptly listening to the record on his radio headphones, the whistling very loud. Ali's lips purse in silent imitation of Ronalde's accomplished and yet, now, to us, comical whistling.

Marlow watches Ali with a puzzled irritation, as we – but not he – continue to hear the headphone imitations and then –

Marlow swiftly turns his head a little – all that can be managed – to face us, exactly as, on record – the cuckoo sounds.

The picture fades. Then –

Night-time in the ward again. A cough here, snore there, deep sigh or mumble elsewhere. Then – plaintively, and not loud enough.

MR HALL: Nurse – !

The night nurse, a very large woman, is deeply asleep on her folded arms under the dim little table lamp.

Finding Marlow, wide awake, unhappily brooding, a gleam of troubled eyes.

CONSULTANT: (*Voice over*) Do you wish to see the Padre? Would that help at all?

REGISTRAR: (*Voice over*) Or a psychiatrist perhaps.

Pause. Snores, grunts, sighs. Then a strangled, desperate little cry.

MR HALL: Nurse – !

Marlow tries to turn his head, and half manages it, to look at the sleeping night nurse.

MARLOW: (*Voice over, whisper*) The captain is asleep. We are drifting off unanchored into the dark. We are lost. All of us. Lost. (*Pause. Mutters out loud*) Rubbish. Stop it. Bloody rubbish. Stop it, stop it.

Pause.

MR HALL: Please! Nurse!

But the night nurse does not stir. Mr Hall, pathologically timid despite the frequent blustering, seems to be in desperate need. It follows that if he manages to wake the nurse at the other end of the ward from his bed, he will also wake some of the sleepers.

(*Softly to himself*) Please. Oh, please wake up. Please. (*His tone changes.*) You big fat dopey bitch. You stupid great cow. I shall mess myself. I – oh God, God. (*Very loud*) Nurse! (*Softly again*) Oh, wake up. Please wake up. There's a darling, there's a love – (*Near sob*) You sodding bitch. You cow. Fat cow. (*Very loud*) Nurse!

So loud that he clasps his hand to his mouth in alarm. In delayed reaction, the big night nurse wakes with a start, peers ill-temperedly into the gloom, and then, with a yawning ill grace, she gathers up her torch and lumbers heavily around the ward. The flickering oval of light flashes briefly across each sleeping face. As it slides on to Marlow he quickly closes his eyes.

(*Hoarse, agitated whisper*) Here. Over here. Here.

The enormous nurse, heavily arriving, shines the beam full on Mr Hall.

NIGHT NURSE: Go to sleep!

MR HALL: (*Whisper*) Bedpan, nurse. Sorry. I need the bedpan.

NIGHT NURSE: Can't you get it yourself?

MR HALL: (*Almost in tears*) I'm not – I mustn't get out of bed – cardiac – oh, please, I need it, the contraption – I need it so badly –

NIGHT NURSE: You got something wrong with your heart?

She says it like someone hearing an unlikely tale.

MR HALL: (*Yelp*) Yes!

ASSORTED VOICES: Shut up – ! Be quiet, willya – ?

NIGHT NURSE: Shh! Shh! You want to wake everybody up?

MR HALL: (*Near sob*) The bedpan!

REGINALD: (*Waking*) Wha – ? Wassamatter – ?

ANOTHER VOICE: Go to sleep for Chrissake!

NIGHT NURSE: See what you done? You woke them up. You woke them all up! I'll get it for you. You only had to ask! No need to make all this noise!

MR HALL: (*Whimper*) Sorry, nurse, but I –

But she is padding heavily away, excessively disgruntled.

REGINALD: (*Bleary*) What the hell's going on – ? Mr Hall?

MR HALL: You. It's you, my boy.

REGINALD: What?

A VOICE: Shut up over there!

Mr Hall leans across to whisper, nastily.

MR HALL: You've been grinding your teeth, Reginald. In your
    sleep.

REGINALD: What?

MR HALL: You woke everybody up. Grinding your teeth. Like
    rocks being rubbed together.

REGINALD: What – ?

MR HALL: Why don't you move your bed? If that's all you can
    say. (*Makes a gasp of pain, clutching at his stomach.*) The –
    ooh, Christ, hurry up – The night nurse is very angry with
    you – And I'll tell you something, Reginald. She's not one
    to make angry. By God, she's not. She's off her rocker for
    one thing. I – (*Gasp*) – I tell you, she's completely round
    the bend. You've only got to look at her eyes to see that –

But there are renewed snoring sounds from Reginald's bed. Mr
Hall has to stop in any case, to clutch at his stomach again.
Then –

    Reginald? (*Plaintive pause.*) You're no sort of company.
    Night nor day. I might as well be in the middle of the
    desert. (*Gasp, then*) Everybody needs somebody to talk to.

A VOICE: (*Loudly*) Shut up! You old fart!

Hours have passed, perhaps indicated on the dimly lit ward
clock, and the large night nurse dozes again, though not so
deeply as before. All is apparently calm, except for the whistles,
grunts and snarls of the regular snorers. Including Mr Hall this
time.

    But slowly find and settle on Marlow. He is still wide awake,
brooding in the half-light, eyes gleaming. The voice overs come
now with an added, more menacing resonance –

CONSULTANT: (*Voice over, resonant*) Do you wish to see the
    Padre? Would that help at all?

REGISTRAR: (*Voice over, resonant*) Or a psychiatrist, perhaps?
Pause.

MARLOW: (*To himself*) Perhaps.

Then suddenly, Noddy – more politely, Mr Tomkey – is
clambering, all skin and bone and obscure, head-nodding
mutters, into Marlow's bed.

NODDY: Mabel.

35

MARLOW: (*Astonished*) What you – Hey! – What are you
    doing – ?
Noddy is now somehow or other in the bed, eyes rolling, mouth
drooling, and his arms trying to enfold Marlow – and so hurting
him, of course.
NODDY: Where you where you been – Eh? Eh? Mabel – ?
MARLOW: Off! Get off! – Ooch! Oof! Stop it you silly old –(*Yell*)
    Nurse! Nurse!
Noddy, drooling 'Mabel!', is on top of Marlow now, muffling
Marlow's cries of pain and his shouts for the nurse. There is
now so much noise from Marlow's bed that the night nurse and
most of the patients awaken.
    Ali, sitting up with a start, sees the odd, grotesquely tumbling
shape in the half-dark and cannot at first make out what is
happening. And then, when he does, the 'Mabels' and the cries
continuing, he clicks on his lamp, eyes popping –
ALI: (*Exploding*) Hoo! Hoo! Hoo–oo!
The night nurse charges heavily down the ward.
NIGHT NURSE: Hey! What's going on! None of that! None of
    that – !
MARLOW: (*In great pain*) Ow! Oooh! Get off – off!
NODDY: Bloody bed.
ALI: Hee Hee Hee Hoo!
NIGHT NURSE: (*Shrill*) You can't do that in here! Stay in your
    own beds! Oh, you naughty boys!
Bedlamp after bedlamp is coming on, and the night nurse
belatedly realizes what is actually happening. Instead of helping
the distressed Marlow, she dissolves into quivering laughter.
Many of the other patients also begin to hoot and cackle.
REGINALD: (*Calls*) You dirty old devil – !
MARLOW: Help! Help me – !
In a desperate effort to settle more comfortably, Noddy rolls off
the helpless Marlow, bump!, on to floor. He gapes up at the
quivering nurse in total, bewildered indignation, his head still
nod–nod–nodding.
NODDY: Bloody – bloody beds – !

On the word processor's screen, the greenish letters blip-blip.
    Binney was like a railway station sandwich. He was playing

36

both ends against the middle. And the middle was one hell of a mess –

In the dark street beyond Skinscape's, Binney, overcoated but cold, waits. He beats his arms, and stamps his feet, as –

MARLOW: (*Voice over, side-of-mouth style*) It was cold waiting for Amanda to come out. The air was like an Eskimo's mother-in-law, bitter and icy. But not as icy as the double-crossing heartbeat under his cashmere coat. He intended to warm himself on her overpriced flesh . . . Work and pleasure, and a kiss before dying.

Click-clack of high heels, and Amanda and Sonia approach, in fur coats.

(*Voice over*) Binney stared. He did not expect to see the two of them together. What was cooking?

AMANDA: (*Nearing*) Aintcha got a taxi, honey?

BINNEY: None around. It *is* half-past three in the morning.

AMANDA: Oh, there'll be one. There's always a taxi. My momma done told me.

And almost as though summoned by her, a taxi comes along.

BINNEY: I see. A magician, are you?

AMANDA: A wizard. I told you.

Binney, waving down the cab, looks at silent Sonia.

BINNEY: Are you – ah – ?

AMANDA: (*Quickly*) You don't mind if we give my friend a lift, do you?

BINNEY: (*Frown*) Well –

TAXI DRIVER: Yeah? Where to, guv?

BINNEY: We'll drop you first, Sonia.

It sounds like an instruction, curtly delivered.

In his hospital bed, Marlow ponders.

MARLOW: (*Voice over*) He wondered whether Amanda was as dumb as she sounded. You never could tell what a dame was up to when she flapped her eyelashes like a –

His thoughts cut out abruptly as the registrar pulls up a chair to sit close to Marlow's bed, leaning in almost conspiratorially.

REGISTRAR: Good afternoon, Mr Marlow. How are we today?

MARLOW: I'm not very happy. I don't know about *him*.

REGISTRAR: Sorry?

MARLOW: Or perhaps you mean *you*?

REGISTRAR: I don't follow –

MARLOW: (*Sigh*) You said 'How are *we* today?' We. I wondered who the other or others –

REGISTRAR: Come, come. A manner of speaking.

MARLOW: And a very tedious one, too.

A little pause. The registrar examines him, not without sympathy. Marlow looks a terrible mess – and worn out as well.

REGISTRAR: Not feeling too great? Well. That's not very surprising, is it? You're going through a tough time at the moment.

MARLOW: Look. I'm impressed with your astonishing powers of deduction, which surpass even those of the great Holmes himself –

REGISTRAR: (*Mildly*) Now, now.

MARLOW: But I am *trying* to do some work –

REGISTRAR: Work? What do you mean?

MARLOW: Are you one of the great majority who thinks that writing is not work?

REGISTRAR: No. Of course not –

MARLOW: (*Severely*) And do you by any chance labour under the delusion that it consists solely and entirely of the act of actually putting words on a page? Without thought? Without planning? As though I were a *Sunday Times* journalist, or something?

REGISTRAR: Ah. I see what you mean.

MARLOW: *Do* you, now?

Pause. The registrar shifts a little under the obvious hostility, but tries again, an essentially kindly man.

REGISTRAR: It must be hellishly ticklish to work out a plot in a detective story, I should think. I suppose you have to scatter clues all over the place.

MARLOW: Yeh. Like throwing grit to the hens.

REGISTRAR: I'd like to read one of your – ah – books if –

MARLOW: (*Bleak*) Out of print. All of them. And why not, say I, why not? The hens wouldn't lay and the cock wouldn't crow.

REGISTRAR: I see.

Pause.

MARLOW: (*Gritting his teeth*) For Christ's sake. For Christ's sake.

Awkward little pause.

REGISTRAR: (*Gently*) Mr Marlow. Do you think you have the right attitude towards your illness?

MARLOW: Do *you*? That's the really interesting question. *Your* attitude.

REGISTRAR: Partly, yes. But you should also consider your own –

MARLOW: (*Interrupting*) Will I ever be free of it?

REGISTRAR: Well, now, that's something we –

MARLOW: (*Cutting in*) Will I ever be able to move properly? Will I ever be able to hold a pen again? Tell me that. Come on. Tell me! Never mind the blather. I can get that from a doctor, doctor.

REGISTRAR: You ask those questions as though someone else was responsible for your condition. But no one is or, at least, in the unlikely event that someone, anyone, is – then that someone cannot be anyone other than yourself. Can it?

Silence. Marlow glares. But the registrar waits.

MARLOW: (*Eventually, reluctantly*) What do you mean? What are you talking about? It's not *your* job to be cryptic.

REGISTRAR: I have occasionally seen patients who are just as bad and sometimes worse than you are. But I think it would be fair to say that none of them react to their condition in quite the way *you* do. With such – aggression, or such –

MARLOW: (*Interrupting*) What do they do? Sing madrigals?

REGISTRAR: Well – they don't rail against the world and all that is in it. They don't behave as though they have fallen into a sewer.

Silence. Then –

MARLOW: Are you trying to say I should take the tranquillizers? Or is it a deodorant you have in mind?

The registrar smiles, and then frowns as Marlow glares.

REGISTRAR: I think you should take them. The tranquillizers. For a little while . . .

MARLOW: No! I won't!

REGISTRAR: That's entirely up to you, of course. Nobody's

going to ram them down your throat. But – where are you
going to find any equanimity?

MARLOW: Oh, I don't know. When you lot have finally turned
me into a potato, I suppose. You *do* mean, 'When are you
going to be a vegetable?', don't you? That's the only
equanimity that interests you fellows.

REGISTRAR: How long can you go on seeing things through a
blinding rage? Mr Marlow? What do you live by?

MARLOW: (*Hostile*) What?

REGISTRAR: I know it's always an embarrassing question. (*Little
smile.*) Even between husbands and wives. But – what do
you believe in?

A small, bristling pause.

MARLOW: Malthusianism.

REGISTRAR: (*Blink*) Come again?

MARLOW: Malthus, but mandatorily. Compulsory depopulation.
By infanticide, genocide, suicide, or whatever other means
suggest themselves. Aids, for example. That'll do. Why
should queers be so special?

REGISTRAR: (*Heavily*) I see.

MARLOW: I also believe in cholesterol, cigarettes, alcohol,
masturbation, carbon monoxide, the Arts Council, nuclear
weapons, the *Daily Telegraph*, and not properly labelling
fatal poisons. But most of all, above all else, I believe in the
one thing which can come out of people's mouths. Vomit.

Little pause.

REGISTRAR: (*Carefully*) I want you to think about what I'm
going to say. There's a very good man here, at the hospital,
very alert and – ah – and sympathetic. I'd like you to talk to
him.

MR HALL: (*Off*) Nurse! Please, nurse!

MARLOW: (*Suspiciously*) What do you mean? Alert and *what*?
What are you talking about? Who is he? He'll get himself
struck off.

REGISTRAR: A Doctor Gibbon.

MARLOW: Doctor of what? Skin? Joints? The Decline and Fall
of the Roman Empire? What's he got to be alert and
sympathetic about?

REGISTRAR: He's a – well, a psychotherapist. Very good man.

You'd get on well with him.

MARLOW: (*Violently*) Get stuffed!

The registrar stares. His face twitches. He goes to stand.

REGISTRAR: You are out of order. I will not be spoken to in this manner.

And yet he hesitates, and he looks at Marlow almost imploringly.

MARLOW: (*Measured insolence*) Then eff–you–see–kay off, sir.

The registrar nods, grim-faced, with a bleak dignity.

REGISTRAR: I will talk to you again. Good afternoon.

Without waiting for a reply, he goes. A moment. Then –

MARLOW: (*Quietly*) Good afternoon.

Pause. His distress is evident. Then –

ALI: Hey. Hey! Hey.

MARLOW: (*Eventually*) What do you want? How are things in Glocomora?

ALI: He say when you *go*?

MARLOW: God Almighty. Go where – Handsworth?

ALI: (*Yearningly*) Did he say *when*? Hey? Get out – Hey?

MARLOW: We're never going to get out of this place, Ali. This is our home on the range, old pal. Well, the hot plate, anyway.

ALI: (*Passionately*) Yes! Yes, we are! Yes, yes! Any bloody time now!

Silence. Marlow takes pity.

MARLOW: One day. We will one day. Arm in arm together, like Alcock and Brown. You can be Brown.

Silence.

ALI: We're never going to get out of this place. You are bloody right. Never!

He sounds so desperately melancholy that Marlow is stung.

MARLOW: Oh, yes we are! We'll break a poppadam together. We'll get out, Ali. I promise.

Silence – except for ward sounds.

ALI: (*Eventually*) Hey! Hey – !

MARLOW: Christ. What is it now? Call the Samaritans, willya?

ALI: You want a sweet?

MARLOW: How about sour? That's more my line.

ALI: You want sweet?

MARLOW: No, thank you. My jaws hurt. Thank you all the
same. Thank you very much, Ali. Some other time,
sweetheart.
ALI: (*Beam*) You have sweet. I have a lot of sweet and I have
sweet and we say up the arse, hey?
Ali pulls himself up to reach for a bag of boiled sweets on his
bed trolley.
MARLOW: (*More to himself*) Yeh. Up the arse.
But as Ali strains forward to get hold of the bag he has a cardiac
arrest. He falls back with a sudden, sharp noise, and his
clutching hand scatters the bag of sweets on to the floor between
his bed and Marlow's bed.
(*Startled*) Ali – ?
Then he realizes what has happened, and starts to shout.
Nurse! Nurse!
Others join in the call. Very quickly, running feet, and sudden,
violently dramatic action. Staff Nurse White, first into the ward,
looks at Ali –
STAFF NURSE WHITE: (*Yell*) Arrest! Arrest!
She puts her hand on his chest, and then delivers a very sharp
blow. The ward, so to speak, holds its breath as, within seconds,
the cardiac arrest team comes clattering into the ward, followed
almost immediately by the oxygen equipment, which plugs into
a wall socket. The curtains are partly drawn around Ali's bed by
a spare hand. A moment. Marlow holds his breath. Then all the
frenzy suddenly stops.
MALE NURSE: Time of death.
STAFF NURSE WHITE: Three – I mean, fifteen thirty-seven.
They complete the drawing of the curtains. And then most of
them troop out. The picture fades to blackness. Then –

Later on the same day, in the ward, there is a stripped and
empty bed where Ali had died. Nurse Mills and Staff Nurse
White arrive to make up the bed for a brand new patient.
Marlow is watching the activity, expressionless. Staff Nurse
White bends and picks up something from the floor between
Marlow's and what was Ali's bed.
STAFF NURSE WHITE: (*To* MARLOW) Oh, you *are* untidy!
MARLOW: Who is? What?

STAFF NURSE WHITE: Dropping your sweeties all over the
    place.
MARLOW: Oh, but they're not –
And then he stops, suddenly. Staff Nurse White dumps a scatter
of Ali's boiled sweets on to Marlow's trolley.
STAFF NURSE WHITE: Try and be more careful, shall we?
MARLOW: Thank you. Sorry.
Attractive Nurse Mills, plumping a pillow for the newly made
bed, gives him a sidelong look.
NURSE MILLS: Do you want me to unwrap one for you?
MARLOW: I'd rather have a cigarette. Please.
NURSE MILLS: Oh, no, I'm not giving you one of those –
STAFF NURSE WHITE: You shouldn't smoke. Especially in bed.
    I don't know why they allow it.
MARLOW: Yes, nurse. Quite right. Quite so. They might make
    me ill.
He falls broodingly silent. Nurse Mills seems affected by his
sadness. She keeps looking at him as they finish making the
adjoining bed. Then – as the nurses turn to go –
NURSE MILLS: Have you been greased yet?
MARLOW: No.
STAFF NURSE WHITE: Oh, but you should have been! Why
    don't you speak up instead of telling us when we're busy?
MARLOW: Did I tell you? Did I say anything? (*To himself*) Jesus
    Christ on a bike.
NURSE MILLS: It's all right, staff nurse. I'll do it before I go off.
Staff Nurse White is already on her way out. Nurse Mills looks
at Marlow.
    (*Again*) It makes you a bit more comfortable, doesn't it?
    Eventually?
Marlow seems to make an effort.
MARLOW: I – All right. I will have a sweet, nurse. Thank you.
She unwraps one of Ali's sweets, looking at him.
NURSE MILLS: What's the matter?
MARLOW: Nothing.
She pops the sweet into his mouth. But as he takes it, the tears
spring to his eyes.
NURSE MILLS: What is it? Do you want something for the
    pain – ?

43

Marlow, choking with grief, stiffly shakes his head.

MARLOW: Very – nice – these sweets. Very – nice indeed –

The tears splash on to his blotched cheeks as he openly cries, as defenceless as a child. Nurse Mills goes to see him, then stops, leaving him be, and, from the outside, draws shut the curtains around his bed. Alone with his misery, Marlow rolls the sweet in his mouth. The Casa Loma Band's version of 'After You've Gone' begins to swell, taking us –

Gliding along the rolling treetops of the Forest to the bounce of the Casa Loma Band.

Peeping out of the foliage of the tall oak, high in the cleft of the topmost branches, the small boy Philip stares out at us. The music dips to allow –

REGISTRAR: (*Voice over*) It must be hellishly ticklish to work out a plot in a detective story, I should think. I suppose you have to scatter clues all over the place.

2

The Thames at Hammersmith slip-slaps and glistens and blobs in the moonlight, and, in stages, the moon itself is half glimpsed, breaks up, and then is fully seen, floating mysteriously in the oily-black water. 'Limehouse Blues', in the Ambrose version, begins to be heard. The gilded bridge is empty and silvered a little in the moonlight. 'Limehouse Blues' now beating out strongly, insistent, raggedly urgent.

Unexpectedly, there *is* someone on the bridge after all. The Singing Detective, in his 1945 garb, is on the pedestrian walk, a hand on the wooden-topped rail, looking at the slow, dark river, and smoking a cigarette.

The music dips under, and he is talking straight at us, in his best, sardonic, 'Side-of-the-mouth' delivery –

MARLOW: The thing about the moon is, it gives you the creeps with a capital K. Am I not right? (*Drags in smoke, blows it out.*) It makes dirty water look like silver, turns flotsam into the crown jewels, and causes poor slobs in the cuckoo-house to think they are Jesus Christ or F. W. Woolworth. Am I right?

He sucks in smoke as though it were oxygen, then throws the cigarette in a glowing little arc into the water. And shivers.

Also, it's cold. The sort of dead of night when lonesome cats cry for empty hours on the broken slates.

He turns, and looks across to the riverside Mall beyond the bridge. It is empty, eerily shadowed and silvered. The music fades out under the voice over.

(*Voice over*) But tonight there isn't a pussy in sight. Not even a four-legged one. All good people have gone home. And some bad ones, too –

In a second floor room of a spacious house which overlooks the river, Binney, stooping, is putting a match to a 1940s gas fire.

BINNEY: This is the sort of night to freeze a pawnbroker's balls.

But it'll soon get warm in here. That's the thing about gas.

He looks across the mustily expensive room at – Sonia. She is

still wearing her fur coat, her hand to the collar at her throat, a
glitter in her eyes, steadily staring back at him.

> I hate the cold. I hate it as much as I hate plots and
> schemes and mysteries. (*Looks at her.*) I didn't think it was
> going to be *you* coming back with me.

He waits for her to speak, or to smile. She shows no sign of
doing either.

> What's going on, eh? (*Contemplates her.*) Mind you. I'm not
> complaining. Amanda's very pretty, but she's as thick as
> shit in the neck of a bottle. You're just as pretty, Sonia.
> You don't talk though, do you? What you trying to be? The
> Snow Queen?

During which, he has advanced upon her, a hard look in his
eyes. He touches her face. She does not move.

> Be the Snow Queen if you like. Pretend you don't know
> anything about anything. I'll find out whether you do or
> not. There's a cupboard at that club with room for more
> than one, Sonia.

He takes his fingers from her face, and then, suddenly, smears
her lipstick with the ball of his thumb, harshly. Amazingly, she
does not react.

> Maybe you're just one of the whores. Maybe. (*Looks, waits,
> moistens his lips.*) Take your clothes off.

Suddenly, in her first movement, her first words, she thrusts out
her hand, palm up, her eyes blazing.

SONIA: *Giff!*

He looks at her, and then laughs.

BINNEY: Maybe you *are*, at that.

SONIA: *Mon–ey.*

BINNEY: You don't have to be quite so bloody Russian, do you?
   Can't you ask with a touch more *grace* – ?

SONIA: *Mon–ey.*

BINNEY: (*Seemingly delighted*) Oh, you bitch. Oh, you greedy,
   suspicious, great big beautiful bitch.
   Da, da, moya luiboff. Konyechno.

SONIA: *Spasseebo.*

BINNEY: My arrangement was with Amanda. I thought it was
   Amanda who was going to warm my lonely little bed. We
   agreed on a price –

46

SONIA: Fifteen pounds.

BINNEY: Oh, no. No, no. Listen, you little tart. It takes a
shopworker a *month* to earn that sort of money. Ten. I
agreed ten. And think yourself lucky.

SONIA: Fifteen pounds.

BINNEY: I see. Very polite, aren't we? Ask me nicely. Go on.
Nicely.

She stares back at him, expressionless. But her eyes are
glittering. The thought occurs that she might be a little crazed.
Binney, a wholly nasty creature, suddenly slaps her face, in a
way that shows he finds it exciting.

Please. Say *please* to Daddy.

But she does not move, does not speak. And then, calmly, holds
out her hand again.

(*Sigh*) I see. It's Stalingrad all over, is it?

But he smacks three big white £5 notes one by one into her
outstretched palm, jeeringly.

One for my baby. Two for my love. Three to come again.

She closes her hand over the money. Her eyes flash.

SONIA: Is shit.

BINNEY: (*Startled*) What – ?

SONIA: Is shit. Mon–ey is.

And then, to his horrified incredulity, she starts to tear up the
three big white banknotes she is holding.

BINNEY: Christ – ! What are you – No! Stop it!

He grabs at her wrists, but she pulls them free.

SONIA: Is shit.

And she laughs, too high, too oddly, making him step back, his
eyes widening in consternation.

BINNEY: You're crazy. You're – Anybody who treats money
like that is round the – (*Then, in a surge of anger*) You
stupid bitch! I've a good mind to stuff it down your throat
and make you choke on it – !

But he stops, for she suddenly stuffs some of the torn pieces into
her mouth – enough to make her cheeks bulge. And chews.

(*Awed*) Are you off your head – ? Are you totally insane – ?

In answer, she opens her fur coat. She has only underwear on
beneath the coat: of the flimsiest, frilliest, most alluring kind.

SONIA: (*Mouth full*) Mon–ey.

47

And she spits out the pulped, chewed banknotes on to his shoes as he advances on her.

BINNEY: (*Hiss*) What are you trying to do? Make me feel small?

A ragged 'Limehouse Blues' takes us back into –

A corridor in Marlow's hospital, stretching ahead of us as we move along it. A slightly odd, almost elasticated perspective, as the music bounces. A view from a trundling wheelchair.

In the chair, discover Marlow, still unsightly and ill, his eyes fixed on the corridor as it unwinds ahead of him, the chair being pushed by the same tall black porter as before.

PORTER: What you say?

There is no answer. The music fades.

What you say, man?

MARLOW: Where is it?

PORTER: What?

MARLOW: The nuthouse door.

PORTER: (*Laugh*) Here you is. You is right upon it, little
    squirrel.

He stops the chair, taps on the wide door marked DR GIBBON. The porter pushes Marlow's wheelchair right up to a table in the middle of a large room which looks as though it were once a substantial side ward. A big window behind the table shows a treetop. There is no one at the table.

Wait for the man. Right?

MARLOW: (*Subdued*) Right.

PORTER: The cuckoo man. Right?

MARLOW: (*Very subdued*) Right.

A disconcertingly shrill laugh from the porter, and then the sound of the door closing as he leaves.

Marlow, alone, swivels his eyes from side to side in his scorched and peeling flesh, trying to examine the room, but unable to turn his head very easily. He seems apprehensive. There are curtained-off, portable partitions in the room. But no sound is coming from within any of them. Traffic noises come from high windows at the far side of the room. Marlow concentrates on the treetop he can see.

(*Voice over*) Poor tree. Poor bloody tree. Fancy having to look into *this* pisshole all day long.

Puzzled, irritated, Marlow's eyes fall on the table in front of him. And there, to his dismay, among other papers, is a lurid cover for *The Singing Detective* by P. E. Marlow. Hunched stiffly in his chair, clearly riddled with pain, Marlow expels his breath in a hiss of hate.

(*Voice over*) Why? What *for* – ? Is this the British Museum? He is unaware of Dr Gibbon suddenly watching him, half in and half out of one of the curtained-off partitions. Gibbon, behind Marlow, where he cannot be seen, makes no move, no sound, and shows no wish to identify himself. Marlow stares at the paperback on the table, unable to reach it.

(*Voice over*) What's going on?

In an otherwise empty dance hall, a small band is running through its numbers. At the moment, 'Cruising down the River'. And the singer is an unafflicted Marlow.

As he 'sings', a door swings open at the far end of the dance hall, and Binney comes in. His eyes narrow. Looking at the band, listening, he edges forward, almost furtively, then stands with his back against the wall, seemingly unwilling to come any closer. Marlow stops singing, in mid-note.

That'll do, fellas. The words break my heart.
The band, trailing off, laughs.

There's a frog about to spawn in this old throat of mine.
Enough's enough. See you later. Keep your whistles dry.
Binney begins to edge forward again, too obviously imitating nervousness, as the band begin to put away their instruments.

BINNEY: (*Nervously*) Mr Marlow – ?

MARLOW: The one and only, pal. I was born that way. Are you the guy I've been waiting for ever since Sax stumbled upon the phone?

BINNEY: Sorry – ?

MARLOW: The gent with the fat contract, and piano keys when he *smiles*. The guy who just loves the way I croon.

BINNEY: I'm very sorry. But I'm afraid I'm not –

MARLOW: But you liked the song. Right? It made a spider crawl up your throat. Yes?

BINNEY: I – yes. Well. Sort of.

MARLOW: It's a tune for old ladies and puppy dogs. You agree?

BINNEY: (*Swallow*) Mr Marlow –

MARLOW: I know what it is. You weren't listening, were you? You didn't take it in, my friend. Other things syncopating, huh?

BINNEY: No. I – Sorry?

MARLOW: Yellow mellow curls at the edges. Breaks. Goes rotten.

BINNEY: (*Lost*) I'm sorry – I don't understand –

MARLOW: Trouble. You're in trouble.

BINNEY: I – (*swallow*) – sorry. Yes. I am.

MARLOW: Dead trouble.

BINNEY: I'm – look. I'm told that you can help me. If anyone can.

MARLOW: Who said so? Why'd you believe him?

BINNEY: John Bordington. My solicitor.

MARLOW: That over-inflated toad. If *he* recommended me, this must be a lulu. He hates my guts. I tend to agree with him. Does he still pick his teeth?

BINNEY: He said you got results.

MARLOW: I get the cases the polite guys pass over. I get the jobs the guys who don't sing don't get. I'm the piano tuner who's heavy on the pedal. OK. OK. So what's the story? Who's the dame?

BINNEY: How do you know there's a –

MARLOW: There's always a dame.

BINNEY: Yes.

MARLOW: Where's the body? There's always a body, too. I know that, you know that. And you're looking a trifle pale, pal. Like you been eating fried eggs and green bananas. Who's trying to swing *you* into this number? And are you as nervous as you seem?

Back in the room in the hospital, the real Marlow is being observed from behind by Gibbon as he sits hunched and still in his wheelchair in front of the table, a forlorn looking figure.

(*Voice over*) Yeh. I'm as nervous as I seem.

DR GIBBON: Yellow mellow curling at the edges. Breaks. Goes rotten.

Gibbon's voice comes from behind Marlow. Marlow cannot turn around, because of his arthritis, and a panic momentarily leaps

50

into his eyes, but is quickly extinguished.

MARLOW: (*Bitterly*) Oh. Very good. Very funny.

Gibbon, feet sounding on the boarded floor, comes up alongside, without a smile – and, indeed, looking oddly menacing.

DR GIBBON: I have a degree of fondness for easily disposable things. Kleenex tissues. Bic pens. Razor blades. Cheap literature.

MARLOW: Prescription forms. Don't forget prescription forms. And medical degrees.

DR GIBBON: He said out of the side of his mouth.

MARLOW: What?

Gibbon suddenly thrusts out a hand.

DR GIBBON: Gibbon. How do you do, Mr Marlow?

MARLOW: I can't shake.

DR GIBBON: Oh? No – of course not. Sorry.

MARLOW: I wouldn't anyway. I wouldn't if I could. I'm here under protest. This is tantamount to a kidnap.

Gibbon seems unduly pleased by this, nodding his head vigorously.

DR GIBBON: I see. I see. An abduction.

And he sits on rather than at the table, eyes bright, staring keenly at Marlow, legs not quite touching the floor.

MARLOW: (*Nastily*) Little men shouldn't sit in places where their shoes don't touch the floor. Don't you think? It kind of demeans them. Makes me think of nursery rhymes.

Gibbon keeps examining him, the twinkle not at all abated.

DR GIBBON: It must be very difficult for you.

MARLOW: More difficult for me than for you, that's for sure. *I* can't creep up on people like I'm in a Marx Brothers film. Where'd you learn that trick?

DR GIBBON: You don't want to talk to me. You don't want this.

MARLOW: Christ. What sharpness. What perception. I've underestimated you.

DR GIBBON: And yet you came. *Not* against your will.

Silence. Bright-eyed Gibbon twinkles at him, relentless. Then – Why? Why did you agree to be wheeled here?

MARLOW: Gets me out of the ward.

Gibbon cups his hand to his ear, pretending not to hear.

DR GIBBON: What's that?

MARLOW: I said it makes a change from the bedpan and sick old farts talking in their sleep. Lets me see The Warp and Woof of Life In All Its Rich Texture. You know – crap like that. Where the cuckoo drops its egg, know what I mean? Someone else's smelly little nest. Yours.

DR GIBBON: This is an act. This is desperate pastiche.

MARLOW: No. I don't like Italian food.

DR GIBBON: You can't keep it up.

MARLOW: Oh, little do you know!

Gibbon laughs. Then taps at the book on the table beside him.

DR GIBBON: I suppose you've noticed that I've gone to the trouble of obtaining a copy of one of your – ah – what do you call them? It's not a *novel* is it, properly speaking? Not what Lawrence would call the one bright book of Life – is it?

MARLOW: Quote me no quotes.

DR GIBBON: But you wouldn't call it a novel. Would you?

MARLOW: Of course not. It has *pages*, that's all. Where did you get it? The Lost Animal Shelter, I suppose. Not in a bookshop, that's certain. And what did you get it for? What casual little cruelty do you have in mind, doctor? Not *reading* it, I hope.

DR GIBBON: Clues.

MARLOW: What?

DR GIBBON: It's a detective story, isn't it? That's what you're supposed to find in a detective story. Am I not right? Or am I right?

MARLOW: (*Jeer*) Oh my Go–o–od. *You* can't do it!

DR GIBBON: I know the clues are supposed to point in the direction of the murderer. But what if they also reveal the *victim* a little more clearly?

MARLOW: Are you going to keep on like this? Is this what you think will start me off talking to you? Well, you're wrong. If you think you're being friendly or reassuring – Ah! I know! You think you're being *interesting*, don't you? You think you're being quite a character! Dear God! You're barking up the wrong trouser leg.

DR GIBBON: So I see.

Silence. Marlow twitches.

MARLOW: May I go back please? I am bored. I wish to be

returned to my bed. I want to go back to the ward. It's
vivid and exciting there.

DR GIBBON: Yes. It must almost seem like home to you. How
long have you been there now?

MARLOW: (*Reluctantly*) Ten, eleven weeks. Something like that.

DR GIBBON: Do you have visitors?

MARLOW: I don't want any. My day is too full.

DR GIBBON: How often have you been in hospital? How many
times?

MARLOW: You must have all this stuff. There's a great army of
you filling in cards, padding out files, poking, prying. Why
don't you look it up?

DR GIBBON: Tell me. How many times?

MARLOW: Thirteen, fourteen. I don't know.

DR GIBBON: Quite an old lag, then. Aren't you?

Silence. Gibbon fingers the paperback *The Singing Detective*, but
as though absent-mindedly.

Does your wife not visit you – or do you –

MARLOW: (*Quickly interrupting*) Not married.

DR GIBBON: – or do you stop her coming?

MARLOW: I'm not married.

DR GIBBON: Oh, but – (*Stops*) – Yes. I see.

Pause. Gibbon is looking too intently at Marlow – who suddenly
seems to snap.

MARLOW: Stop it! Stop staring at me! Put your little piggy eyes
somewhere else! You hear!

DR GIBBON: Now, now, now.

MARLOW: (*Violently*) Call for the porter! I want to go back to
the ward! I'm not talking to you. I'm not going to talk to
you!

Gibbon, taking no notice, taps the spine of the well-worn
paperback with his thumbnail.

DR GIBBON: You don't like women. Do you?

MARLOW: Which sort do you mean? Young ones. Old ones. Fat
ones. Thin ones. Faithful ones. Slags? Sluts? Try to be
more specific.

Gibbon permits himself a grim little smile.

DR GIBBON: All right. Let me rephrase that. I'm reasonably
sure that you think you *do* like them. That you even think

53

they are – well – capable of being idolized, or – You don't like *sex*. You probably think you do. I mean, we spend a great deal of time thinking about it, don't we?

MARLOW: (*Snarl*) *You* do. You dirty little sod.

DR GIBBON: (*Smile*) Yes. I do. But – listen to yourself – isn't it clear that you regard sexual intercourse with considerable distaste – or what is more to the point, with *fear*. Would you not regard that as a fair statement?

No answer. Comically, Marlow will not look at him.

Would you say that I was totally wide of the mark? Is it not the case that you regard sex with fear and distaste, even – loathing?

MARLOW: (*Jeer*) My God. Oh, my God. This is so–o–o sick.

Gibbon riffles through the paperback, then, finding the passage he wants, runs his thumb down the page.

DR GIBBON: Ah. Here, for example.

Marlow watches him as the prey watches the predator.

MARLOW: I can't believe this. I just *can't* believe this!

Gibbon looks at the page, then looks up, to meet Marlow's fearful gaze.

DR GIBBON: I will read you a passage. If I may.

MARLOW: (*Evenly*) I'd rather you shoved it up your arse.

Gibbon stares, then closes the book, stands, and walks away from the table, with a decisive manner, as though to go to the door and call for a porter. Marlow sits tense and still and even a little frightened as he realizes that Gibbon has not in fact gone to the door. Instead, the doctor is walking up and down, up and down, on the woodblock floor behind him. His feet are going click-clack-clock on the wood of the floor. Rather weirdly. And Marlow, who can only hear and not see him, is unable to turn. Click-clack-clock. Marlow visibly holds his breath.

Bring up music: the rather strange, edgy, harmonica, non-vocal version of 'Peg o' My Heart' by the Harmonicats.

In the Mall beyond Hammersmith Bridge, it is dead of night, with fleeting silver from glimpses of moon through low, moody, scudding cloud. And the strange, multi-harmonica beat of 'Peg o' My Heart' swelling –

And then two shapes, not much more than silhouettes: the

54

two mysterious men.

SECOND MYSTERIOUS MAN: (*Whisper*) You got the gun? You going to use the new silencer?

FIRST MYSTERIOUS MAN: (*Whisper*) Keep quiet.

SECOND MYSTERIOUS MAN: (*Whisper*) But are you? Eh?

FIRST MYSTERIOUS MAN: (*Whisper*) What do I want it for? What are my hands for? Eh? God gave me good hands, didn't he?

He flexes and unflexes his hands in the air. Silence. They look up at the one oblong of lighted window in the row of houses, enviously.

SECOND MYSTERIOUS MAN: (*Whisper*) Jig. Jig.

FIRST MYSTERIOUS MAN: (*Out loud*) Yeh. Jig bloody jig. And us stuck out here in the cold.

SECOND MYSTERIOUS MAN: (*Urgently*) Shhhhh!

In a bedroom in Binney's house, at an angle, from a wardrobe mirror, half-lit, Binney is glimpsed making love to Sonia, with much grunting. Her underwear is tangled on the floor, with her coat, and high-heeled shoes.

DR GIBBON: (*Voice over*) Would you say I was totally wide of the mark?

The real Marlow endures the click-clack-clock of Gibbon behind him, and then Gibbon's hands falling on the back of the wheelchair and Gibbon's face looming into view as he leans close in.

DR GIBBON: I don't wish to upset you, Mr Marlow.

He pulls back as Marlow flinches.

No. Let me be more precise. I do not wish to upset you *unnecessarily*. I think you *know* that you need help. And you're too intelligent or too aware of your own condition to deny it.

Marlow makes no attempt at a reply, but he is very tense. Gibbon comes around to the front of the chair, and once again perches sparrow-like on the edge of the table, arms folding, legs swaying, eyes twinkling.

Most chronic dermatological patients are on tranquillizers or antidepressants, you know. Almost as a matter of routine. The skin, after all, is extremely *personal*, is it not? The temptation is to believe that the ills and the poisons of the mind or the personality have somehow or other erupted straight out on to the skin. 'Unclean! Unclean!' you shout, ringing the bell, warning us to keep off, to keep clear. The leper in the Bible, yes? But that is nonsense, you know. *Do* you know? Well – one part of you does, I'm sure.

At no response –

You–can–be–helped! Moreover, Mr Marlow. Moreover. I think *I* can help.

Pause.

MARLOW: You can. Yes, you can. If you give me a couple of hundred barbiturates you can. Otherwise (*Mimics*) – 'Moreover, moreover' – Otherwise stop pissing into the wind. Stop listening to the sound of your own voice. Stop confusing wisdom with smugness. And send me back to my bed. 'Moreover.' Jeez – moreovovover –

DR GIBBON: I can't say I care too much for your manners, Mr Marlow.

MARLOW: (*Side-of-mouth*) Yeh. I've had complaints. Sorry about that. But I never went to Sunday School. You thank your stars I don't crack my knuckles into the bargain.

Gibbon smiles, jigs his folded arms, swings his little legs.

DR GIBBON: You didn't set out to mimic that sort of stuff, now did you?

MARLOW: What sort of stuff?

DR GIBBON: It not raining in the foothills sort of stuff. Down these mean streets sort of stuff.

MARLOW: (*Mock innocent*) *What* sort of stuff?

DR GIBBON: All right. All right. (*Mimics the style*) So you won't play ball –

MARLOW: I've heard that psychiatrists, psychotherapists or whathaveyou are very, very peculiar people – but, really, I find it almost impossible to understand a single word you say!

DR GIBBON: My contention is, now that I've read some of your prose –

MARLOW: Hah!

DR GIBBON: – my feeling is that you did not set out to write like that – What sort of things would you rather have written about?

MARLOW: If I had the talent, do you mean? Come on! Be a critic. You have the face for it.

DR GIBBON: If you like. If you had had the talent.

Pause. Marlow glares at him, hurt.

MARLOW: One-liners in Christmas crackers. Speeches for Mrs Thatcher. Obituaries. Or is that the same thing? Verses in birthday cards, captions for Prince Andrew. There's no telling what I could have done. It's all a matter of putting one word after another, that's all. That's where all the troubles of the world spring from. The next word. In case you hadn't noticed.

DR GIBBON: (*Quietly*) It won't be used in evidence, you know.

MARLOW: What won't?

DR GIBBON: You telling me what it was that you wanted to write.

MARLOW: Forget it. I have. Long ago.

DR GIBBON: Tell me.

Marlow stares. And then, all at once, mysteriously, some sort of hostility, some level of tension, seems to leave him.

MARLOW: I would have liked to have used my pen to praise a loving God and all his loving creation.

DR GIBBON: Really?

MARLOW: (*Gratingly*) *Moreover* – I would have liked to have seen hosts of radiant and translucent angels climbing along spinning shafts of golden light deeper and deeper into the blue caverns of heaven. Ho. Ho. But, then, I'll tell you something even more unlikely – I also wanted to play what used to be called inside right for Fulham and England –

DR GIBBON: Fulham? Why *Fulham*?

MARLOW: That's right. Be rude. I don't care. We're used to slander at Craven Cottage. Goals, no. That's something else.

Gibbon leans back, picks up the book again. Marlow instantly tenses.

DR GIBBON: I'm not very interested in football –

MARLOW: You should be. If you're really a psychiatrist. Because that's where all the nutters are nowadays. On the terraces. Except at Fulham, of course. That's where you go to be alone.

DR GIBBON: There's a paragraph here which sits rather oddly on the page. It doesn't seem to belong in a detective story – not in my opinion –

MARLOW: Oh, I see. Psychiatry is not nasty enough for you. You *still* want to get into literary criticism, do you, running down that slope, with swine to the left of you, swine to the right of you, grunt grunt.

DR GIBBON: Listen to this. A purple passage.

MARLOW: No. A blue one, I hope.

DR GIBBON: (*Reads*) 'Mouth sucking wet and slack at mouth, tongue chafing against tongue, limb thrusting upon limb, skin rubbing at skin – '

MARLOW: Oink. Oink.

DR GIBBON: ' – Faces contort and stretch into a helpless leer, organs spurt out smelly stains and sticky betrayals. This is the sweaty farce out of which we are brought into being – '

MARLOW: (*Savagely*) Oink! Oink! Oink!

DR GIBBON: ' – We are implicated without choice in the slippery catastrophe of the copulations which splatter us into existence – '

He half waits for another jeering 'Oink!' but it does not come. Without looking up, he continues to read –

'We are spat out of fevered loins. We are the by-blows of grunts and pantings in a rumpled and creaking bed. Welcome.'

He closes the book, looks at Marlow, questioningly.

MARLOW: (*Jeer*) Yeh. The Milk of Paradise.

Binney rolls off Sonia, face gleaming with sweat, panting, and stares up at the ceiling. A moment, then –

BINNEY: Good. Now we can talk.

Sonia lies still and expressionless, the sheet around her, eyes fixed on Binney. Binney, in his socks and underpants, standing away from the bed is getting a cigar from a humidor. He lights it.

(*Puff.*) What was it Kipling said about women and cigars – ? Never mind. How would *you* know. (*Looks at her, contemplatively.*) *What* do you know? Mmmmm? How much do you know?

She doesn't answer, doesn't move. His expression hardens. He advances upon her, puffing on the cigar, then takes it from his mouth.

You see this? It can make a very unpleasant burn. And you have such nice skin, Sonia. Porcelain. Do you by any chance know the origins of the word 'porcelain'? No. I suppose not. (*Stares at the silent girl.*) Doesn't it disgust you, what you do? Being paid to stretch yourself out, and let a stranger enter you? They must have trained you well, the NKVD. Do you think I don't know who you work for?

She still does not answer, her melancholy eyes fixed on him. He stares, then lowers his eyes, and turns away, his face twitching.

This is the dead time, isn't it? Dead time in a dead city. You can feel Nothingness pressing down on you. Pressing down on the whole dirty place.

There is a sudden gleam of disdainful amusement in her eyes, but still she says nothing. By contrast, his whole mood and manner seem to have changed. He flicks aside the curtain, to look out, talking more to himself than to her.

It looks cold out there. The river looks as though it's made of tar, sludging along. Full of filth. (*Then, suddenly*) Who's that out there? There's two men out – who are they? Are they the same as – ? There are two men out there looking at this house!

SONIA: (*Intense*) Are you sure?

Holding the curtain just a little aside, Binney stares down.

BINNEY: If those are the same two who were at the – (*Sucks in his breath.*) It's half-past four in the morning. They can't be there by accident. They must be up to –

He drops the curtain, agitated, and turns to see that Sonia is dressing, in a frantic hurry.

SONIA: Is there back way?

BINNEY: What – ?

SONIA: Another way *out*?

BINNEY: (*Angry*) I *knew* you weren't just one of the girls – Who are they? Sonia! What do they want?

She has thrown on her fur coat, eyes wild. He grabs at her arms, no less scared himself.

59

SONIA: Way out. Quick. Quick.
BINNEY: Are they after you, or are they after me?
SONIA: Let go!
BINNEY: Who are they!
SONIA: (*Struggling*) Let me go!
BINNEY: You're not going anywhere until you – Ooch!
This because, with a crisply precise nod of her head she cracks him full in the face with her forehead, forcing him to let go of her arms. He spins away, his nose spurting blood, yelping out with the pain as she hurtles out of the room.

Binney is telling Marlow the tale in the empty, daytime dance hall.

> – and my nose started to bleed. I wasn't – ah – well, I wasn't fully dressed, you see. I couldn't go after her. I think she must have been not quite right in the head, you know?

MARLOW: Who is?
BINNEY: Yes. Well. There you are. Who is? Who, indeed.
MARLOW: Why should she butt you like that? What did she *say*?
BINNEY: She was too frightened to speak. She kind of gabbled something in Russian as she ran out of the room, but –
MARLOW: (*Cutting in*) Where'd you pick up that lingo?
Binney hesitates, too obviously. Marlow registers it.
BINNEY: The Army. Intelligence Corps. I was one of the team who interviewed Red Army soldiers who got tangled up with us at the end of the war.
MARLOW: You're not in the Army now.
BINNEY: No. I – no.
MARLOW: So six months ago you were interviewing the comrades. And then a Russian girl goes missing after having just called at your house. Question. Did this dame know something about you? Is that it?
BINNEY: I don't know.
MARLOW: You're holding out on me. Don't waste my time.
BINNEY: I don't know. Really don't. The point I'm trying to – Mr Marlow. I swear before God that she left my –
MARLOW: (*Cutting in*) Swear before something you *believe* in, good buddy.

BINNEY: I swear on my mother's grave that Sonia left my place
 alive and unharmed.
MARLOW: So who says different?
BINNEY: (*Apparently scared*) I think I'm going to be arrested.
 The Police. They're at me all the time. They've told me not
 to leave town. There's a man watching me. They're – they
 say that the girl has vanished, but I can tell that they think
 she is dead. They don't seem to believe me about there
 being two men outside the house that night. In fact, my
 telling them that has made them even more suspicious of
 me. It seems the girl never went back to her flat –
MARLOW: And where's that?
BINNEY: Queensway, apparently. She lives with Amanda, if
 that's her name.
MARLOW: Who's she?
BINNEY: The girl in the nightclub.
MARLOW: Another whore?
BINNEY: I – yes. If you want to put it like that, yes, she –
MARLOW: How else would you put it?
BINNEY: Well. I don't think I'm all that interested in calling
 them names, or –
Marlow snaps back at him, firmly in the tradition of the mid-
Atlantic, snap-brimmed, honest but tough private eye.
MARLOW: Dogshit by any other name smells just as foul, my
 friend. And it still sticks to the bottom of your shoe no
 matter what you call it. Be as mealy-mouthed as you like,
 but not around *me*, OK? You've stepped in something
 nasty, and you want me to clean it up. Isn't that right? I'm
 the scoop. I'm the brush and the shovel.
BINNEY: What I want is someone to find that girl, or the
 men who were outside the house, or to prove that nothing
 nasty happened to her from *my* hands when she was with
 me –
MARLOW: But it did.
BINNEY: What?
MARLOW: Something nasty *did* happen to her at your hands.
BINNEY: (*Hotly*) I'm telling the truth, Mr Marlow!
MARLOW: I didn't say you weren't, Binney.
BINNEY: Then I don't –

MARLOW: All I said was something nasty did happen to her when she was with you. Wouldn't that be the way her mother would see it?

BINNEY: (*Snort*) Her *mother* – for God's sake –

MARLOW: You just swore on your own mother's grave, Mr Binney.

Binney gives him what used to be called 'an old-fashioned look'.

BINNEY: Mr Marlow. Aren't you being unduly censorious for this day and age?

MARLOW: What's the day? What's the age?

BINNEY: Money is not particularly one of my problems, and I'll pay you well –

MARLOW: I haven't told you what I want yet. I'm not as cheap as I look.

BINNEY: I'll pay you whatever you ask. My good name is important to me. But I'm not paying you to make me feel small, am I?

MARLOW: Oh, you don't have to do that. That's thrown in without charge.

BINNEY: I don't see why I should pay for cant or for humbug, do you? Why are you so bloody rude!

Marlow fixes him with his hard-eyed stare.

MARLOW: You'll pay me when I get results. You don't have to like me, and I don't have to like you. Maybe the cops are fixing to put a rope around that stiff neck of yours, and maybe you deserve it. And maybe you're playing some deeper game. We'll find out.

BINNEY: Mr Marlow –

MARLOW: You'll pay me – and you'll pay me double for the cant and humbug, Mr Binney. Part of the service. Take it or leave it. And let me know. I can't wait for the mail. Not in this day and age.

In the ward, the same porter lifts Marlow very tenderly out of the wheelchair, and lays him on the bed. Marlow is not quite able to stifle a cry of pain.

PORTER: Hey, man. That's bad. You got it bad.

MARLOW: (*Gasp*) Thank you. Thank you very much.

PORTER: What bring this on? What you do?

MARLOW: Camay.

PORTER: What?

MARLOW: That perfume. Worth a few guineas an ounce.
Camay.

The porter stares. Then roars with laughter.

PORTER: I tell you something. I tell you something for free.

MARLOW: That's right. Be like the Health Service used to be.

PORTER: (*Very earnest*) No. Listen. This is news. This is real
important news. *Don't eat tomatoes.* You read me?

MARLOW: (*Wearily*) I hears you.

PORTER: You try it. You see. No—o—o tomatoes. I'm telling you.

MARLOW: Yeh. I'll try.

PORTER: They don't be telling you that sort of good tiding here.
But *I'm* telling you. You ever shit?

MARLOW: What?

PORTER: You ever shit?

MARLOW: Occasionally.

PORTER: You look down at it after tomatoes. The pips. They
there, man . . . They ready to grow. The pips in your
poop.

MARLOW: Waste not, want not.

PORTER: Lay off them love apples. Tomatoes. That's the truth.
They nothing good. I'm telling you. You register?

MARLOW: Registered. Thank you.

PORTER: Be seeing you!

And he goes. Marlow stares up at the ceiling, with a pained and
exhausted resignation.

MARLOW: (*Eventually*) Tomatoes. Yes. Of course.

Time passes in the ward. Then –

A new patient is arriving, reluctantly, at what was Ali's bed
next to Marlow. He is a very worn and old East-Ender, George
Adams, being escorted by his wife. George looks much too weak
to walk, but that is what he is doing. His wife is toting 'his
things' in a couple of brown carrier bags. Sister Malone is with
them, as they pass by Marlow's bed.

GEORGE: Gawd. Somebody must have thrown boiling fat over
that one.

SISTER MALONE: Now, now, Mr Adams. We don't make those
sort of remarks about each other in *here*.

63

MRS ADAMS: Shut your mouth, George, and watch your ps and qs.

SISTER MALONE: This will be your bed –

MRS ADAMS: Nice clean sheets, George.

GEORGE: Yeh, but I'm not getting in it, am I? I'm not staying –

SISTER MALONE: Now, now, Mr Adams –

GEORGE: (*Gasp.*) Never bin ill in me life. And I'm not ill now. I'm not getting in that bed, and that's all there is to it. It's *my* life, ennit, not nobody else's –

SISTER MALONE: I'll just draw the curtains around your bed, Mr Adams. And then you undress in privacy.

GEORGE: In what?

MRS ADAMS: In your pyjamas, dad.

GEORGE: Pyjamas? Whatchamean – ? I'm not wearing bleed'n pyjamas, now am I? You're not getting them things on me, I'm telling you now! I'm not having it!

As she pulls the curtains around the bed, Sister Malone rolls her eyes complicitly at Marlow. But she fails to notice that he is in more than usual distress, sheened above his lesions with sweat, eyes hot, throat trying to swallow.

MARLOW: (*Voice over*) Hot. Hot. Why is it so hot?

The curtains are now closed off around the adjoining bed for the admission of George Adams.

MRS ADAMS: Come on, George. Stop it. No more messing about.

GEORGE: (*Behind curtains*) Can't bloody wait, can you?

MRS ADAMS: George!

GEORGE: Can't wait. Can't bloody wait. You'll be in the first carridge, won'tcha? You'll be right up behind the bleed'n 'earse, laughing your bleed'n 'ead off – !

Inside the curtained-off bed space, Mrs Adams, none too tenderly, is dragging at George's shirt, to pull it out of his trousers, and begin to get it off. He is so weak that she easily presses him down to a sitting position on the bed.

SISTER MALONE: (*Mildly alarmed*) Gently does it, Mrs Adams.

MRS ADAMS: Come on, George. Stop mucking about –

GEORGE: (*Protesting*) But I'll bloody 'aunt you, I will. I'll be back, mother. I'll be back!

At the next bed, unseen by them, Marlow's physical stress is growing. His temperature is zooming up out of control.

MARLOW: (*Faint croak*) Heat – the heat –

But the comedy continues from behind the drawn curtains at George's bed space, next to Marlow.

GEORGE: Christ, what's this then? What do you call this then? What sort of pillow is this? Put yer bloody 'ead on that and you'll suffocate – *Gitorff*! No! No, no, no – No!

MRS ADAMS: George! I'm warning you! George – if you don't stop – !

SISTER MALONE: Come along now, Mr Adams. There's no need for all this fuss –

GEORGE: Git off! You bloody old cow – leave me alone –

There is a sudden loud *smack!* from behind the curtains, as of a hand on flesh, very hard.

SISTER MALONE: (*Behind curtains*) Mrs Adams! – ! – What on earth – !

GEORGE: Oooo! You hard-hearted – *Oooo* you bitch! – That bleed'n '*urt* – ! (*Starts noisy weeping*.) Oooo you bitch oooo!

MRS ADAMS: (*Behind curtain*) 'Sthe only way, sister. Give him one. The only way to deal with him. I know. I've had it for long enough, years and years of it – Give him one! He's not strong enough to give you one back, not no more he ain't.

The sound of poor George's plaintive, child-like weeping comes from the adjoining, curtained-off bed space. But over Marlow's badly lacerated and disfigured face, the sound is mysteriously distorted and elongating. Marlow's eyes look hot and wild, and he no longer seems able to locate the source of the weeping, which, amplified, continues to distort. The weeping gets unnaturally loud.

At the same time – without losing the weeping sounds – fade up the over-resonant voice of Gibbon.

DR GIBBON: (*Voice over*) 'Mouth sucking wet and slack at mouth, tongue chafing against tongue, limb thrusting upon limb, skin rubbing at skin, skin, skin, *skin* – '

In the Forest, the small boy is climbing the special tree, his face contorting with effort, concentration, and perhaps a little fear as hand over hand, grappling, branch upon branch, he ascends higher and higher into the magnificent old oak.

(*Voice over*) ' – Faces contort and stretch into a helpless leer,

organs spurt out smelly stains and sticky betrayals. This is
the sweaty farce out of which we are brought into being.
We are implicated without choice in the slippery
catastrophe of the copulations which splatter us into
existence – '

The voice has been slowly fading, and now disappears. Birdsong
takes over, liquid, slightly amplified. And the soft, sea-like
Hush–u–shush–hh of a breeze stirring through the myriads of
summer leaves. Philip, the boy, has reached his treetop perch,
and is able to look out and around at the forest spreading in
every direction. There seem to be no other sights but the
undulating treetops, no other sounds but the trilling birds and
the wind in the branches. Philip's face is troubled. It is streaked
with recent tears.

PHILIP: (*Strong accent*) Our Father which art in Heaven
Hallowed be thy name Thy kingdom come Thy will be
done . . .

Music, quickly swelling, drowns his frightened, intense voice: it
is from a wireless set.

In a small room in a cottage in the village, there is one tiny sash
window, in the sill of which sits an accumulator-charged
wireless, loudly playing 'Don't Fence Me In'. Listening, and too
crowded, are Grancher, hunched in a sagging chair by the coal
grate; Gran, pinafore-ed; Mr Marlow, and Mrs Marlow, an
attractive young (30-ish) woman. All except Grancher are at the
table, eating bread and jam.

GRAN: (*Forcefully*) Putt thik racket, off, ut?

GRANCHER: Oy. Tis, yunnit? Get on thee wick.

Mr Marlow gets up and switches the wireless off. But he looks at
his wife, slightly timidly, as he comes back the two paces to the
table.

MRS MARLOW: I like the Andrews Sisters. I like Bing Crosby.
Unlike the others, she has a London accent.

MR MARLOW: (*Nervously*) Oh ay. Well. And I do.

End of conversation. Black looks around the table. Grancher has
a tin-tack rattle in his chest caused by silicosis. He suddenly
gasps and wheezes into a truly awful hawking cough from
somewhere deep in his diseased lungs and – phlop! – a nasty

gobbet of phlegm lands on the bars of the grate, where it sizzles, oozes, and elongates. An entirely matter-of-fact expectoration. Mrs Marlow has just taken a mouthful of bread and jam. She stops chewing. Distress, distaste, on her face, she looks sidelong at her husband, who, although painfully aware of her feelings, affects not to notice.

GRAN: Lovely bit o' plum, yunnit? Thou costn't byut [*beat*] plum, not for jam. I don't care what nobody d'say . . .

Once again, the tin-tack chest rattle, the preliminary to another foul performance. But Grancher momentarily holds it back.

GRANCHER: (*Gasp*) Cosn't cook a plum. A plum don't like cooking. Him a' got too much skin. Give I stro'bry jam any day of the wik – I'd rather have me a –

But his observations have to remain unfinished. The rattle gets too much for him. The hawking cough starts all over again, and concludes with an equally emphatic spit into the grate. Crash! Mrs Marlow, flushed, throws her knife down on to her plate, with an exaggerated clatter, and pushes back her chair with loud scrape.

MRS MARLOW: God Almighty.

MR MARLOW: What – ? What's the matter?

MRS MARLOW: What's the matter – What's matter – ! How can anybody eat with *that* going on?

GRAN: (*To* MR MARLOW) What's up wi' her *now*?

MR MARLOW: (*Mildly, to* MRS MARLOW) Him cont help it, now can 'a? It chunt no joke, mind. That coal dust in the lungs. What's our Dad supposed to do – ?

GRANCHER: (*Offended*) Eh? What? What's that?

MRS MARLOW: He can go outside! When we're *eating* –

GRAN: Oh, aye. Whose house is it? Tell me that! Have him got to go *outside* for a bit of a cough in his own whum!

There is an obvious tension and dislike between the two women.

MRS MARLOW: A bit of a cough. You call *that* a bit of a cough! More like a bleed'n avalanche!

GRAN: Langwidge.

GRANCHER: (*Plaintive*) You try it o'butty. Thou try a chest like mine!

MR MARLOW: (*Unhappily*) It's all right, Dad –

MRS MARLOW: It's *not* all right!

MR MARLOW: All right. All right.

MRS MARLOW: It turns me right off, and you know it does! I'd just put some food into my mouth. It was as much as I could do to get it down.

GRAN: Fuss! Fuss!

The door opens and the boy Philip stands looking at them, pale, withdrawn, anxious. And not coming any further into the room. His father, Mr Marlow, notices him with relief, hoping for some sort of distraction to halt the brewing row.

MR MARLOW: Where's thou been, our Philip? Tea's bin ready half-hour agoo.

MRS MARLOW: It's not fuss, not at all. It turns me up.

GRAN: (*Nastily*) Then thee's know what thou can do – doosn't!

MR MARLOW: (*Unhappily*) Now, our Mam.

MRS MARLOW: (*Jeer*) 'Now our Mam.' 'Ooh, our Mam.' Why don't you stick up for *me* for a change! Christ Almighty.

GRAN: Langwidge!

The boy is watching, wide-eyed, his back against the latched door.

GRANCHER: Let's have no an–i–mos–ity. Not in my house. I don't want it.

GRAN: Whose house is it – that's all *I'da* want to know? Whose feow sticks of furniture – ? Have Dad and me got to be told what to do at our time of life in our own place – Whose house! Tell me that!

MRS MARLOW: Is that all you can say? Do you ever say anything else? Can't you change the bloody tune sometimes?

Grancher half rises from his sagging fireside chair, greatly offended.

GRANCHER: No cussing! No cussing here! If you please!

GRAN: I won't have you talking to *me* like that, my girl – Not in my own –

MR MARLOW: (*Sharper*) Mam!

GRAN: We never wanted this. Never wanted to end up like this!

MR MARLOW: Oh, let's have our bit tea. For goodness' sake, don't let's have all this squabbling! I be sick at heart with it all.

A small, hostile pause – and, almost simultaneously, they all seem to turn their eyes to Philip.

MRS MARLOW: (*Sharply*) Where have you been? Why are you always late for tea?

MR MARLOW: You heard your mother. Where've you bin?

MRS MARLOW: I've been calling all over for you. Didn't you hear me?

PHILIP: (*Barely audible*) No–o.

MR MARLOW: You bin mooching about in them woods agyun – on thee own? Is that it? Stuck up top of a tree.

GRAN: Chunt natural.

MRS MARLOW: I never know where you are. Wanted you to go to the shop. Calling, calling! I'd a good mind you wouldn't get any tea at all, if you can't come in on time –

GRAN: Oh, him a got to have his little bit of tay –

GRANCHER: 'Course him have, a growing lad like Philip – (*To the silent boy*) Got to put some gristle in them arms, antcha o'butty?

GRAN: Come th'on. Sit up at table. There's a good boy. Make a soldier of tha, eh?

Mrs Marlow, made edgy, and already very unhappy with her situation in this tiny squabbling-box of a house, all but yells out –

MRS MARLOW: *I'll* decide that! That's for *me* to say! He's my son! Philip! No tea for you!

MR MARLOW: Oh now Betty – doosn't say –

MRS MARLOW: (*Yell*) You gutless bugger!

GRAN: I've never heard the like! Not in all my born days! Ted – bist thou going to put up with *that* or – I'd smack her one, that I 'ood!

MRS MARLOW: (*To* GRAN) Shut up! Keep your nose out of it. You interfering old cow!

Gran rises from the table, utterly shocked.

GRAN: What? What did you – ? Get out! Get theeself out! Get out of this house – !

MR MARLOW: (*Desperate*) Don't, our Mam – don't – holt on!

MRS MARLOW: (*Shrill*) I would! I would! If *your son* was any sort of man –

MR MARLOW: Betty.

MRS MARLOW: – It's *his* job to find us a place, his wife and his son – Instead of being squashed up in this poky hole –

GRAN: Hole!

GRANCHER: Poky! You calling it poky!

69

MR MARLOW: Her don't mean it –
MRS MARLOW: Yes, I do!
Philip stays with his back flat against the latched door, his eyes
wide in his pale, freckled face, the angry adult words sinking
under his unhappy thoughts.
PHILIP: (*Thinks*) *My fault. Me. It's me. Me. It's all my doing.*
      Me. It's me. My fault. Mine. Our Father which art in heaven
      Hallow'd be Thy name . . .
The boy's gabbled voice is quickly fading over the face of the
distressed man he is to become, in the hospital ward.

Sweat now beads and drips, drenching the lesions which cover
Marlow's face. His eyes are burning hotly in his skull, almost
like those of a crazed man. Marlow tries to call out, turning to
look across at the new patient, George Adams.
    The old Londoner is propped up in bed against his pillows
and his back-rest. Above his stiffly starched striped pyjamas, his
eyes are sunk into his pallidly exhausted face. His liver-spot
hands are folded together on the turned-over sheet in front of
him, almost in an attitude of mournful prayer. George looks as
thoroughly miserable as miserable can be.
    Burning up, his temperature shooting out of control, Marlow
is trying to catch the weak and sad man's attention – but not
very effectively.
MARLOW: (*Croak*) Please – hey – please – call the – hey – Call
      the nurse – Please – I need the – I'm burning – burning –
      I'm – call the –
He gives up, but his fiercely, insanely glittering eyes remain
fixed on George, who is lost in his own sickly melancholy, his
stringy old hands beginning to lace, unlace, lace together. Then
he turns his head, and stares vacantly at Marlow.
    Slack-mouthed George, empty of expression, looks at the hot,
mad eyes that are fixed upon him. A moment. Then –
    Click! Without warning, George begins to 'sing' 'It Might as
Well Be Spring', as sung by Dick Haymes in the 1945 film hit
State Fair, his lips synchronized with the smooth crooning.
    Everything else in the ward is unaffected by this obvious and
excessive abnormality.

The Dick Haymes song carries over from the ward, across time and space, to a long, low, converted Nissen hut of a building, smoke-filled, absolutely Saturday-night-packed. A Forest working men's club, as they were once called.

At a small raised platform against the wall, half-way down, Mr Marlow is standing by the upright piano, which is being played by his wife. All the drinkers, at little round tables that have wrought-iron legs, or standing almost shoulder to shoulder at the bar at the top end, are extremely attentive for Mr Marlow, who is now the one lip-syncing the continuation of the song.

Philip, the pale boy, hemmed in at one of the crowded tables, a glass of lemonade and a bag of Smith's crisps (salt in a twist of blue paper) at hand, is staring wide-eyed across the smoke-filled room at his 'singing' father, glowing with pride.

Mr Marlow half raises his arms in a finishing flourish, 1940s style, the Brylcreem glinting and glistening in his wavy hair. And Mrs Marlow, well lipsticked, playing the upright piano at which the singer stands, appears also to finish, with a few elaborate trills. A storm of wildly enthusiastic applause.

The confident, pub-style, 1940s performing manner of Mr Marlow's 'singing' changes instantly. In reaction to the excess of applause, full of sharp whistles, feet-stamping and raucous cries of 'Encore! Encore!', he becomes suddenly very shy, full of an awkward, grinning, rather charming diffidence.

All around Philip, big hands are banging together in the prolonged, loudly enthusiastic applause. Philip is pleased, impressed. A man in cloth cap leans forward to speak to him.

CLOTH CAP: There yunt nobody round here as can hold a candle to thee fayther as far as the warbling is concerned, my boy. Your Dad is too good to belong down the pit o'butty. Him ought to be up there in lights somewhere – You see if I byunt right!

He leans back, as suddenly as he had leaned forward, with the air of a man who has delivered some long-awaited and conclusive announcement of immense significance. Mr Marlow, returning back-slapped to the table, pinkish with embarrassment at the applause, ruffles his son's hair.

MR MARLOW: Bist thou all right, o'but?

CHAIRMAN: Order – order – Come on now. Let's have a bit of

Arder, then. We've heard the husband, now for his missis. Mrs Marlow ool now play 'The Rustle of Spring'. And that chunt nern a cowboy song, mind!

Laughter and applause. The piano notes begin, and die over –

George's curtained-off bed space in the ward, where the same rather pompous houseman, Dr Finlay, is running through the standard admission tests and procedures with the weak, confused, but still potentially hostile old Londoner. Dr Finlay is holding up his index finger in front of and a little to the side of George.

DR FINLAY: Pay attention. I want you to look at my finger –

The old man is blank.

Mr Adams. Please. Give me your attention – Look at my finger. I want you to look at my finger.

GEORGE: (*Indignant*) *What for?*

Nurse Mills, the prettiest of the nurses, arrives at Marlow's bed, in order to grease him again. She stoops to his locker, where the big tub of ointment is kept, not yet particularly noticing the extremity of his condition.

NURSE MILLS: Time for your greasing, Mr Marlow – sorry to disturb you.

Her attention is caught by the voices coming from the adjoining, curtained-off bed space.

DR FINLAY: (*Behind curtain*) Oh, for goodness' sake, Mr Adams. Don't be so – Of course I didn't hit you – !

GEORGE: (*Behind curtain*) 'Ammers. Bleed'n '*ammer*! Smack on my bloody knee!

DR FINLAY: (*Behind curtain*) I am simply – oh, goodness me – Your reflexes, I'm testing your –

GEORGE: (*Behind curtain*) Hit me again and I'll have the Law on you!

Nurse Mills puts her hand to her face, to stop a gurgle of incredulous laughter.

NURSE MILLS: We've got a right one here, by the sounds of it.

Standing, she takes the thermometer out of its wall-holder, pops it automatically in Marlow's mouth, and takes hold of his wrist, for the pulse. She still has not registered the deterioration in his condition. Inside George's curtained-off bed space, the flustered

72

houseman is entering up an admissions form.

DR FINLAY: And your next of kin is your wife, presumably?

GEORGE: (*Mildly*) The cow.

DR FINLAY: (*Ignoring this*) Her first name. Your wife's first
　　name is – ?

George looks at him, puzzled.

GEORGE: Um.

DR FINLAY: Yes? What is her name? Her Christian name – Mr
　　Adams?

GEORGE: Buggered if I know.

DR FINLAY: But you – surely you – What do you call her? You
　　must call her *something* –

GEORGE: Yeh – and I won't tell you *what*, will I?

He cackles, sharply, and disconcertingly – then sinks back a
little, exhausted by his own joke.

DR FINLAY: Mr Adams. This is only a small matter, and then
　　I'm done –

GEORGE: No tablets?

DR FINLAY: Sorry?

GEORGE: What sort of doctor are you?

DR FINLAY: (*Sigh*) Just tell me, if you would be so kind, Mr
　　Adams, what name you give your wife – Come on, now.
　　What do you call her? What name do you use when you
　　want her attention – ?

GEORGE: What?

DR FINLAY: Do you say, for instance, 'Mary, may I have some
　　tea – ?'

GEORGE: *What?*

DR FINLAY: Her name, man! Her name! What–do–you–call –
　　her?

George stares at him, as though the young man is an object of
wonder and interest.

GEORGE: Mum. I call her Mum. What the bleed'n hell do you
　　think I call her!

At the next bed, beyond the closed curtains, Nurse Mills,
laughing, takes the thermometer out of Marlow's mouth.

NURSE MILLS: Life is a cabaret, old chum. In here it is.

MARLOW: (*Croak*) Drink –

NURSE MILLS: Hang about.

But her expression changes as she reads the thermometer.

MARLOW: (*Croak*) A drink –

NURSE MILLS: (*Changed tone*) Are you in more pain – ? Are you in much pain? Do you understand what I am saying? Mr Marlow?

She is already pouring some water from the carafe on top of his locker. He does not answer – nor even seem to hear. She holds the glass to his lips, frowning now.

> Here. A drink. Please. You *must* drink. Come on. There's a good boy.

He gasps a helpless, involuntary gasp of pain.

MARLOW: The – oh – the piano –

NURSE MILLS: What? Pain, do you say – ?

MARLOW: (*Gasp*) Piano.

NURSE MILLS: (*Firmly*) Come on. Take some water. Drink! Never mind the piano or whatever – Drink this. Philip – drink – Then I'm going to fetch your doctor – Come on. Come along –

He takes a little water, and spills more.

MARLOW: Spring.

NURSE MILLS: No. Tap water.

He starts to laugh as she gently lowers his head back on the pillow.

MARLOW: 'Rustle of Spring'.

She looks at him, but he stops laughing, not returning her look, his eyes raking the ceiling in an obvious fever.

NURSE MILLS: Mr Marlow – ?

He does not reply. She havers, unsure. Then leaves, quickly. A fevered moment. Marlow is alone.

MARLOW: Yeh. Water.

On the cold river, at daybreak, grappling hooks and nets from Police launch are pulling at, pulling in, the body of a young woman, as 'Peg o' My Heart' sounds on the harmonica.

A stiff-armed, old Army great-coated, ominous-looking scarecrow in a battered hat stands in the middle of a sloping, sour little field. Dream-like, it looks at us, and lifts its stiff, straw-tufted arms to its mouth and seems to join in 'Peg o' My

Heart' on the harmonica.

Suddenly we are moving fast along a narrow, twisting, brambled
path, deep into the massed trees of the Forest. It is from the
perspective of someone running, but the lower branches of the tall
undergrowth whip and lash and crowd in. On either side, the trees
are apparently endless, jostling together, darkening almost to
black in the distance. The sounds of the running feet stop, and a
hand pulls aside the foliage, to look into a grassy, woodland dell.

An attractive woman – later identified as Nicola – is on her back
on the grass, her skirt pulled up to her hips, her stockinged legs
open, her high heels digging into the soft earth, her long black hair
spread, being made love to, with crude and hurried vigour, by
some man who cannot be identified, his bare backside gleaming.
Nicola, aware of a watcher, twists her head to look, and gives a
jeering laugh.

NICOLA: Caught me, have you, Marlow?

The branch snaps back, obscuring the dell, and the running
continues, as the woman calls mockingly –

> (*Off*) Phil–ip! Phil–ip! Why don't you look! Philip! Don't be a
> spoilsport! Why don't you join us! (*Receding*) Philip! Come
> back! Come back! Don't be so sill–y!

Pant-pant-pant, amplified, rasping. And between the trees,
children stand, watching, each child alone, staring out of the
foliage, like dream children, almost dead children. Terrifying.

Frightening enough, indeed, to make Marlow's fevered eyes
swivel, as he sweats in his hospital bed.

> (*Voice over, a receding call*) *Phil–ip! Phil–il–il–ip! Come back!*
> *Come back!*

The twisting Forest path, brambled, ferned, foxgloved, is
plunging yet deeper into dense woodland, but normal now,
without the watching children. And the runner is now seen to be
the thin, pale, freckled boy Philip.

OLD WOMAN: (*Voice over*) Why is it only *this* boy who knows the
answer? Why is it only Philip who has his hand up? Always
Philip. The capital of Iceland.

The question has been asked in what was once a typical country primary school, which has windows set too high in the brown walls for a child to see out of. A crowded class of 9-year-olds. And one boy with his jerseyed hand up. Philip.

PHILIP: Reykjavik, miss.

OLD WOMAN: Correct! Good boy. Very good! You put the others to shame.

But on the Forest path Philip is running, running, as though all the devils in hell are after him.

(*Voice over*) And who can tell me the name of the very brave and good man who wrote the *Pilgrim's Progress*? Who was it?

Behind him now, in the dell, Nicola, on her back, skirt up, heels digging into the soft ground, twists her head around the man on top of her, to address us.

NICOLA: John Bunyan!

OLD WOMAN: (*Voice over*) Correct! Good girl. Very good! You put the others to shame.

The boy plunges on and on through the clutching branches and thickening foliage. His classmates are once again standing in the trees, at the side of the path.

(*Voice over, faster*) The new President of the United States of America?

PHILIP: (*Voice over*) Harry S. Truman.

The children in the trees step forward to the edge of the path, and he has to run through them. They jeer and point as he passes.

JEERING CHILDREN: Clever Dick! Clever Dick! Makes me sick! Clever Dick! Clever Dick! Give her arse a lick!

Marlow, feverish in his hospital bed, hears the mockery as though it were newly minted.

(*Voices over*) Clever Dick! Clever Dick! Makes me sick!

Faintly greenish letters blip-blip on to the word processor screen, which has the suggestion, or the merest hint of, the subdued grey reflection of a shimmering tree in its glass.

H–e–l–p.

The letters slowly fade on the foliage of the special tree. Philip, the boy, is once again securely lodged in the saddle-like cleft of the upper branches of the tall old oak, able to stare out over gently moving, undulating acres of green, most of the trees being at a lesser height. He turns his head very deliberately to look straight at us, challengingly.

PHILIP: When I grow up I be going to be the first man to live for ever and ever. In my opinion, you don't have to die. Not unless you want to. And I byunt never going to want to. Not me. (*Pause.*) When I grow up I be going to leave the light on *all night*. I be! No matter bloody what. (*Pause.*) I be going to have *books*. I be going to have *books*. All over the – on shelves, mind. I be going to have a *shelf just for books*. (*Pause.*) When I grow up I'm – (*Savagely*) I be going to have a *whole tin* of evaporated milk on a *whole* tin of peaches I be! I bloody be, mind! I bloody buggering bloody damn buggering be! Oy. And I shall cuss. (*Pause.*) I'm going to – I'll tell tha what – When I grow up I'm – When I grow up –

He stops, distressed.

Everything will be all right. When I grow up, *everything* – There'll be none of – there'll be no – Everything ool be *all right*. (*Tiny, uncertain pause.*) Won't it? Won't it, God? Hey? Thou's like me a bit – doesn't, God? Eh? (*Longer pause.*) When I – When I grow up, I be going to be – *a detective*.

The birds are loud, insistent, varied, clear above the slightly mysterious, almost dream-like sound of a slow, steady breeze sighing and murmuring as it shifts through the dense woodland.

Philip is now just a tiny figure, way up in a tree, alone in the middle of the Forest. Then – as from a long way off, or a long way up –

I'll find out. I'll find out. I'll find out things! I'll find out. I'll find out who did it!

Silence. Except for the insistent birds. Then, startlingly near, and distinct, a cuckoo begins its throaty, traditionally mocking call, *Cuck–oo! Cuck–oo!*

Marlow is in a bad way in the hospital bed, his temperature clearly racing out of control, his eyes the hot eyes of a madman.

Cuck–oo! Cuck–oo!

The repeated cry of the cuckoo, with its extra edge of mockery, is used as the prelude for the sudden, startling jump into the full pitch of Ronnie Ronalde's 'Birdsong at Eventide' as once heard by Ali on his headphones.

In the village club, a packed and attentive audience of beer-drinkers at the little tables, listen to what happens to be Mr Marlow's brilliant finger-to-lips rendering of the whistling and whooping Ronalde recording. Mr Marlow is a picture of concentration as he stands beside his wife at the piano, his fingers vibrating at his mouth as he lip-syncs from one bird-call into another.

The listeners, too, seem rapt, absorbed, even entranced. Sitting at one of the tables, in his greased-blotched pyjamas is the disfigured, lesion-covered Marlow, like one stiff with pain, carefully avoiding movement, listening like the others to Mr Marlow's whistling. Nobody takes any notice whatsoever of this oddity, this grisly near- apparition.

'Birdsong at Eventide' reaches its crescendo, and ends to rapturous and prolonged applause – clapping, whistling, feet-stamping, calls of 'Encore! Encore!'

As in a bad dream, where limbs cannot move and desires are ossified beyond possibility of action, Marlow makes a struggling attempt to join in the hand-banging, foot-stamping applause for his father. But he finds that he can move his arms only with Herculean effort. And even then, even managing to do so, the twist and curl of his arthritically bent and crippled and skin- flaking hands make it literally impossible for him to bring his palms together.

MARLOW: (*Shocked*) I can't – I can't seem to – (*Immensely puzzled*) I can't clap my hands – I *can't do it* – ! Not even for my dear old Dad.

The same man in cloth cap as before, in the same way as he had earlier with the boy, suddenly leans in, looming across the pint-littered table. But this time his expression is full of malice.

CLOTH CAP: Ah. But thee doosn't *want* to – doost?

MARLOW: What – ? Don't *want* to – ?

CLOTH CAP: You byunt interested in clapping thee fayther, now be ya? Thou's never did give the poor bugger credit when him was alive! Got too big for thee boots, disn't?

78

Marlow stares at him, sick with horror.

MARLOW: Wh–what do you mean – ?

CLOTH CAP: Thee's know very well what I'd mean! You cocky
bugger.

MARLOW: Are you trying to say – now listen – Are you saying
my Dad is *dead* – ?

CLOTH CAP: (*Cackle*) Dead? Aye! 'Course him is! Dead and
gone! And nobody to care yuppence.

MARLOW: But – no – but you see – There's so much I want to
say – I need to talk to him, very badly. (*Then, indignantly*)
Don't be so stupid! He can't be! Not my Dad!

CLOTH CAP: (*With great satisfaction*) Oh, him's dead. Him's
dead, all right. Dyudd and buried long since.

MARLOW: Listen! Listen, you! That was *him* wasn't it! That was
my Dad doing the birds! That's my Dad up on the platform
– (*Shouts*) Dad! Dad! Over here, o'butty! Come over here!
Dad! Thee's know how much I'd care about tha –

But as he looks across the club room, his voice trails off. It is
empty, and poorly lit. The upright piano on the platform is
draped with long, dusty cobwebs. Some of the windows are
broken. A chair lies on its side. A few pint glasses are crusted
with mould.

(*Distressed*) But he was there – he was! – My lovely dear old
Dad was there – That was him whistling. I heard him – I
heard him! All the birds in the trees – all the love in the
world – I heard him. I *saw* him.

Again, the man in the cloth cap looms into view, leaning in
across the table.

CLOTH CAP: What's that? What are you saying, old chap? What
are you trying to say – ?

But these are the educated tones of a very different voice. We
are not now in the club at all.

The registrar, who had been leaning in, and whose voice it was,
straightens from Marlow's bed and addresses Nurse Mills.

REGISTRAR: Nothing – just a babble – but he's more or less
asleep now. Everything is under control. You did right to
call me, but he'll sleep now for quite a while. Don't let him
be disturbed – never mind the topical applications this

evening. Forget supper. Just leave him be, all right?

NURSE MILLS: Shall I close his curtains, doctor?

REGISTRAR: Yes, why not?

Out of the sudden blackness, slightly glowing letters blip-blip across a word processor's screen.

> *'You've stepped in something nasty,' he said, 'and you want me to clean it up . . .'*

Sound of heavy knock–knock–knocking. Binney is opening the door of his house on the riverside Mall to the insistent knocking.

BINNEY: All right! You want to break the –

His expression, voice changes.

> Who are you? What do you want?

The two mysterious men are glowering menacingly at him on the doorstep.

FIRST MYSTERIOUS MAN: The Police found her this morning.

BINNEY: W–what – ?

SECOND MYSTERIOUS MAN: They found the poor little thing. Your little piece of fluff.

FIRST MYSTERIOUS MAN: Your harmless bit of fun.

SECOND MYSTERIOUS MAN: She's turned up.

BINNEY: I don't know what you're –

FIRST MYSTERIOUS MAN: (*Interrupting*) In the river.

SECOND MYSTERIOUS MAN: Naked.

FIRST MYSTERIOUS MAN: Poor soul.

SECOND MYSTERIOUS MAN: Poor little girl.

They stare at him, eyes like marbles, shoulders hunching. Binney looks scared, but holds his ground.

BINNEY: Who are you? You sound like strays from a bad film. What do you think you're playing at?

FIRST MYSTERIOUS MAN: It comes to all of us in the end. But it didn't oughter come like that.

SECOND MYSTERIOUS MAN: Not even her knickers on her. Not a stitch.

FIRST MYSTERIOUS MAN: Whatchado with her clothes?

SECOND MYSTERIOUS MAN: Especially the fur coat. That was sable, you know. Did you know it was sable? Do you know how much sable is worth?

BINNEY: You make me laugh. Do you know that? I can guess who you clowns are. It's written all over you.

FIRST MYSTERIOUS MAN: Don't keep us on the step. I'd advise you very strongly not to do that.

SECOND MYSTERIOUS MAN: Ask us in. Go on. Be polite.

FIRST MYSTERIOUS MAN: That's what I'd do if I were you.

SECOND MYSTERIOUS MAN: It's only civilized. Ennit?

Binney looks at their hard faces, and then, in a sudden frightened whirl tries to slam shut the door –

BINNEY: Get lost!

But the second mysterious man has got his foot hard in the door.

FIRST MYSTERIOUS MAN: Now, now, now, Mr B.

SECOND MYSTERIOUS MAN: That's not very friendly, is it?

BINNEY: (Scared) What do you want from me? Who sent you – ? (Then, despairingly) All right. All right. You had better come in – we'll talk it over.

FIRST MYSTERIOUS MAN: Thank you.

SECOND MYSTERIOUS MAN: Thank you, sir.

The three go up a stair to the living room. There are pictures on the walls. The first mysterious man stops on the stair, to look at a painting. It is a large portrait of a naked woman, provocatively posed. The woman is recognizable as the woman (Nicola) seen making love in the woodland dell.

FIRST MYSTERIOUS MAN: Goodness me. Look at this. What do you call this?

SECOND MYSTERIOUS MAN: This is what I would call a provocative picture. (Sniff.) I'm provoked.

FIRST MYSTERIOUS MAN: It tells us a great deal about the woman, does it not? A slut, I'd say.

SECOND MYSTERIOUS MAN: It also tells us a great deal about the man who hung it there, surely? A pimp, would be my guess.

They have a peculiarly formal, stilted way of speaking, and their faces are like flint. Binney is both puzzled and frightened by them.

BINNEY: It's only a painting. A decoration for the wall.

FIRST MYSTERIOUS MAN: A very attractive girl. As a decoration for a wall.

SECOND MYSTERIOUS MAN: Splendid breasts.

FIRST MYSTERIOUS MAN: (Sigh) Yes. Yes. Splendid.

The nude portrait is staring back, very erotic, glossy, life-like, with a certain brazen arrogance and a hint of mockery. Dance music begins.

And Marlow, the Singing Detective, fronts the dance band for the last waltz of the evening in a 1940s ballroom. He is again lip-syncing to the most appropriate version of the number he had been 'rehearsing': 'Cruising down the River', but this time the floor swirls with dancers. The song dips under his 'thoughts' as his eyes rake the dance floor, watching the couples.

MARLOW: (*Voice over*) I like to snap my eyes around the hall when I'm crooning this sort of stuff. Study faces. Watch the feet. You can learn a lot about life when you size up ballroom dancers. It helps my think-box to send out sparks. And my head has got to fizz–zz – ! on *this* case . . .

The song momentarily reasserts itself, then dips under again.

(*Voice over*) This ol' river I'm cruising down. I knew they'd fished out a body. And I knew it wasn't a mermaid. But there *was* something fishy about it, that's for sure. Yes, sir, the Thames can be all sleaze, no flow. And talking of flotsam and jetsam, who were those guys threatening Binney? Was he playing his own game with me? What's this with the Russianski lingo? Is it *Da* or is it *Nyet*? I had some visiting to do. To the sort of places where you don't leave a calling card –

In the ward, there is an air of expectancy. Then –

MR HALL: The Charge of the Light Brigade, Reginald.

REGINALD: The hordes of Genghis Khan, Mr Hall.

MR HALL: If only they knew how we suffered, Reginald.

REGINALD: And what we had to put up with –

And then, in a mob, the visitors all come flooding in, in a rush. The sudden hubbub of voices from the visitors, heard from outside Marlow's curtains, seems not to disturb the still deeply sleeping patient. But then the curtains are opened a little to admit Nurse Mills and a woman –

NURSE MILLS: He was running a very high temperature, but it's back under control now. The skin, you see. I'm afraid he had to be sedated, and he's been asleep most of the day.

She is talking to an attractive, black-haired woman, Nicola – the
nude in the portrait, the woman in the dell. Nicola seems
nervous, or unsure.

NICOLA: But I'd rather he wasn't woken if he needs to –

Her expression changes as she looks at him, as the Nurse flicks
on the lamp.

> Oh, my God. Oh, the poor thing. I had no idea he looked
> as bad as *this* –

NURSE MILLS: Yes – it must be at its absolute peak now. One
> hundred per cent of the skin –

NICOLA: But *surely* something can be done – Heavens above –
> this is *ghast–ly* – It looks as though he's been scalded –

NURSE MILLS: They're trying him on a new drug. One of the
> retinoids – but you must know that, of course.

NICOLA: (*With edge*) Of course.

Nurse Mills gives her a searching look, and then –

NURSE MILLS: Mr Marlow! A visitor!

NICOLA: (*Nervous*) Oh, I'm not so sure we should wake him, are
> you? He'll probably send me away with a mouthful of
> abuse, anyway.

Nurse Mills gives her another swift, coolly appraising look.

NURSE MILLS: They wanted to know if and when you came.
> The doctors, I mean. They're not here now – but sister
> would like to speak to you.

Nicola contemplates sleeping Marlow, with pursed lips.

NICOLA: I don't know that I want to get too – (*Stops herself.*) All
> right. I'll see her. I suppose I ought to speak to *somebody*.
> At least, I won't get a lot of abuse –

NURSE MILLS: Sorry?

NICOLA: Boy, if this one wakes up and sees me, you'll find out
> what I mean! (*Turns away, decisively*) In fact, I can't face it.
> I don't want it.

NURSE MILLS: Are you sure you –

NICOLA: I shouldn't have come. I shouldn't have even tried!

She steps quickly through the curtains, into the ward, followed
by the nurse. A moment. Then Marlow opens his eyes. In a way
that shows he has actually been awake for the last few minutes.

MARLOW: (*Sardonic, softly, to himself*) Farewell, my lovely.

He considers things, expelling his breath in a venomous hiss.

(*Shout*) Nicola! Come here! Come back, you bitch! Nicola! Marlow's is the only curtained-off bed, like a tent in the ward, which is crowded with chattering visitors at almost each bed –

(*Loudly, behind curtains*) Come back! Come back, you bitch! You filthy little slut! Nicola! Come here!

The buzz of conversation slowly dies, all around the ward. Into astonished silence. Comically, every aghast eye turns to look at the curtained-off bed.

(*Yell, behind curtains*) You disgusting tramp! Nicola! You two-bit, rutting whore! Come here! Come here, you heartless bitch!

Patients and visitors, all stare at the curtains. An expectant, watching, waiting, comical silence. Then, just as they all seem to decide that there is going to be no more entertainment, and that they are not going to be shocked any more –

(*Yell, behind curtains*) Who are you opening your legs for now, you rutting bitch? You stinking bag of filth!

This is too much. There is a sudden babble of shock and protest, with some calling for the nurses. Staff Nurse White, the tough one, comes charging through the double doors.

(*Yell, behind curtains*) Nicola! You whore! Nicola! Come here! Come back! You filthy, heartless, rutting, rotting piece of –

The curtains are violently jerked open, all the way round, by a thunderously furious Staff Nurse White.

STAFF NURSE WHITE: Mr Marlow! What do you think you are doing! Where do you think you are!

Mrs Adams is visiting George.

MRS ADAMS: Wash his mouth out! He wants his mouth washed out with soap and water. The dirty bleeder.

Marlow is astonished to see the ward full of people in their outdoor clothes.

MARLOW: What – ? What's going on – ?

STAFF NURSE WHITE: You! That's what! Stop this shouting! Stop this at once!

Everyone is staring, enthralled. Marlow, considerably embarrassed, looks around the ward. Silence. Then he makes, or tries to make, a helpless little gesture. And, in a husky croak of a voice, his real voice, he manages to sing a few lines of

'Cruising down the River'. An inapt performance followed by an incredulous, comical little silence. Then –
MARLOW: (*Sigh*) That's all, folks.

3

A small branch-line steam train is huff-a-puffing laboriously out of the country railway station, in 1945.

Mr Marlow stands forlorn on the unroofed platform, where milk churns are stacked, and wartime posters ask, 'IS YOUR JOURNEY REALLY NECESSARY?' He stands in a light drizzle of rain under a lowering, slug-coloured sky, his face heavy with misery. His arm is up in a stiff farewell.

Leaning out of the third-class carriage window, as the train slowly pulls away, is the 9-year-old boy, Philip. He is waving frantically.

The Mills Brothers' 1940s version of 'Paper Doll' begins to throb.

The Singing Detective fronts the band in a London dance hall, his eyes on the dancers, singing the 'Paper Doll' song. The music dips under his thoughts.

MARLOW: (*Thinks*) There are songs to sing. There are feelings to feel. There are thoughts to think. That makes three things. And you can't do *three* things at the same time. The singing is easy. Syrup in my mouth. The thinking comes with the tune –

Thoughts which are heard as the country railway station returns to view.

(*Voice over, continuous*) – so that leaves only the feelings. Am I right? Or am I right? I can sing the singing. I can think the thinking. (*Suddenly savage*) But you're not going to catch me feeling the feeling. No, sir.

Mr Marlow waits abjectly on the edge of the platform, his arm up, oddly stiff and not actually waving. He waits, melancholy in expression and posture, until the little train has puffed out of sight. And stays there, his arm still upraised. Like a statue.

The boy Philip comes from the train window, steps awkwardly over his mother's feet, and sits opposite her. The rocking, crowded, corridorless carriage is full of soldiers, in uniform, with kitbags. Philip looks anxiously, questioningly, at his mother. But she has hidden herself behind the *Daily Mirror*: deliberately, it seems. He looks up at their bulging, shabby case, the one civilian bag among the kit on the sagging, string-meshed rack.

PHILIP: Mum. Dad was waving. Our Dad were a-waving all the time. All the time, mind. Mum?

She does not answer nor emerge from behind her protective newspaper. Clicketty–clacketty–clack, and the soldiers hungrily eyeing pretty, shapely Mrs Marlow, especially noticing the peep of petticoat at the edge of her skirt.

Philip keeps staring at her, too. The black banner headline of her newspaper, facing him, insistently draws attention: 'THE WAR IS RUSHING TO AN END! GERMAN ARMIES SURRENDERING ON ALL FRONTS.'

Clacketty–Clacketty–Clack–Clack.

Philip looks sideways at the soldiers, not wanting to be overheard, but clearly waiting for the chance to cross-examine his mother.

(*Eventually*) Mum? Our Mum?

It looks as though she doesn't intend to answer. One of the soldiers winks at him, and he looks away, concentrating on the newspaper Mrs Marlow is holding: 'THE WAR IS RUSHING TO AN END! GERMAN ARMIES SURRENDERING ON ALL FRONTS.' His small, pale, wide-eyed freckled face is puckering in concentration, trying to work something out.

(*Thinks*) That's bloody old Hitler done for, then. So everything ool be all right. That's what um do say, yunnit? It'll Be A Lovely Day Tomorrow. Whatsits – blue birds and that, over the – *Everybody* says – 'When the war is over – ' Lights. Flowers. Butter. Eggs. The lot. Comics. Sweets. Everything. It'll be all right – all right – all right – The War Rushing to an End exclamation mark. I da like me a good exclamation mark, mind.

But he shifts and sighs, as though his body and his expression are less hopeful. He looks out of the window of the slow, clack–clack–clacking train at the damp, passing fields. In the middle of a slowly passing, scrubby, sloping field, in the slow drizzle, stands a scarecrow, garbed in a long old Army greatcoat, with a battered trilby hat pulled well down over its 'face'.

The nighttime ward has dimly lit beds in a row, with the patients fast asleep, whistling and bubbling. It is eerily still, like a scene in the mind, or an image formed on the edge of a dream's slow prelude.

As, indeed, is the damp field, no longer seen from the train, because the train is glimpsed laboriously huff-a-puff-chuffing out of sight. Caw–caw–caw of rooks. A slow, damply clinging drizzle. A grey light. A vague, but growing sense of unease, or even of menace, compounded by the way the wind bends the long grass, and then tugs and flaps at the battered hat and the long greatcoat of the stiff-armed, more than half human scarecrow.

Marlow is the one who is not asleep in the night-time ward. In the dim light, his eyes gleam a little, as he lies very still, looking up at the ceiling.
    Caw–ca–a–aw! – caw! sound the rooks, in his mind.
MARLOW: (*Thinks, softly in awe*) The rooks gather in the lost
      trees comma like premonitions of the night full stop Why
      do they cry question mark

The scarecrow suddenly swivels around on its central pole and looms straight at *us*. And its mouth (the only part of the 'face' visible under the pulled-down trilby hat) is exactly like a human mouth, opening and shutting. Half a beat, then, weirdly it appears, this mouth, to break into the 1940s Mills Brothers' version of 'Paper Doll' which Marlow had been 'singing'.

Mr Marlow stands alone on the small, unroofed station platform in the slow but thickening drizzle. His hand is still raised in pointless farewell, for the little train has long since disappeared from view. It is now Mr Marlow who takes up the Mills Brothers' song.

On the train, the 'Paper Doll' song continuing as Mrs Marlow, signs of a held-down distress on her face, hides herself rather too obviously behind the thin wartime newspaper.

Philip, opposite, is watching her all the time, wanting to talk to her. His face twitching a little.

And the soldiers in the carriage are also looking at her, or at her shapely legs, with covert, sidelong, potentially lascivious glances. One of the soldiers takes out a packet of Woodbine cigarettes and offers them around, looks at Mrs Marlow as though to include her, but seems to lose his nerve.

The boy notices. The rain splatters sideways against the carriage window.

At the country station, Mr Marlow, as he takes up the 'Paper Doll' song again, forlorn, lowers his arm at last, peers up at the brimming skies, turns up the collar of his rough jacket, and turns away, shoulders drooping. As he 'sings', turning away in the rain, he looks at a tattered wartime poster on the rain-soaked wooden wall behind the Milk Churns: 'IS YOUR JOURNEY REALLY NECESSARY?'

On the train 'Paper Doll' rolls on without interruption, over the crowded carriage.

Philip watches the way the soldiers wink at each other as they smoke and look at his mother's crossed legs and take up the change of voice and tempo in the Mills Brothers' original recording, lip-synchronized.

Mrs Marlow, during this 'singing', unaware of any abnormality, so to speak, at last lowers her protective newspaper and looks steadily and yet almost questioningly at Philip.

Philip seems unable to hold her look, even though he has been waiting for it. His face twitches in some sort of stress, and he looks away, to the carriage window. There is a grey, subdued, fleeting reflection of the boy's face, barely discernible, ghost-like in the window as the slow train hoots and clanks into a tunnel.

The Mills Brothers' version of 'Paper Doll' continues, without interruption, as the ghost-like reflection slowly fades to blackness. The soldiers are 'singing' it.

Gradually emerging out of the dark, the song, and the clack–clack–clacketty–clack of the train, is the glow of a lamp in

89

the otherwise night-dark hospital ward. The night nurse is once again, improperly, dozing heavily at the table at the far end of the ward. The small glow is now, clearly, the dim lamp beside her on the table.

The song and then, moments later, the clack–clack–clacketty–clack of a slow train in a long tunnel, fade away.

In the ill-lit ward, stretching away into darkness, the snores, grunts, and whistles of the sleeping patients reassert themselves. But then –

PHILIP: (*Voice over*) Mum? Mum. Why – Mum? – Why can't our Dad come wi' us to London? Why do him have to stay back whum [*home*] – ? Eh? Mum?

Around Marlow's part of the ward, away from the night nurse's table and the small glow, it is very poorly lit. But it can nevertheless be seen that Marlow remains sleepless.

MRS MARLOW: (*Voice over*) Questions. Questions. Because they won't let him out of the pit, that's why.

PHILIP: (*Voice over*) Then why don't *we* stay? Why do *we* goo?

MARLOW: (*Faintly*) I know. Oh, I know. I know. *I* know. Questions. Questions.

MRS MARLOW: (*Voice over*) I wouldn't stay in that house for a hundred pounds! Not if you put it in my hand right here and now – !

The voice seems to be coming from a long, long way away.

On the train, Philip is looking through the carriage window at the damp, slowly darkening landscape. He does not seem happy. His eyes narrowing in thought, like a child trying to work out a difficult piece of arithmetic. As though summoned by the same mental difficulty, the same scarecrow as before stands stiffly and disturbingly near-human in the middle of the scrubby, sloping field by the side of the single and now empty railway track.

Caw–caw–caw of rooks, nearby.

The light is thickening and darkening into a wet and miserable dusk, and the now stronger wind is billowing and tugging at the scarecrow's pulled-down trilby hat and long Army greatcoat. And then a particularly strong gust of whistling wind snatches off the scarecrow's hat. It rolls and bowls and bounces away across the sodden, bending-in-the-wind grass, like a ball.

The scarecrow suddenly turns its exposed head and stiff neck to look straight at us.

Startlingly, comically, the blazing black eyes of a very indignant Adolf Hitler stare out, with his moustache and cowlick of black hair slicked down across his forehead, and he is screaming with comic-strip rage.

HITLER: (*Bellow*) Mein hat! Mein bloody hat! Englander
pig-dogs! This is Biggles' doing! Bloody Biggles!

From the edge of the dusk-gloomed field, under the overhanging hedges, and by the small embankment of the single-track railway, British soldiers, on their bellies, with their rifles, open fire on the scarecrow in the middle of the field. The Hitler effigy slumps over, and more or less disintegrates, its innards exploding outwards.

A big 'Hip–hip–hooray!' comes from the raucous children's throats, heard from within the crumbling old village school. The old woman is in front of the class, as before, and the class includes Philip. She is glowing with an almost evangelical fervour. There is a long pointer in her hands, held like the actual instrument of conquest, and a big coloured map of Europe unrolled and draped over the blackboard. The map has, pinned to it, tiny Union Jacks, Stars and Stripes, and Hammer and Sickle flags clustering deep into a purple Germany, with now only the narrowest of 'unoccupied' strands left between them. The class of 8–9-year-olds is sitting bolt upright, with arms folded behind backs in what was then the recommended manner – but their faces, too, are as rapt and proudly glowing as teacher's.

OLD WOMAN: Deeper and deeper – look at it now! – Deeper
into the black heart of the Evil Land! See! Oh, boys and
girls. Oh, it will be a very great day, the day that is coming.
Better by far and away than any you have ever known.
Better even than Christmas or your birthday! It will be a
wonderful day. Yes? Rita?

As a hand shoots up.

RITA: Will the bells ring, miss?

OLD WOMAN: Oh, indeed, the bells! The bells will ring out, yes.
The church bells, starting with Westminster Abbey in

London, and then all across the country, everywhere, from John o' Groats to Land's End. Yes? Brian?

As a hand shoots up.

BRIAN: Ool there be bonfires, miss?

OLD WOMAN: (*Correcting*) *Will* there.

BRIAN: *Will* there, miss?

OLD WOMAN: Indeed, yes indeed, oh yes. And on top of each one, there'll be not Guy Fawkes, not this time, but old Hitler himself! He can stick his arm out and shout 'Heil', but, whoosh!, makes no difference – crackle, crackle, up in flames he goes!

A ripple of laughter around the class, of great pleasure, becoming excessive.

(*Eventually*) Enough. That will do!

The noise stops instantly: this was another age. She looks around the silent and once again attentive class. Her voice changes, becoming almost lyrical.

When darkness falls on that day, Victory Day, all the lights will begin to glow again, to beam and to twinkle again. All the lights will go back on, boys and girls. All the lamps in the streets! All the lights in the shop windows! (*Almost, now, like one a little crazed*) Lights! Lights! Lights! Lights everywhere a-shining!

THE CLASS: (*Together*) Ooooooooooh.

OLD WOMAN: (*Eyes glistening*) Ah. But can you even begin to imagine what that will be like, boys and girls? Can you remember? No. Of course you can't. You none of you can recall the days of peace.

She looks at them, then points at the map again.

But it won't be long now, the way things are going. Thanks to our brave soldiers and sailors and airmen – God bless their hearts. Oh, it certainly won't be long, boys and girls. The big day is coming! So–o–o–o, chests out, shoulders back, eyes bright! Shape each word loud and clear with happy hearts! We will sing the song that is at last, at long long last, going to come true! A-one, a-two – !

She beats out time with her pointer, then, as evocative as the Ovalteenies, the children sing 'It's a Lovely Day Tomorrow'.

On the train, the song still in our ears, Philip looks at the newspaper headline: 'THE WAR IS RUSHING TO AN END! GERMAN ARMIES SURRENDERING ON ALL FRONTS.'

He makes small-boy-guns-and-explosion sounds, to himself. *Kerrrr–bang! Pshloop!* Mrs Marlow lowers her paper. She looks across at the self-absorbed but noise-making Philip.

MRS MARLOW: Stop it, Philip.

He does. She looks out of the window, and his attention focuses intently on her again.

PHILIP: Mum? Our Mum – ?

MRS MARLOW: (*Sigh*) What is it now?

Philip darts an anxious look at the soldiers in the carriage, but they are decidedly more interested in his mother than in him, so –

PHILIP: Why won't they let him come wi' us? Why won't they let our Dad out of the pit?

Tiny pause.

MRS MARLOW: Direction of labour.

PHILIP: What? Wos that?

One of the soldiers laughs.

A SOLDIER: It's doing what we're told as makes us free.

Mrs Marlow does not want general conversation.

MRS MARLOW: Why don't you just sit quiet? Be a good boy. You should have brought your *Hotspur*. Sit quiet and look out of the window, before it gets too dark to see anything.

PHILIP: (*Sigh*) It's a long time. It chunt half a long woy. England yun half a big country, mind.

She doesn't respond, so he sighs, and looks out of the window. Mrs Marlow snaps open a small compact, looks at herself in its little mirror, and starts to put on very bright red lipstick. The soldiers are watching her, hungrily.

SAME SOLDIER: Would you – excuse me, would you like a fag – ?

She looks at the soldier, evenly.

MRS MARLOW: Don't smoke.

They momentarily hold glances, with some sort of spark.

SOLDIER: Oh, dear. No vices, eh?

MRS MARLOW: I wouldn't bank on it.

And she snaps shut the compact, with one sidelong glitter of a glance at him as he laughs. Philip notices, and frowns, then looks out of the darkening window again at a passing field.

Puzzlingly, as though formed out of the boy's anxiety and unhappiness, it seems to be the same field as before, miles back, except for the much poorer light. That is, there is a stiff, oddly near-human scarecrow in the middle of the scrubby, sloping patch, in the same long old greatcoat, the same battered trilby. Philip looks back from the window, upset, puzzled.

PHILIP: There's a –

He checks himself, and frowns, knitting his brows, and looking around the crowded carriage.

MRS MARLOW: (*Voice over*) *Seeing things again, are we?*

He looks at her, but decides she has not really spoken.

PHILIP: (*Swallows*) Our Mum – ?

But she does not reply. Clacketty–clacketty–clack–clack.

Philip thinks the soldiers are staring at him. And they do: staring, staring, hard-eyed, accusing. He shifts, and swallows, nervously.

Clacketty–clacketty–clack–clack, hypnotically. The rhythm of the train seems amplified over the boy's scared, worried little face. Then –

> (*Thinks, an intense whisper*) *Summat's wrong! This yunt right! This yunt never right. Where's our Dad then? Do him know about the woods – ? What be thoy looking at I for? Is it my fault? I a' gone and done it agyun!*

Staring, staring at him, hard-eyed and accusing, no longer the soldiers, but the patients in the ward, pyjamaed, in the carriage. And also staring at him, with cool mockery, not Mrs Marlow, but the woman Nicola.

> (*Thinks, intense*) *Perhaps they be German in disguise – but – but – I thought everything was supposed to be all right when we have byut* [beat] *them buggers. But – but – where are –*

MARLOW: (*Voice over, same accent*) *– Where we goo–ing? Mum? Our mum? Round and round I reckon. Round and –*

PHILIP: (*Thinks, intense whisper*) *– Round and bloody round. The same bits all the time. Summat's wrong. Summat's bloody wrong, mind!*

Clacketty–clacketty–clack–clack.

Then Philip's eyes go even wider at another sound within the

94

carriage. Mrs Marlow has started to cry. It is a suppressed, embarrassed, snuffling sound, from held-in beginnings growing into open weeping, her hands going to her face.

(*Shocked*) Mum! What is it, our Mum? Mum – ! What bist thou crying for – ! Mum!

The soldiers, looking at her, are obviously awkward and embarrassed.

THE SOLDIER: Is there anything we can do, love? What's the matter? It can't be as bad as that, can it?

PHILIP: Mum! Doosn't!

MRS MARLOW: (*Choke*) It's – I'm all right – It's – Leave me alone – I'll be all right in a – in a – in a minute –

Grim-faced, tense Marlow is in his wheelchair, facing Dr Gibbon's table, as the last echoes of Mrs Marlow's held-in sobs seem to die in the room. Gibbon is walking up and down behind him, in his mildly eccentric manner, his shoes once again going click–clack–clock on the wooden floor. Then he stops.

DR GIBBON: Irreducibly beyond elucidation.

MARLOW: (*Surly*) *That* wins a prize. A year's subscription to the *Reader's Digest*.

DR GIBBON: Impossible to unravel, I mean.

MARLOW: You think so?

DR GIBBON: Oh, yes. There are *always* things which puzzle us as children, Mr Marlow. Accept it. Do you?

MARLOW: Accept the sky. Accept the birds. Accept birdshit.

Click–clock–clack again. Then –

DR GIBBON: The point is there are always things from our childhood that we can never properly work out, surely? They are mysteries. They remain so. Even to a writer of detective stories!

MARLOW: You know something?

DR GIBBON: Yes?

MARLOW: You're not a character in *The Maltese Falcon*. You're more like something in *The Archers*.

DR GIBBON: Sorry?

MARLOW: The way you walk about behind me, where I can't see you. The way you walk up and down on this wooden floor – I mean, are you pretending to be eccentric? Or are

you genuinely cuckoo? Do you think it helps? If so, let me
    tell you it is simply ve–r–y irr–it–at–ing –
Gibbon, who has stopped during this, solemnly listening,
resumes the offence, walking loudly up and down behind
Marlow's wheelchair, as though considering the point.
DR GIBBON: Mmm. Mmmmm.
MARLOW: (*Hiss*) God in heaven!
DR GIBBON: (*Suddenly*) Has your wife been to see you, yet?
    Oops! So–rry. You *said* you were not married, didn't you?
Gibbon waits, behind Marlow, his head cocked, a glint in his
eye. But Marlow makes no reply, and does not so much as
twitch. The doctor half-sighs, and comes to the table, in front of
Marlow, and perches sparrow-like on its edge, and peers keenly
at him.
MARLOW: Ah. There you are.
DR GIBBON: (*Smile*) You are beginning to look better. Do you
    know that?
MARLOW: (*Edgy*) Am I?
DR GIBBON: Your posture would seem to indicate that you are
    in less pain. Is that so?
MARLOW: (*Half-reluctant*) It's not hurting so much, no.
DR GIBBON: Then let go of those neck muscles a little.
MARLOW: What do you mean?
DR GIBBON: I wondered if you would look around, you see.
MARLOW: What – ?
DR GIBBON: I wanted you to turn your head. You'll get fewer
    headaches that way.
MARLOW: Who said I – ?
DR GIBBON: (*Cutting in*) But you do, don't you? Severe ones.
Marlow does not reply.
    I have little doubt that – partly as a result – your
    perceptions are a little – distorted? Mmm?
MARLOW: (*With irony*) Minute by minute, we make the world.
We make our own world.
DR GIBBON: The point is –
MARLOW: (*Snap*) *That's* the point!
DR GIBBON: The point is you are, without perhaps realizing it,
    using your body just a little more freely. Leaving aside the
    skin for a moment, I take it that the arthropathy is less

pronounced?

MARLOW: (*Slight pause.*) Maybe.

DR GIBBON: Wouldn't you be better off in a side ward? More or less a room on your own.

MARLOW: (*Suspicious*) Why?

DR GIBBON: Because it might well be time for you to consider starting work again, might it not? And with more privacy, of a sort –

Marlow holds out his scabbed and brutally buckled hands, bitterly.

MARLOW: How can I do that?

DR GIBBON: I never write anything myself. I dictate. Ever tried it?

MARLOW: Who to? (*Slightest pause.*) To whom?

DR GIBBON: Oh, there are people. Agencies.

MARLOW: (*Suspicious*) Has someone been getting to you? Someone talking to you about me? Have they?

DR GIBBON: What do you mean?

MARLOW: Has a certain high-class whore of my former acquaintance been thrusting her hard little nose into my affairs? Eh?

Gibbon stares at him, astonished by the degree of the venom. Then – in a decidedly harsher tone –

DR GIBBON: Mr Marlow. Perhaps I've misunderstood. But – you *do* intend to get better?

MARLOW: (*Surprised*) What?

DR GIBBON: You do *want* to?

MARLOW: (*Indignant*) What do you think!

Gibbon drops off his perch on the table edge, like one challenged, looking, for the moment, almost comically fierce.

DR GIBBON: Chronic illness is an extremely good shelter. Have you ever seen it in those terms? A cave in the rocks into which one can safely crawl?

Marlow scowls, but makes no immediate comment, and Gibbon starts walking about on the wooden floor again, click–clack–clock, moving behind Marlow again.

A retreat. Is it not? Illness. A cave in the rocks.

MARLOW: (*Growl*) Not much of one, I can assure you. A very poor bloody cave, if you want to know.

DR GIBBON: Oh, no, not very comfortable, of course – There are bats in it. Squeaking rodents with wings of skin, and fur, and eyes that see in the pitch darkness – creatures that hang upside down. But, then – you know about those. You know about *bats*.

Marlow whirls his head all the way round, or nearly so, spontaneously.

MARLOW: (*Indignant*) What you mean – ?

Gibbon points at him in a boyish sort of triumphant glee.

DR GIBBON: You see! You turned! You *turned*. Virtually all the way round.

Marlow blinks at him, so astonished by himself that he does not even hear the faint tap–tap on the door, though Gibbon clearly does.

MARLOW: Yes. I did. I did! I mean – I *am*!

Then he realizes that Gibbon is hissing urgently at the quarter-opened door.

DR GIBBON: Not now! Not *now* –

Nicola, at the partly open door, looks startled, then nods, and quickly closes the door. Gibbon expels his breath, as Marlow, too slow, manages to get his head around again to look at the closing door.

MARLOW: What is the m– ? Who was that?

But Gibbon has bounced jovially in front of him, beaming his congratulations, diversionary.

DR GIBBON: (*Excessive*) Progress, Mr Marlow! Undoubted progress! Who knows how far it will go, eh? Tomorrow can be a much brighter day.

Marlow appraises him, coolly.

MARLOW: I never went to see Billy Graham. But there *is* someone you remind me of!

The sardonic memory is, in fact, of the old woman teacher in the village school. She beats time in front of the class with her long blackboard pointer, glowing. The children are singing their hearts out, in the middle of the optimistic 'It's a Lovely Day Tomorrow'.

Each bright 8- or 9-year-old face in turn glows through the song, and before the finish, when they all fold their arms behind

98

their backs again, eyes alive, but now absolutely still and completely silent, Marlow's side-of-the-mouth style observations creep in.

> (*Voice over*) Swing it. Jazz it. Drag it. Howsoever the beat, I tell you I know *hoods* when I see them. And you don't play nursery tunes to hard-faced pugs with marbles where their eyeballs should be.

The last face in all the classroom faces to be examined is that of Philip, at his desk.

> (*Voice over*) I knew I was ankle-deep in the mess. What I had to do now was to decide whether to let the ooze get up to my knee bones. Something needed doing. I had to do it. And I don't mean dropping the toast to see if it landed butter side up –

Marlow's words end on the night-time Thames at Hammersmith. Moonlight on dark water, ornate bridge, lower river wall, and house fronts.

A figure is waiting by the river wall, very still, looking up at Binney's windows. It is a female silhouette.

And then we see she is a blonde woman, steady-eyed, and wrapped in a luxurious, dark fur coat, her hand holding the collar to her throat. It would be Mrs Marlow, except for the colour of the hair and the luxury of the clothing. It is, in short, the same actress. Now, she is called Lili. Her eyes are fixed in a watchful glitter on Binney's house.

Inside, Binney is pacing up and down, looking surly, even malevolent. The Singing Detective lounges unconcerned in an armchair, a half-full glass and a bottle of single-malt Scotch on the table beside him.

> Don't get a kick out of it myself – but you ever go to the zoo, Mr Binney?

BINNEY: What?

MARLOW: Maybe the reptile house is more in your line, but you ever watch a tiger in its cage?

BINNEY: What are you talking about, Marlow?

MARLOW: Up and down, up and down, pad, pad, pad. You'll get sore paws, my friend.

BINNEY: I'm thinking. And *you're* no help, are you?

MARLOW: Looking for a way out. Any way to get through those
bars. But do you know what that dumb creature hasn't
worked out, for all its stripes?

BINNEY: What?

Marlow takes a slow drink, swishes it around his mouth,
swallows.

MARLOW: (*With satisfaction*) There *is* no way out. Not through
the bars. They never get out. Period.

Binney, standing in the middle of the room, stares at him, with
bitterness.

BINNEY: Thank you. That's very profound.

MARLOW: Don't mention it. I like to share my observations
with my clients.

BINNEY: And what else are *you* doing? Apart from making these
silly, second-hand remarks?

MARLOW: You wouldn't be meaning my unhelpful,
paperback-soiled, mid-Atlantic, little side-of-the-mouth
quips by any chance, would you?

BINNEY: Precisely!

MARLOW: I'll have to change my toothpaste. It's too late in the
day to change my style.

BINNEY: You'll have to change something! So far, I've not got
much out of you, Marlow. What have *you* come up with,
may I ask?

MARLOW: As yet? Nothing. Zero. Nix. *Nichevo*.

BINNEY: (*Startled*) What?

MARLOW: Russian. For the same big O.

BINNEY: I know it's Russian. How – (*Stops, changes tack.*) Mr
Marlow. You can't deny that I'm paying you good money,
and –

MARLOW: (*Cutting in*) Money. You're paying money. Why put
'good' in front of it. Who knows its virtue? *I* don't know
where it's been. Do you?

BINNEY: Good money. Bad money. What-the-hell-money. I'm
paying you enough, that's for sure, because I was told you
were the best – But – please! – Tell me! – *What*, precisely,
are you doing – ?

Marlow takes a drink, measures him, sardonic.

MARLOW: Vamping.

BINNEY: What – ?

MARLOW: Vamping till ready.

BINNEY: (*Exasperated*) I have no idea what you mean. Really.
No idea of what you are talking about. Isn't it possible for
you to talk properly, in ordinary, decent English?

MARLOW: (*Sigh*) Vamp till ready. That's what the piano player
does. No big deal. That's what the ivory tickler does while
he's waiting for the band. Or the singer or whatever to
come in with the theme. (*Sniff.*) Jesus. The standard of
education today. You'll be telling me next you don't know
Hoagy's surname.

BINNEY: What – ?

MARLOW: Carmichael. It's Carmichael.

BINNEY: For God's sake!

Marlow twirls his glass, looking at the Scotch inside it.

MARLOW: Yellow. Mellow.

BINNEY: Now listen here, you – !

MARLOW: No curling at the edges.

He drinks, relishes it, then looks at Binney.

So far, the intro does not tell us what sort of song we're
going to hear. We *have* to vamp. Until things start –
unravelling – a bit.

BINNEY: Wait, you mean?

MARLOW: Wait.

BINNEY: (*Agitated*) That may not be possible. What if the
Police arrest me? They might! Or what if those two
creatures come after me?

MARLOW: Forget the cops. If they had got enough, they would
have nabbed you already. They're not broody hens. They
don't sit on their eggs. Know what they do?

BINNEY: No – what do you – ?

MARLOW: (*Cutting in*) Break the shells straight away. And then
fry what's inside.

BINNEY: (*Swallow*) I'm the – they say I'm the last person to see
her alive –

MARLOW: Last but one.

Binney stops short. Looks at him.

BINNEY: Yes. Last but one. Of course.

MARLOW: (*Insolently*) You've got some expensive things in this room, Mr Binney.

BINNEY: I have some *nice* things, if that's what you mean.

MARLOW: No. That's not what I mean. Nice, I did not say. Expensive, I said. Hideously expensive things.

BINNEY: (*Aloof*) Tastes differ. You're more at home in dance halls.

MARLOW: Either way – you're not groping in your pockets for the last penny, are you? You're weighed down with half-crowns.

BINNEY: I do all right.

MARLOW: Oh, I can see you do. But what do you do all right *at*?

BINNEY: (*Shrug*) I buy. I sell.

MARLOW: So does the rag-and-bone man. *What* do you buy? What do you sell?

Binney looks at him, his disdain showing.

BINNEY: I rather think that is *my* affair, isn't it?

MARLOW: Sure. But maybe there's a connection if you're buying and selling the wrong sort of stuff for the wrong sort of people. Some trades are not healthy.

BINNEY: No, no.

MARLOW: Or – maybe the gap is too big between what you pay for the goods and what you get for them. There's a word for that. Begins with T.

BINNEY: No.

MARLOW: No?

BINNEY: (*Angrily*) No!

Marlow shrugs, swirls his whisky, drinks, smokes, then looks at Binney as though he is about to play games with him.

MARLOW: *Sprechen Sie Deutsch?*

Binney stiffens, and stares at him.

BINNEY: Why do you ask? What's that to do with it?

MARLOW: Well, now. I know you speak the Slav. And when somebody gets their tongue around those sorts of syllables, Mr Binney, I'd make a guess that they were pretty nifty with the larynx in other lingos. I'm the same with English, in case you hadn't noticed. But I've asked you a question. How's your German, *Kamerad*?

Binney watches him with narrowed eyes. He hesitates, then, half reluctantly –

BINNEY: I speak it. A little.

MARLOW: How little? I mean, can you say *Auf* but not *Wiedersehen*, or what?

BINNEY: A little. Enough to find my way around the rubble.

MARLOW: Or to say *Guten Tag* to some fat old Nazi on the run, maybe?

BINNEY: (*Sharply*) What do you mean? What are you getting at?

MARLOW: Well, now am I right? Or am I right? (*Sips his drink, with deliberation.*) I'm a slow sort of guy. The neon doesn't flash on my forehead. I can't even keep up with a retired tortoise. (*Sips again, with the same sort of deliberation.*) But I do have funny little tunes that make me tap my toes. And I get there. I get there in the end. *Tum–tee–tum–tee–tiddly–tum.*

Binney stares at him, troubled, but speculative.

BINNEY: I think I – I think I've underestimated you.

MARLOW: That's no new experience.

BINNEY: Mr Marlow.

MARLOW: I'm listening. Don't you see my ears swivelling?

BINNEY: (*Hesitant*) I – well, I've slightly misled you. I didn't go to that nightclub *totally* by accident.

MARLOW: I'm still listening.

BINNEY: A club like that, you see – well, it's not just a sort of, sort of high-class brothel, or – it's an exchange market for girls, yes. But not all those girls are what they seem.

MARLOW: Girls are never what they seem.

BINNEY: I wish I'd never got mixed up in it. Murder is not my cup of tea, I can tell you. But I think somebody or some organization is trying to pin this girl's death on me. And I wouldn't be totally surprised if it was a counter-intelligence thing – (*Stops.*) Have you any idea what I'm talking about?

MARLOW: Go to the window.

BINNEY: What? (*Blink.*) Why?

MARLOW: Take a peep, Mr Binney. Pierce the murk and gloom. I'll lay you any odds there's one of those girls who are not what they seem watching this place. It's a cold night. I hope she's wearing some dead animal or other. (*Sips his drink again, in the same deliberate manner.*) Sable, at a guess. And *they're* nasty little shits, believe you me. Sharp teeth is one thing. But they *stink*, too.

BINNEY: (*Nervous*) There's a girl – ? What sort of girl?

MARLOW: Take a look. I'm only guessing. I might even be
wrong. Am I wrong? Or am I wrong?

Agitated, Binney goes to the window, and twitches the curtain
aside, just a little, and stands side on so that he cannot be seen.

The widening chink reveals, down below, the blonde woman
in a fur coat, her hand holding up the collar to her throat, the
river glinting cold and dark behind her. There is something
about the tableau which evokes some long-gone illustration on a
song-sheet cover, of the romantic but melancholy kind. So, of
course, the opening notes of a particularly haunting song begin,
of the period.

The beautiful girl, this Mrs Marlow masquerading as a
mysterious blonde, so to speak, and now called Lili, turns to us,
forlorn, mysterious, the moonlight gleaming on her long blonde
hair. She 'sings' a 1940s recording of 'Lili Marlene', throatily,
mysteriously. The song ends, almost in mid-note, as Binney,
eyes bright with alarm, lets the curtain fall back into place and
looks back across the room at Marlow. He seems to know who it
is.

BINNEY: Why is she there? What does she want – ?

Marlow looks at him with sardonic amusement.

MARLOW: I'll be the pickles. You be the ham.

BINNEY: (*Changed tone*) What are you getting at?

MARLOW: I'm saying in my subtle way that you're not too hot as
an actor, Binney. I think you know who it is out there with
a pistol in the pocket of her fur coat. I think you know *what*
she is.

BINNEY: All right. What is she?

MARLOW: She works for a place with onions on top of its
towers. She's as red as a London bus. She doesn't trade in
Nazis. And she wonders why *you* do.

BINNEY: Me?

MARLOW: Yes. You.

Binney's face twitches.

BINNEY: Get out, Marlow. Get out. And don't let me see you
again.

MARLOW: And what about my fee?

BINNEY: Fee? What fee?

MARLOW: I sing for people who dance, Binney. Tell me the
tune you want. I'll croon it for *your* dance. When your feet
go through the trap door. I'll enjoy that. Believe me.

Marlow picks up his trilby hat.

BINNEY: You're cheap, Marlow.

Marlow, already at the door, looks back.

MARLOW: Ten cents a dance, fella.

And he puts on his hat.

Revolving on its spindle under the antiquely fat needle head, a
thick old 78-rpm record is shiny as it turns. 'Lili Marlene' is
being played.

In the hospital, the real Marlow is being pushed back to the
ward, in his wheelchair, from Gibbon's door, by the same porter
as before. The record of 'Lili Marlene' continues to be heard. A
troubled memory in his head. After Marlow passes, Nicola steps
out from the shadow of a doorway, and watches the wheelchair
recede down the long corridor. There is an undoubted gleam in
her eyes: *What is she up to?* is the question.

The gramophone record is in fact coming from a crowded room
in a terrace house in Hammersmith, back in 1945. Listening
with an almost excessive respect to the big wind-up
gramophone, which is encased in a fluted and whorled walnut
cabinet the size of a modern cabinet freezer, are the boy Philip,
Mrs Marlow, and the new characters Grandad Baxter, Aunt
Emily, a lodger called Mary, and in Army uniform (lance
corporal), Uncle John.

A hugger-mugger, oppressive, working-class intimacy.

'Lili' waits in the riverside Mall, alone in the dark. She is
fleetingly illuminated by moonlight, like a figure on a song
sheet, as the song continues.

Binney has gone back to his window, where he holds aside the
curtain just enough to stare down at the Mall below, his eyes
cold, his face menacing. The song is continuing.

At the river wall, the waiting girl (as on the original record) turns and delivers a sensually throaty, painful evocative, bitter-sweet German version.

German words on the gramophone record for the over-attentive listeners in the Hammersmith house. As the song continues on the gramophone, Grandad Baxter, old and fat, and leather-belted, with boots with tabs on, and a walrus moustache (Mrs Marlow's father) looks at Philip.

GRANDAD: That is *German*, Philip. That is yer actual bleed'n German that tart is singing!

MRS MARLOW: (*Mildly*) Watch your language please, Dad.

GRANDAD: What?

MRS MARLOW: Don't say tart.

GRANDAD: Don't you tell me what to say, gel. (*Then, puzzled*) Whatchewmean – It is a tart, ennit? Singing.

MRS MARLOW: It's not nice.

AUNT EMILY: Ooh. Come over posh now you come back, Bett.

MRS MARLOW: He won't understand. Philip doesn't understand words like that.

GRANDAD: Then he'd better bloody well learn, then, hadn't he?

In the hospital ward, there is the normal hustle and bustle of the daytime activities as the song, in German, continues without break.

The old Londoner, George, looking just a little perkier or more used to the ward, is leaning across, trying to attract the attention of the man in the next bed, Marlow. He has his eyes on the packet of cigarettes on Marlow's bedside locker. But Marlow is totally abstracted or self-absorbed, exactly as though he is listening to the Lili Marlene song. He gradually, and reluctantly, becomes aware that the old man in the next bed is seeking his attention.

GEORGE: Oy. Oy, there. Bloody 'ell! Oy–oy, Char–lie!

MARLOW: What?

And he reaches to his locker, like someone returning to life, to get a cigarette. This is something which, even though accomplished with some difficulty and a tiny gasp of pain, we have seen that he was unable to do before. And he lights it, holding the lighter in both clenched, damaged hands.

GEORGE: Blimey. Wiv us now are you, mate?

MARLOW: What?

And he blows out smoke.

GEORGE: Fought you was dead! Like being in the bleed'n
　　waxworks.

MARLOW: What is it?

GEORGE: (*Still indignant*) Bloody miles away, you was.

Marlow looks at him, with a frown, not wanting conversation.

MARLOW: Well, that's better than being *here*, isn't it? And a
　　sight more *private*, I'd say –

GEORGE: Oh, oh. Be like that.

MARLOW: Yes. Sorry. I don't want to talk.

GEORGE: Christ All Bloody Mighty.

Pause. George stares. Marlow smokes. Then –
　　(*Changed tone*) It's the fags, y'see. It's the fags, ennit?

MARLOW: (*Sigh*) What – ?

GEORGE: A fag.

MARLOW: You want one?

GEORGE: I'm gasping for one. I tell you. I'm dying for one.

Marlow blows out a column of smoke, a nastily amused glint in
his eye.

MARLOW: That's probably more true than you'll ever know.

GEORGE: Bloody old doc. Off his coconuts. I smoked all me life,
　　I have, and it ain't never done me no harm. (*Wheedlingly*)
　　Give us one. Lend us one. Eh? Give us a drag, for Gawd's
　　sake . . . It's bloody crool. That's what it is. (*Coughs,
　　gratingly.*) Eh? *Eh*?

MARLOW: I can't throw. And I can't get out of bed.

GEORGE: Nor me.

MARLOW: Why's that, then?

GEORGE: Me chest.

MARLOW: Your heart.

GEORGE: Me *chest*. Got this bleed'n awful pain in me chest.
　　(*Slaps it, feebly.*) Right here. And down me arm.

MARLOW: And you want a cigarette. You must be off your
　　head.

GEORGE: Clear me chest, won't it? A fag clears yer lungs out.
　　Give us one, there's a pal.

MARLOW: (Sigh) I can't get out of bed.
GEORGE: (Sigh) Nor me.
Marlow loses whatever interest he had in the conversation, and,
propped up against his pillows, tries ineffectually to blow smoke
rings. Then –
> It's like being back in the bleed'n war.
No response.
>> Like gold, they was. Fags was. Like little gold bars. You
>> could get anyfink wiv a fag. You could hump a lovely young
>> girl for a couple of fags.
Marlow becomes interested again, but with a frown.
MARLOW: What?
GEORGE: Yeh, you could. Nice bit of skirt, if you had a packet
of Player's in your pocket. Not half!
MARLOW: When? Where?
GEORGE: When we come into Hamburg. 1945. Phew – bloody
place was flattened. They'd come out of *holes*, these krauts,
wouldn't they? Holes in the grahnd. In the rubble and that
– know what I mean? And some of them women – Cor
bloody hell, whatchacallits – ? *Frow Lines*. Blonde, ent
they? But – nice. Know what I mean? I'm talking about no
slag, am I? Lovely bits of stuff. Good knockers on 'em.
Well – couple of fags it was for a shag. Couple of fags, eh?,
and up wiv their dresses, dahn with their knickers – Eh?
Cor – !
George, running out of wind, nevertheless cackles lasciviously,
like a cartooned dirty old man, but the cackle, and the gasping
for air that it entails, evidently causes shooting pains in his
chest. The lascivious, over-stimulated cackle ends in a little yelp
of pain, followed by a helpless series of shuddering gasps.
  Marlow is looking across at him, without sympathy. Indeed,
with every sign of a fierce, puritanical disgust.
MARLOW: (Gratingly) What's wrong, George? What's the
matter?
GEORGE: (Faint gasp) Chest –
MARLOW: (Gratingly) Hurting, is it? In pain, are you?
GEORGE: (Barely audible) Nurse – call the –
It is glaringly obvious that Marlow should press his dangling
buzzer or yell for help, for no one else seems able to hear

George's feeble struggles. But –

MARLOW: Are they coming up out of their holes in the ground, George? All those helpless little blonde girls with frightened eyes. Are they coming up out of the rubble? Are they pointing at you, George? Are you going to give them a couple of fags?

GEORGE: (*Croak*) N–ur–se –

Very faint, almost like a valedictory croak.

MARLOW: Oh? And what would *you* do with a pretty young nurse, Georgie Porgie Pudding and Pie? Would you call her an angel, my old mate? Think of her as a saint, eh? The pure. The undefiled.

George half rallies for a final, desperate plea.

GEORGE: Call the – Call –

Pitiless Marlow watches George's agonized struggles with a terrible glint in his eyes. He lets out more smoke, deliberately slowly. Then –

MARLOW: (*Mimics*) Up wiv their dresses. Dahn with their knickers.

George is no longer trying to call, as he loses consciousness. He makes the peculiar noise of a man on the edge of a cardiac arrest. Marlow watches, cruelly, and still makes no attempt to call for help.

(*Eventually, and to himself*) Time has come for roll-call.

But he seems upset.

You can't say you haven't asked for it, George old son.

Time for us to part. The old lamp is due to go out –

He stops. He turns his head to stare at the apparently dying George. Then –

Nurse! (*Loud yell*) Nurse! Quickly! Nurse!

But George has a bubble on his lips, and a small, odd gurgle comes from his mouth.

In the Forest of long ago, wedged in the uppermost cleft of the old oak tree, the boy Philip looks out thoughtfully on the surrounding woodland, which is full of singing birds. A blackbird trills, liquidly. Philip listens to it, then looks straight at us, and speaks in a conspiratorial, half-frightened near whisper. A characteristic intensity.

PHILIP: Thoy won't find out who it was. Na! Thoy'll never ever-ever – find out. Na! (*Thinks about it.*) Thoy can give I the worst Chinese burn ever. The worst in the history of the world. (*Thinks about it.*) Thoy can tie me down on a hill of cruel, poisonous black ants, with my shirt off my back. And I'll never tell. Not ever! (*Less certainly* –) Thoy'll never find out – Not if I kip my mouth sh–

He stops abruptly, startled, in mid-word. He has heard something, down below in the woods. From way down below, and some way off, a woman laughs. The laugh is coming from a path that we may perhaps recognize from before – very narrow, twisting and turning its way through the densely packed trees and the fern and foxglove undergrowth of the thickest, leafiest and most remote part of the Forest.

It is pretty Mrs Marlow who laughs. And the young man with her, Ray, feels nervous about the noise, looking about in the dense woodland foliage.

RAYMOND: Highsht, mind, Betty, o'butt – thee's never know who's about in these 'oods.

Appalled, the boy Philip recognizes the voices, as the two people get nearer. He strains to listen. The path below is so narrow, so overgrown, that the two are virtually in single file, Mrs Marlow a little behind.

MRS MARLOW: Don't be such a ninny, Raymond. There's nobody about.

RAYMOND: Didn't say there *was*, but –

MRS MARLOW: Christ, we've been going into this stuff for ages. We must be half a mile from *anywhere*. And we haven't seen a soul.

RAYMOND: Ah. But thou bisn't from round here. You don't come fram here, doost?

MRS MARLOW: No – but what's that got to do with it – ?

RAYMOND: Just that round here there's eyes and ears everywhere. Oh, I d'know, mind. Tha' cosn't be too careful.

MRS MARLOW: (*Slight mockery*) I didn't know you were so nervous –

Puzzled, obscurely frightened, Philip listens on his perch as the voices come so close that they are almost directly below.

RAYMOND: (*Below*) I byunt nervous at all. Just careful.

MRS MARLOW: (*Below*) There's nothing to worry about. There's only *trees* – lots and lots of bloody trees and brambles and God knows what – !

And she laughs again. But the laugh is just a little too shrill, showing that she, too, is nervous and on edge.

RAYMOND: Oh, thik laugh of thine – No wonder thou's make I nervous – I'll have to shut thy mouth, won't I?

But he is grinning as he says this, and he pulls her into him, his mouth searchingly eager for hers.

MRS MARLOW: Raymond – Hang on. Hang on, there's –

A trailing of bramble or briar has caught in the flimsy material of her dress, at its skirt.

RAYMOND: Ho. I see – holt on, holt on, let's get'n off – No damage done as I can see –

He starts to pull the briar away.

MRS MARLOW: Don't tear my dress, whatever you do –

RAYMOND: Christ, these is sharp! Kip still a minute –

MRS MARLOW: Don't tear my dress!

But he has got the bramble clear, almost.

RAYMOND: Tear'n *off* ya, Betty, my babby!

In releasing the thorn, holding the bottom of her thin, flowered dress very carefully, Raymond has had to raise her skirt. He now lifts it higher, enough to expose her thigh.

MRS MARLOW: That's right. Get an eyeful.

RAYMOND: And lovely 'tis, too! I could look at tha all the live-long day.

He clasps her thigh, vigorously.

MRS MARLOW: Hey. Steady –

RAYMOND: What's the matter?

MRS MARLOW: No marks, Raymond. No bruises.

But it does not sound like a genuine admonition. Indeed, the opposite. He keeps her dress in his hand, and bends, kissing her thigh.

RAYMOND: Hey. Hey. No sense in wasting time, chick – This is what we come for, yunnit? I cont hold back no more!

Philip perched in the treetop, listening to the voices below, is trying to work out dark and threatening mysteries.

MRS MARLOW: (*Off*) Ooh, God. Don't. Don't touch me there.

Not yet. I can't – oh, Raymond – wait – we can't lie down
here – Jesus Christ, Ray – oh – don't –

A mysterious pause. Philip strains to listen, leaning right out
from the branch.

RAYMOND: (*Below*) There's a – by God, you be summat – !

MRS MARLOW: (*Below*) Don't get me going yet!

RAYMOND: (*Below*) There's a little hollow up here always, Bett
– a sart of dingly dell – better'n a double bed, eh – ?

Down below, Mrs Marlow and Raymond have broken apart a
little.

MRS MARLOW: You've been here before, haven't you! This is
not the first time –

RAYMOND: (*Leer*) I byunt saying nothing.

MRS MARLOW: Oh, you dirty devil, Ray. You're not good,
Raymond.

RAYMOND: Ah. But that's what you d'like, yunnit? You don't
want no angel doost?

MRS MARLOW: Don't think so much of yourself. There's always
another apple in the barrel.

He laughs, pulling her away.

RAYMOND: Come th'on, then. Let's see the pips!

In the treetop, Philip is still not totally sure about what is going
on, but his face shows that he knows it is frightening and illicit.
The voices below begin to recede a little – and Mrs Marlow's has
a slightly different tone now.

MRS MARLOW: (*Below*) Have you got the thing – is it going to
be all right –

RAYMOND: (*Below*) 'Course I have. Listen – don't start getting,
you know – A bit of fun never hurt nobody.

MRS MARLOW: (*Below*) I'm not so sure of that.

RAYMOND: (*Below, laugh*) Not if nobody'd find out, it don't.

MRS MARLOW: (*Below*) You wouldn't say anything, would you?
You'd never breathe a word – would you?

RAYMOND: (*Below, indignant*) What sart of bloke do you think I
be!

The voices are getting further and further away, so that the next
comment is just on the edge of all audibility.

MRS MARLOW: (*Below*) Oh – I know what sort of bloke you are,
all right!

There is some receding laughter, of that distant, mysterious, half-heard order which is always the most difficult to deal with. Whatever remaining conversation is now out of Philip's reach – and yet it is there, threateningly, and the worse for being increasingly far off.

Philip waits. He does not move. Then the birds seem to break into his attention, with their trills and chirrups. He stares at a beetle or a slug or a ladybird on the bark of the branch. His eyes narrow, and he brings the ball of his thumb hard down on the slug or insect, squashing it flat. Philip looks at the mess on his thumb. He tries to blow it off, and fails, and sighs. Then he wipes it off on the bark of the tree.

PHILIP: I cont abide things that creep and crawl and – (*Stops, thinks, works his face.*) They got to be got rid of, an' um? (*Stops, thinks, works his face.*) I cont abide dirt. It d'get everybloodywhere, doan it?

A moment. He cocks his head, listens intently, hears nothing. Then, cautiously and quietly, hand over hand, feet reaching for the next and then the next foothold, he begins the slow climb down.

Some way off, in a space between the trees, the sheltered and grassy hollow is the same place where – in Marlow's hospital fever – Nicola was seen. And, in the same configuration, her hair spreading on the tufty grass, Mrs Marlow is flat on her back. The skirt of her thin and flowered dress is pulled up to her waist. Her legs are apart. Her heels are digging into the soft ground. And Raymond, his bare backside more visible than his face, grunts and labours on top of her, his trousers down around his ankles.

Philip approaches the dell as a commando might, slithering forward on his stomach, using his elbows, inch by inch through the lush undergrowth. He reaches a fringe of tall ferns on a slight bank of wild flowers that overlook the couple.

The strange sounds from the lovers make Philip stop, dead still, hardly daring to breathe. He looks, and he looks – and he looks. From the boy's incredulous point-of-view, the love-making seems akin to violence, or physical attack. Mrs Marlow's legs have tightened in a fierce clench, and she begins to cry out, uninhibitedly.

The thrashing limbs of the lovers, and their sounds, yield slowly to the urgent anxiety around George's bed in the hospital. At first, too, the words of Raymond and Mrs Marlow overlay the activity.

MRS MARLOW: (*Cry, voice over*) Oh!

RAYMOND: (*Voice over*) Shhh! Shhh!

MRS MARLOW: (*Voice over*) Ray – !

RAYMOND: (*Voice over*) Oh–h – lovely – lovely, lovely –
    Wonderful o' butty – lovely my babby –

The emergency team for a cardiac arrest are clustered around George's bed, in a violent struggle. As George dies –

The Forest lovers are at their climax.

In the hospital, George is dead. 'It's over,' says a voice from the Emergency Team.

The Forest lovers lie still, love-making finished. Philip, in cover, is watching with wide-eyes, puzzled and scared. Raymond begins to pull himself off Mrs Marlow.

MRS MARLOW: Oh, stay! Stay!

In the ward, Marlow is watching rather as the boy has watched, with a similar expression, as somebody is starting to pull the curtains completely shut, and George lies dead on the bed, the oxygen tubes attached. Raymond's sniggery sort of laugh is heard, over.

RAYMOND: (*Voice over*) One more done, then!

MRS MARLOW: (*Voice over*) Don't laugh like that!

In the woods Philip watches and listens in an agony of conflicting thoughts.

RAYMOND: I byunt laughing – Not in the way thou's think –

MRS MARLOW: Yes, you were!

RAYMOND: Hey – hey, now –

Mrs Marlow seems resentful. Her whole mood appears to have changed. She pushes at him.

MRS MARLOW: You're heavy, Raymond –

RAYMOND: Pressed tha' right down into the ground, have I?

But he laughs the wrong sort of laugh, too close to a leer, and
she hates it.

MRS MARLOW: Off. Get off! Get off me – Raymond!

The watching Philip is alarmed, his face poking out of the
protective covering of the ferns.

PHILIP: (*Terrified whisper of thought*) *Wos him a-doing? Wos him
   doing to our Mam? Mum! Mum! Shall I go and fetch our
   Dad? Mum –* ?

RAYMOND: All right – All right! Doosn't thou start getting
   funny now. You liked it, didn't you? Got no complaints in
   thik de–partment – hast?

Mrs Marlow is now sitting upright on the tufty grass. She has
pulled her flowered little dress back down over her legs, but the
top is still unbuttoned and askew, half exposing her. Raymond,
who has pulled up but not yet buttoned his trousers, looks at
her, a flare of sexual interest fast igniting in him again.

   Oh, Betty. Bett. Thee's got lovely titties, mind. Real
   beauties. As good as I ever sid –

MRS MARLOW: Don't say that.

RAYMOND: No, mind. The best!

MRS MARLOW: Don't make comparisons –

RAYMOND: Well, they be. You should be proud on' um.

MRS MARLOW: You go on about it as though I'm a – (*Pushes his
   hand away, a little.*) I ain't a sow, Raymond. The way you
   go on about my –

RAYMOND: Aw, now! Who said 'sow'? (*Laugh.*) Hast thou ever
   sid one? Eh?

MRS MARLOW: I don't like crude talk, that's all.

RAYMOND: Sorry. Sorry. I'll wash my mouth out, shall I?
   (*Looks at her, grins.*) But all the same –

MRS MARLOW: What?

RAYMOND: All the same, my beauty. Thee's *still* got lovely 'uns!

Again, his hand moves up to cup her breast. It looks for a
moment as though she is going to protest or to stop him. But,
suddenly, in a spasm of quick feeling, she covers his hand with
her hand. They look at each other. Other feelings, other
emotions, appear to be engaged, rather than simple desire.

MRS MARLOW: Raymond?

RAYMOND: (*Tenderly*) Oh, my babby. My babby.

MRS MARLOW: Do you – mean it?
RAYMOND: My lovely soft babby.
He gently presses her back on the grass again, and begins to lick her face.
MRS MARLOW: But Raymond – ? No. Listen. List–
The watcher's eyes have not moved in his head.

Marlow, silent in his hospital bed, not dissimilarly broods, enmeshed in a complicated melancholy.
   And then he becomes aware of a strange chink–chink–chink sound. From behind the closed curtains of the next bed, the odd, yet familiar chink–chink turns out to be that of George's small change being counted, from the top of his bedside locker. Inside the curtains, withered old George lies dead and naked on top of his already stripped bed, looking peaceful, a crumpled pillow case casually or even accidentally over his genitals. Staff Nurse White and Nurse Mills are completing the inventory of his bedside locker.
STAFF NURSE WHITE: (*Counting coins*) Thirty-five – thirty-seven – forty-seven – fifty-two, three, five – um – sixty-five – seven – Sixty-eight pence. Right? Two pounds sixty-eight.
Nurse Mills enters it on a chart.
NURSE MILLS: Two pounds sixty-eight. Right.
STAFF NURSE WHITE: And one packet of mints.
NURSE MILLS: What – ?
Marlow listens intently to the conversation from behind the closed curtains immediately adjoining his bed.
STAFF NURSE WHITE: (*Behind curtains*) Packet of mints.
   They've not been opened. We don't want any fuss over those. She's the type to ask, his wife.

In the Forest dell, Raymond is sliding his mouth down from Mrs Marlow's mouth to her neck to her breast.
MRS MARLOW: (*Near-whisper*) Oh, what are we doing – ? What do we think we're –
RAYMOND: I could bite a piece out of tha', and that's the trooth – Bett? Oh, Bett, love – I wish this was – (*Stops himself.*)
   Thee's know what I d'wish. I ood give half my life for't.
She looks at him, measures him, considers –

MRS MARLOW: It can't be. It'll never happen.

RAYMOND: Why!

MRS MARLOW: (*Upset*) Oh, God. Oh, Jesus.

RAYMOND: (*Passionately*) I could, though! I could!

She looks at him, steadily.

MRS MARLOW: You could what?

The moment of dangerous bravado leaves him. He turns his declaration into something else.

RAYMOND: Bite tha'. I could bite tha', my babby. (*Clutches.*)
    Sweet as an apple. As sweet as –

His head drops to her breast again, but she suddenly twists her head, and starts to cry.

MRS MARLOW: Oh, don't – don't please – oh Ray – Raymond –
    (*A real sob.*) I don't know. I don't – I can't stand what's
    going on or –

RAYMOND: Hey, now. There yunt nothing to cry about. Now,
    is there? Betty? Hey. Hey. Stop it now. Stop it. It's only a
    bit of fun, yunnit?

Philip is once again in the train which took him to London, sitting alongside the pale glimmer of his own reflection in the darkening window. Clacketty–clacketty–clack. But Philip's eyes widen as another sound in the carriage makes him realize that his mother, opposite, is crying.

THE SOLDIER: Is there anything we can do, love? What's the
    matter? It can't be as bad as that, can it?

PHILIP: (*Shocked*) Mum! Doosn't!

MRS MARLOW: (*Choke*) It's – I'm all right – It's – leave me alone
    – I'll – I'll be all right in a – in a – in a minute –

But the one particular soldier, the one who has spoken, and who had earlier offered the cigarette, lurches to his feet, and says, almost *sotto voce* to the soldier who is actually next to Mrs Marlow –

THE SOLDIER: Move down.

SECOND SOLDIER: What? Oh. Right.

And the soldier slides into the seat, close up against Mrs Marlow in the crowded carriage.

THE SOLDIER: (*To her*) Now, now. We can't have this. Things
    can't be as bad as this, love. Now you blow your nose in

this big hanky – it is clean – Come on, now.

Controlling her tears more successfully now, she hesitates a moment, then accepts the handkerchief.

MRS MARLOW: (*Thickly*) Th–thanks –

Something about his face, his posture, crushed up close against her as he is, more than suggests that at any moment he is going to sneak his arm around her shoulders, ostensibly to comfort her. Then, suddenly, shrill, unexpectedly –

PHILIP: Leave her alone!

THE SOLDIER: (*Startled*) Now, now, sonny Jim –

PHILIP: (*Near Scream*) Doosn't thou touch her! Kip thee hands off our Mum! Leave her alone!

MRS MARLOW: (*Astonished*) Philip – ?

THE SOLDIER: Nobody's going to touch your Mum, sonny –

PHILIP: (*Sob, near hysteria*) Leave her leave her! I shall tell our Dad! Him ool kill you! Him ool!

MRS MARLOW: Philip!

PHILIP: I shall tell him! And the man in the woods! And the man!

An awful silence. Everyone stares.

Mr Marlow is on the small raised platform in the middle of one side of the crowded working men's club, 'singing', with Raymond standing 'humming' beside him, and Mrs Marlow at the piano. They are 'performing' a 1940s Inkspots' hit, 'Do I Worry?' to the original recording, and to an initially rapt audience of working men and women and servicemen.

The boy Philip is at one of the tables, with a bag of crisps and a glass of lemonade. At first, he is watching the presumed singer, his father, but as the words roll out he begins, almost in fear, to switch his attention to the people around him.

And in an exaggerated, half-parodied or even pantomimic fashion, the drinking and smoking adults start to behave like extensions of the boy's thoughts and feelings and anxieties. That is, their heads begin to lean together in a conspiratorial way, whispering an evidently poisonous gossip. They leer, and snicker, and nudge, and wink. Philip, sick with shame, looks towards the platform. But suddenly it is transformed, as in a bad dream. The physical expression of a disturbed mind.

The lighting has dipped to a ghostly dim, not unlike the hospital ward in the dead of night. The customers have all gone. The little tables are empty, except for the occasional half-full pint glass, in which the beer faintly gleams brown. Mrs Marlow is not at the piano, and Raymond is no longer standing beside Mr Marlow. And Mr Marlow stands alone and forlorn on the platform, in his singing stance, peculiarly half-lit in bluish tones, 'singing', with a slightly echoing resonance, like a voice from the dead, the high-pitched Inkspot tenor, a song of sexual anguish.

And then, the club is no longer dream-like, but normally lit, smoke-filled, crowded. The Inkspot song continuing, without interruption. Of the two 'performers', Raymond is the one standing nearest to Mrs Marlow at the piano. Almost accidentally, it seems, or absent-mindedly, like one not quite aware of the implications of what he is doing, he lets his hand fall on her shoulder. It is when he gives the tiniest of squeezes that Mr Marlow, standing alongside him 'humming', notices with a fleeting, sidelong frown. And her eyes blaze in swift warning or annoyance, and she tries to give a little shrug of the shoulders to shake off Raymond's rather too proprietorial hand.

The same man in cloth cap looms forward to Philip, across the littered table, in an ugly intrusion, openly tittering at the boy, whose eyes are now welling with tears.

CLOTH CAP: (*Whisper*) There – y'see? Do you see o'butty? Heh! Heh! Look at where him have got his hand, eh? And that yunt the only place him have been, neither! Heh! Heh! Heh!

And the nasty, crude, knowing sort of cackle is quickly taken up by first one and then another and then others at this table and then the next table. The mocking, nasty 'Hee! Hee! Hee!' continues to spread wider and wider until everyone in the crowded, smoke-filled room is laughing and tittering. Amplified, distorted, extended beyond any possible reality, the mocking laughter, almost completely drowning the song, comes at the boy from all sides, from everywhere.

In his hospital bed, Marlow, distressed, hears the end of the club song in his head, and then –

DR GIBBON: (*Voice over*) 'Mouth sucking wet and slack at

119

mouth, tongue chafing against tongue, limb thrusting
upon limb, skin rubbing at skin – '
Gibbon is reading from the paperback of *The Singing Detective*.
MARLOW: Oink. Oink.
DR GIBBON: (*Voice over*) ' – Faces contort and stretch into a
helpless leer, organs spurt out smelly stains and sticky
betrayals. This is the sweaty farce out of which – '
In the ward, behind closed curtains. The two nurses have
completed the inventory of George's bedside locker, and Staff
Nurse White is sealing down the envelope containing the money
she counted.
NURSE MILLS: That's it, then, more or less – Can you carry on
here?
STAFF NURSE WHITE: I suppose. Why?
NURSE MILLS: Mr Marlow should have been greased an hour
ago –
STAFF NURSE WHITE: (*Pulls face.*) You're welcome.
Complained, has he?
NURSE MILLS: Well – no – not exactly –
STAFF NURSE WHITE: Well, *that's* a change – Yes. All right. I
can manage.
NURSE MILLS: Thanks.
Staff Nurse White puts the envelope on George's spindly chest.
STAFF NURSE WHITE: You going to the Italian later? For a
pasta – ?
NURSE MILLS: (*Half reluctant*) I expect so – I'll let you know.
And she pulls the curtain a little aside, just enough to come
through to Marlow's bed, which adjoins. She smiles at him.
I expect you're wondering when we're going to get to
you.
MARLOW: I hope he's left more than that.
NURSE MILLS: Sorry – ?
MARLOW: Two pounds sixty-eight.
NURSE MILLS: Oh, I expect so. That's only what's in the locker
– Anyway. What are you doing listening to things that don't
concern you?
MARLOW: Yes. I've done too much of that. I need a Sony
Walkman or something.
She is bending to the lower shelf of his locker to get the tub of

ointment, showing her knees.

NURSE MILLS: Anyway. I can do you now.

MARLOW: (*Slight mimicry*) Anyway.

NURSE MILLS: (*Frown*) What?

MARLOW: Anyway. Anyway. Anyway.

NURSE MILLS: What's the matter?

MARLOW: Death.

NURSE MILLS: Yes.

MARLOW: There's a curse on that bed –

NURSE MILLS: (*Faint smile*) No, no.

MARLOW: You think it'll be many things, our grim old friend, and that it'll come in many guises. Enemy. Friend. Terrorist. Liberator –

NURSE MILLS: Oh, goodness.

He looks at her, registering the slight sarcasm, but continues –

MARLOW: But somehow – never quite so matter of fact. Quite so insulting. That's two people so far in the next bed – and each time it's been like waiting for a number 52 bus on a cold morning.

NURSE MILLS: We don't think about it. We can't.

MARLOW: No. Of course not.

NURSE MILLS: I'll draw your curtains.

MARLOW: And count my change.

NURSE MILLS: Now, now.

MARLOW: Now, now.

She looks at him. This is the second time there has been this faint mimicry. He sort of smiles a sort of apology.

NURSE MILLS: You know, you might get out of this place all the sooner if –

MARLOW: (*Cutting in, abrupt*) Yes!

NURSE MILLS: I'll draw your curtains.

MARLOW: And count my change!

She draws the curtains. Marlow watches her. His expression softens. Two all-white clad, tall, ebony-skinned mortuary attendants arrive, in soft rubber boots, and pushing a noiseless, rubber-wheeled vehicle not unlike a laundry trolley. They pass in front of Marlow's closed curtains.

FIRST ATTENDANT: (*Expressionless*) Which and what?

SECOND ATTENDANT: (*Expressionless*) Old guy. Nine–teen.

FIRST ATTENDANT: (*Expressionless*) This?

SECOND ATTENDANT: (*Expressionless*) That.

Watched by all the ward, except for the now curtained-off Marlow, they open George's curtains just wide enough to admit themselves, then the ominously quiet rubber-wheeled trolley, and then they close up the gap in the curtains again. Inside Marlow's curtained space, Nurse Mills is once again pulling on the polythene gloves.

NURSE MILLS: Where would you rather start? Legs up, or neck down – ?

MARLOW: I – this is a bit embarrassing –

NURSE MILLS: (*Crisp*) Has to be done.

MARLOW: Does it?

NURSE MILLS: You'd soon know the difference if it wasn't. Count your blessings.

MARLOW: (*Gloomily*) Oh, God. This stuff. This stuff. This filthy stuff. You'd think I was getting ready to swim the channel.

She pulls back the bedclothes.

NURSE MILLS: (*Unexpectedly*) Well, then. Lie back and think of England.

The two white-clad ebony attendants in their softly squeaking rubber boots emerge expressionless from the adjoining curtained-off bed space, pulling the rubber-wheeled trolley. George's body cannot be seen. It is in the hammock-like sag of the trolley, and the trolley has a lid, or a sheet-like cover. The two attendants, terrifying figures, smoothly wheel it towards the double doors of the ward exit, passing in front of Marlow's closed curtains.

(*Through curtain*) I hope this stuff doesn't sting too much – but hold on – I have to grease around your private parts now –

The two attendants break stride. They look at each other. They say nothing. And, comically, they continue on their way, pushing the corpse. Within the curtains, Marlow is a picture of embarrassment, or delicious distress. Once more, he is listing all the most boring things he can imagine, but not without an intensity of expression that, ultimately, rises to a near-hysteria of suppressed physical excitement –

MARLOW: (*Thinks*) John and Yoko. Ethiopian Aid for pop stars. Mark Thatcher in the desert. Dust to dust. Pyramids. Christ, no. Not pyram– *Gardener's Question Time*, chaired by Peter Hall. Plastic pitch at Queen's Park Rangers. Fog Philips on a horse. An evening's viewing from the National Film School. Elvis' birthday. No. Something else! Quick! Quickly! What's the most – (*Gasp*) – the most boring – ! The Fifth Beatle. David Owen and Shirley Williams and and – oh. Oh! How–we–yomped–across–the–Falklands. Oh! *Ludovic Kennedy*! Think Ludovic. (*Out loud*) Oh – !

NURSE MILLS: I'm sorry – I'm trying to be as gentle as I can – but, sorry, there's no way this can be done properly without lifting your –

Marlow tries to close his eyes, with a soft comical whisper, and his thoughts increase in speed, almost to the point of incoherence –

MARLOW: (*Thinks*) The Court page. Jimmy Savile OBE. Wimbledon fortnight. No good – it's no good – Ludovic Kennedy, no, no, Archer, not a penny more whatisname Archer no Geoffrey Howe no a sheep flock of sheep colour supplement special offer oh – oh – (*Gasp of pleasure*) work! (*Gasp.*) Think! Think! (*Gasp.*) The story – *The story*!

And he is released into the cheap paperback, at Binney's riverside house.

BINNEY: You're cheap, Marlow.

Marlow, already at the door, looks back.

MARLOW: Ten cents a dance, fella.

And he puts on his hat, leaves the room. Left alone, Binney's face twitches. Then he rushes to a bureau drawer, takes out a revolver.

HOSPITAL MARLOW: (*Voice over*) No! Don't think of the pistol – ! Not a pistol. Not a – oh. Oh!

Marlow comes down the elegant stair which leads from Binney's living room to the Mall outside. His attention is caught by the erotic painting of Nicola, naked, on the wall. He stops. He looks at it, with an expression of puritanical disdain. Binney appears on the landing above him, looking down. He does not have the gun in his hand, but his hand *is* menacingly inside his jacket. He

123

stares down, hard-eyed, dangerous-looking. Marlow's eyes flick
to show that he knows Binney is above him, but he continues to
examine the painting.

MARLOW: (*Calls up*) Who is this, Binney? Someone for real. Or
just your dirty mind?

BINNEY: (*Calls down*) That's art, Marlow. Which means it's
beyond you.

MARLOW: You call it what you want. But I'll tell you one
thing –

BINNEY: I'm all ears.

MARLOW: If you try to use that gun, you're a dead man.

BINNEY: Gun? What gun?

But he takes his hand away from his jacket pocket. Marlow has
not moved his eyes from the 'Nicola' painting, not once looked
up the stair.

MARLOW: I think I know this dame. Her name is – Her name is
E. Lucy Dation.

BINNEY: (*Snarl*) What are you talking about?

MARLOW: Am I right? Or am I right?

And, with an enigmatic smile, he moves quickly, suddenly, on
down the stair. Binney takes out his gun. He hesitates. Then,
when he speaks, his voice is actually that of a reproving Nurse
Mills.

BINNEY: (*Nurse Mills's voice*) Really, Mr Marlow! I would have
thought you had better control of yourself!

A prettily flustered Nurse Mills becomes real.

NURSE MILLS: Wouldn't it be more sensible to try and think of
– well – something else?

A brisk slam of Binney's front door exactly on the 'else', and
Marlow leaves. He walks into the surrounding darkness. His
eyes are swivelling about, like one expecting trouble.

MARLOW: (*Voice over*) Yeh. Something else.

He stops to cup his hands over a match, lighting a cigarette, the
flame illuminating eyes alertly darting from side to side. As the
flame dies, and he tosses away the dead match, a husky woman's
voice comes from somewhere behind him.

LILI: Mister Marlow – ?

A German accent. Marlow sucks in smoke, not turning, not hurrying. He speaks in a low, side-of-the-mouth voice.

MARLOW: That's my handle.

LILI: I vant to talk –

Marlow resumes walking. But as he does –

MARLOW: (*Quiet urgency*) Not here. Keep back. Keep out of sight. Meet me outside the Laguna in half an hour!

He increases the pace of his walk along the dark Mall towards the bridge. But behind him, also, quickening, comes the tip–tap–tip of Lili's high heels.

(*Hiss*) Little fool!

He keeps walking. She keeps walking. Then phut!, the spit of a gun with a silencer. The tip-tap of the high heels suddenly stops. Marlow turns back and runs, pulling his own gun. He gets a fleeting glimpse of two shadowy figures, but before he can fire, they are gone. He has to pocket his gun to see to the fallen girl. He cradles her. There is blood coming from her mouth.

(*Gently, upset*) Oh, I tried to warn you – I tried to tell you – oh, you silly, you poor . . .

LILI: (*Gasp*) Skinscape's –

He has to lean close to hear.

MARLOW: What? Lili – ? What about Skinscape's – ?

LILI: (*Gasp*) Skinscape's – a front for – a front –

MARLOW: A front for what? Lili – ? The Nazis they haven't caught yet, right?

She sort of nods. He holds her close.

The Nazis the British and the Yanks don't *want* to see caught. Is that it? Lili. Just nod.

But she tries to speak again.

LILI: Rockets –

MARLOW: Rockets? You mean, V2s and – You mean the rocket scientists? Lili – ? And you Reds are trying to stop it. Is that it?

She looks at him imploringly, and dies. He holds her close a moment, deeply upset, then looks along the dark and empty Mall.

(*Hiss*) I'll get you. Whoever you are. Whatever you are. Wherever you are.

Greenish letters finish their blip-blip progression across the small screen of a word processor.

  – it landed butter side up.

Nicola is looking at the monitor screen. She speaks to someone we cannot see.

NICOLA: (*Laugh*) My God! If only he knew! If only that poor sick slob knew the half of it!

'Peg o' My Heart' begins to throb on the harmonicas.

The River Mall is dark. Empty. There is no sign of Marlow, or the girl. Moonlight, and 'Peg o' My Heart'.

MARLOW: (*Voice over*) Something needed doing. I had to do it. And I don't mean dropping the toast to see if it landed butter side up.

4

As before, with what seems a deliberate artifice, the moon
gradually forms itself in a wavery, silvery globe on the slow,
dark water. 'Bei mir bist du Schön' in the almost equally wavery
version by Guy Lombardo and His Royal Canadians begins to be
heard.

A 1945 ambulance has pulled up in the roadway, where Lili
was shot. Two Ambulance Men are covering Lili's body with a
blanket, in the same movement and the same feel and almost the
same configuration as the manner in which the drowned girl was
dealt with on the Police launch.

In the half-dark of the nighttime hospital ward, Marlow broods
and smokes, like one listening to distantly evocative music. 'Bei
mir bist du Schön', in fact.

The Guy Lombardo record is heard over a dispiriting seedy
terrace of houses, whose front doors open straight on to the
pavement. Marlow's thoughts have plunged through the artifices
of his cheap fiction to the real memories of the London house,
forty years ago.

Inside, Philip, Mrs Marlow, Grandad, uniformed Uncle John,
Aunt Emily and the lodger Mary are crowded into the shoebox
of a room, listening to the gramophone record.

GRANDAD: (*Loudly*) Rungs!

The fierce glare leaves Philip in no doubt, and he quickly takes
his feet off the rung of the hardback chair on which he is sitting.
During the evocative, painfully sweet music –

What do you think of it, then, Philip? All right, eh?

UNCLE JOHN: Let's hear it, Dad. Let's hear it, if you please.

AUNT EMILY: Mournful, *I* calls it.

GRANDAD: Open the lid. Lift the lid, John.

UNCLE JOHN: Blimey – you do keep on!

Distinctly surly, unshaven, his tunic undone, and in his socks,
Uncle John crosses to lift the lid of the gramophone cabinet.

GRANDAD: Well, the nipper won't have seen it, will he? He

won't have clapped eyes on nothing like that, not in them bleed'n trees, will he?

UNCLE JOHN: Come here, then. Philip. Look at this –

Philip, not at ease, goes half-reluctantly to the cabinet and peers in.

PHILIP: (*Unimpressed*) Oy. Him d'go round and round. Good, yunnit?

UNCLE JOHN: (*Mimics him*) Oo arrrr!

MRS MARLOW: John!

UNCLE JOHN: Only pulling his leg, eh, Sonny Jim?

He ruffles Philip's hair. But his manner is more menacing than jovial.

GRANDAD: Look at the hole. Watch the hole, Philip.

UNCLE JOHN: (*Wink.*) That's right. Always keep your eyes on the hole.

Aunt Emily sniggers. Mrs Marlow frowns.

MARY: That all depends *whose*, don't it?

GRANDAD: Stop that!

UNCLE JOHN: See – look – the needle is going on, round and round – to the hole in the middle – a–a–a– and – hey presto!

PHILIP: (*Unimpressed*) Yeh.

UNCLE JOHN: Well? What do you think of the gramophone – eh?

PHILIP: (*Unimpressed*) 'S good, yun it?

UNCLE JOHN: 'Yun it?' 'Yun it?' You don't come from 'Ammersmith by any chance?

MRS MARLOW: He's very bored sometimes.

AUNT EMILY: We shan't be able to understand a word he says.

PHILIP: (*Suddenly fierce*) I byunt going to talk much! I byunt going to talk at all! I be going to kip my mouth shut!

They all laugh, except Mrs Marlow.

MRS MARLOW: I don't know. Some of the things he comes out with.

MARY: You won't get very far pointing at things.

UNCLE JOHN: Not in the dark, you won't.

MRS MARLOW: He didn't want to come. I don't think Philip likes the idea of London.

AUNT EMILY: Oh, he'll change his tune. It's the best place there is, Philip.

PHILIP: (*Fiercely*) Chunt like whum though, be it!

MARY: (*Puzzled*) What – ? What's he say?

MRS MARLOW: He says it's not like home.

PHILIP: There yunt no place like the Forest! Where cost thou go up here? Where be the trees? Where be the oaks? The elms. Where the beech, you tell I that!

He seems near to tears, standing, his fists clenching and unclenching against the sides of his short trousers.

UNCLE JOHN: Ravenscourt Park. There's a couple of trees there.

AUNT EMILY: And Barnes Common.

MARY: I can't understand a word he says.

Grandad has been staring at Philip. Then –

GRANDAD: Show him the gas. The gas taps. He won't have seen that!

UNCLE JOHN: Christ, you want him to put his head in the oven, already?

Mary lets out a suddenly shrill laugh.

GRANDAD: No. Show him. It'll be new. All new. Open his eyes it will.

AUNT EMILY: *And* the flush. Out back.

UNCLE JOHN: No burying the shit in the garden up here, young Phil.

MRS MARLOW: (*Mildly*) John. Language.

AUNT EMILY: No garden.

UNCLE JOHN: (*To* MRS MARLOW) If he don't hear no worse than that –

GRANDAD: Never seen gas, I'll bet. Have to be careful you don't just turn it on. Never seen a WC, come to that. And what about the trolley buses? Eh?

AUNT EMILY: And the underground. Philip. Trains running under the ground.

Philip turns and looks at her steadily, as though she is a liar. That's true. Right under us, right under your feet. (*Then, uncomfortable*) The way that boy looks at you. He doesn't *blink* –

MRS MARLOW: Philip. It's rude to stare. Stop it.

He turns and looks at her, steadily.

You'll be able to go to the pictures, and everything, Philip.

There'll be so much to do. You'll see.
MARY: Now them V2s have stopped coming over. It'll be all
nice again.
UNCLE JOHN: You watch him. He'll be a proper little Londoner
by the time he's done. Philip – do you like football – eh?
Philip turns and looks at him, steadily.
Cat got your tongue?
MRS MARLOW: Philip! Answer when you're spoken to!
But he stays silent. They all look at him, puzzled.
PHILIP: Our Dad. When's our Dad a-coming? *When?*
Small silence. They all seem to look at each other.
GRANDAD: What you going to say, Betty? What you going to
tell him?
MRS MARLOW: (*To* PHILIP) Soon.
AUNT EMILY: Wha–a–at?
Mrs Marlow frowns and shakes her head at her, but a little too
obviously.
MRS MARLOW: Soon, Philip.
The boy stares at her, challengingly.
PHILIP: When?
MRS MARLOW: Soon. Sometime soon. (*Guiltily*) I expect.

The darkened hospital ward reverberates with the drones and
groans and snores of the sleepers. The large night nurse
slumbers at the table at the far end. Marlow is still awake, still
brooding.
MARLOW: (*Thinks*) A good detective doesn't go by the book.
No, sir. But he has to have a few rules to help him chew the
cup-cake – First off, never trust your client –

Binney's house by the river, at night, looms out of Marlow's
shop-soiled prose. Binney is staring down at the Mall, and the
river, with a brooding and troubled expression in his cold eyes.
(*Voice over*) – Bankers have the same good sense. That's
how they stay rich and you stay poor. Binney looked as
though he'd got more dough than a tray of croissants. But
they'd gone hard. Crusty. And the crust was maybe just
maybe about to crack –
Binney smiles a small, rueful, almost shamefaced twist of a

130

smile, and speaks, but to whom we do not know –

BINNEY: Doesn't *any* of it seem peculiar to you? I tell you, it gives me the creeps! I mean – I half expect him to be out there somewhere, looking at me –

And there, across the billowing trees, the boy Philip is in the cleft of the topmost branches of a stately old oak.

(*Voice over*) – And I'll tell you another thing – He seems to *know* too much. He's got hold of too many details. Where's it coming from? How does he get it? (*Hiss*) *What's his game?* The boy's face stares out through the foliage. The birds sing. Then –

PHILIP: (*Desperate*) Listen. God. I promise to be good if you'll let I off. I'll be without nern a spot and without nern a sin. (*Pause.*) I didn't mean to do it, God. Honest. Honest!

In the ward, the adult Marlow watches as they push out what was George's bed, stripped down, and wheel across 'Noddy' in his bed, to replace it. Marlow seems troubled. The old man – nod, nod, nod – is now next to Marlow, who speaks to Nurse Mills, one of the bed-pushers.

MARLOW: They come and they go, don't they? They certainly come and go.

NURSE MILLS: Hush. We don't talk about that. Do we?

MARLOW: Why not? Is the working assumption here that none of us is mortal?

MR HALL: (*Down the ward, calls*) Nurse!

MARLOW: (*Sudden urgency*) Listen – if that squad of people had got to him thirty seconds earlier – old George there – would it have made any difference?

MR HALL: Nurse! Please! A word, nurse –

NURSE MILLS: (*Leaving*) Who knows?

Marlow watches her go, speculative. His expression changes. Then –

MARLOW: (*Softly*) Oh, Nurse Mills. Sweet Nurse Mills. I love –

He frowns, stopping himself. Then, with distinct signs of improved mobility, he pulls himself around to get hold of the cigarettes on his locker.

Sorry about that, George.

He smokes sadly contemplative.

    Sorry, George.

NICOLA: Still talking to yourself, are you, Philip? Who is
    George?

Standing at the end of the bed, as he looks up startled, is Nicola,
not totally sure of herself. Marlow seems to take time to register
her presence, with a blink, and then a kind of scowl.

MARLOW: Of course I talk to myself. It's more civilized than the
    conversations I *used* to have. What do you want? Why are
    you here?

She stares down at him.

NICOLA: What a disgusting disease.

MARLOW: Thank you.

NICOLA: You look like some kind of scabby leper, Philip –
    What's all that *grease* – ?

MARLOW: They get it from a garage.

NICOLA: But they said you were getting better –

MARLOW: I *am* getting better.

He is measuring her, seemingly not yet sure what line to take.

NICOLA: Would you like some – (*Nervous little laugh.*) Well,
    some grapes or anything?

MARLOW: Yeh. To tread.

NICOLA: Sorry?

He fixes her, beadily, and repeats his questions, more harshly.
She has remained standing off.

MARLOW: What do you want? Why are you here?

She hesitates, and decides to try a kind of humour –

NICOLA: I'm not entirely sure, actually. Perhaps I've just come
    to gloat.

MARLOW: Well. This is *not* the visiting hour.

NICOLA: I know.

MARLOW: I had the impression they were very strict
    about that.

Because he seems at least half willing to talk, she moves closer.

NICOLA: Well, they didn't stop me. Mind you, I smiled very
    sweetly.

MARLOW: (*Edge*) As ever.

NICOLA: What do you mean?

He deflects it.

MARLOW: There was a patient in here and his wife wanted to visit him after *she* had swallowed three hundred and sixty four asprins. This was at twenty-past six –

NICOLA: What?

MARLOW: They asked her if she'd mind waiting another ten minutes.

NICOLA: (*Blank*) What?

MARLOW: (*Sigh*) Visiting time is six thirty.

NICOLA: Oh. I see. A joke.

They look at each other. Poor or unsuccessful jokes can reveal old degrees of intimacy. She decides to sit on the standard hospital bedside chair.

MARLOW: Sit down. Yes. By all means. Keep the laughs coming.

NICOLA: I did come once before, you know –

MARLOW: Yes.

NICOLA: They told you?

MARLOW: I wasn't asleep. I wasn't really asleep. I knew you were there.

NICOLA: I see.

He contemplates her. She takes his steadily examining gaze with the beginnings of a half-hesitant smile.

MARLOW: You are without any shadow of doubt an exceptionally beautiful woman. At the very peak of her nubility.

NICOLA: That sounds exactly like a death sentence.

MARLOW: It *is* a death sentence.

NICOLA: Philip. Listen to me –

MARLOW: (*Interrupting*) Do you know how long I have been in here, in this bed? Three months. Guess what you do over that sort of period flat on your back.

NICOLA: Go off your head?

MARLOW: (*Bitterly*) You *think*.

NICOLA: Yes. But – about what?

MARLOW: About *everything*.

NICOLA: Yes. But –

She stops.

MARLOW: (*Jeeringly*) But what?

NICOLA: But can you think straight? In here, I mean. Like this.

MARLOW: Oh. I mildly hallucinate now and then – But that's a perspective, too. Past and present. They're only measuring devices. Pooh.

NICOLA: And do you think about us?

MARLOW: (*Edge*) Us?

NICOLA: You and me.

MARLOW: Sex. Do you mean?

Tiny pause. He is staring hard at her.

NICOLA: Amongst other things. (*Then*) Yes. If you like.

MARLOW: Sex.

NICOLA: (*Wry, smile*) Well. That has been known to happen between us. Yes. And I miss it. (*Slightly awkwardly*) With you, I mean.

Staring at her, his expression changes. He seems suddenly moved.

MARLOW: Nicola.

NICOLA: (*Softer*) Yes?

MARLOW: (*Quietly*) The plain fact is that you are a filthy, predatory and totally wanton bitch who is always on heat. And I do not wish to see you. Not now, and not ever.

She considers the matter. Calmly.

NICOLA: (*Statements, not questions*) What if I said I loved you. What if I said I wanted you back.

MARLOW: (*Quietly, still*) Liar.

A pause. She smiles.

NICOLA: There are some things to discuss.

MARLOW: No.

NICOLA: You're hard up. You haven't got a penny. I know that. You haven't put pen to paper for at least fifteen months. I know that for certain.

MARLOW: (*With contempt*) I don't need a pen. I don't need paper.

NICOLA: You write on water, do you?

MARLOW: (*Sudden flare*) Shut your mouth!

NICOLA: My God.

MARLOW: (*Between his teeth*) Go, will you? Just go.

NICOLA: There are some things to discuss.

MARLOW: No!

NICOLA: (*Calmly*) A production company – a film company – wants to take some sort of option on your – on that first book of yours, the –

MARLOW: *What?*

NICOLA: The one about the detective who sings in a dance band.

He stares at her, unable to suppress the eager immediacy of his interest – but trying to be suitably contemptuous or sardonic.

MARLOW: They want to set it in Hartlepool. With Al Pacino and Max Bygraves. Right?

He is still busily putting down his own very real interest.
    Options. Options. That simply means they offer you a pittance now for the right to rip you off later on. Like an election manifesto.

NICOLA: They're very keen – apparently.

The 'apparently', too much a cautious qualification, arouses his suspicions.

MARLOW: But what has this got to do with you? What business is it of yours? Why do *you* know about it?

NICOLA: I want you to be able to support yourself.

MARLOW: (*Snort*) You what?

NICOLA: I'm worried about you.

He stares, then starts to laugh, nastily.

MARLOW: Ah. I see. You still consider that I owe you money, do you?

NICOLA: (*Firmly*) No. I don't.

MARLOW: I should imagine that you would work it out at two hundred pounds a screw. The top rate for hookers nowadays.

NICOLA: Is it? *I* wouldn't know.

MARLOW: Who are – (*Half looks away.*) Tell me. Who are you sleeping with at the moment?

NICOLA: Myself, mostly.

MARLOW: Mostly.

NICOLA: Mostly. Yes.

His strain is showing.

MARLOW: Mostly means not always.

NICOLA: If you want it to be that precise. Yes. It does.

He shows an unexpected spasm of emotion, and his voice degenerates into a near sob.

MARLOW: Nicola. Please –

NICOLA: (*Stiffening*) No. Stop.

MARLOW: (*With effort*) Please, I was trying to say, Please go.
Piss off.

NICOLA: You bet.

MARLOW: (*Half-sob*) Bitch.

She gets up, or nearly so, then sits down again, with a tightening
determination. He notes this, very upset, and seems to drag his
head around in order to look away from her, like a sulking child.

NICOLA: (*Firmly*) I've talked to your consultant. I've talked to
the registrar. They say that you should try to do some
work. No matter how little. They say that you can be
moved to a side ward, away from other people, but only if
you show signs of being – less introspective. Philip. It's up
to you now. Look at me.

But he won't. She sighs. Continues.

You can go into a side ward and we can get someone to
come in for, say, an hour or two hours a day, to take
dictation. We could at least try it, couldn't we?

He doesn't turn back. She cannot see his face.

MARLOW: (*Indistinct*) We?

NICOLA: What – ?

MARLOW: (*Not turning*) We. You said we. *We* can get someone
to come in – *We*.

NICOLA: Me. *I* can. A temp or somebody. From an agency. I
can afford it. I'd like to help. If you'll let me. If you will
please, please let me.

He slowly turns his head back again, to look at her, his eyes
fierce.

MARLOW: What are you up to? (*Hiss*) What's your game!

NICOLA: For goodness' sake – !

MARLOW: You're not a very good actress on the box, Nicola.
And you're an even worse one in real life.

NICOLA: Thank you.

MARLOW: It's called *The Singing Detective*.

NICOLA: Yes. That's the one.

MARLOW: And it has nothing whatsoever to do with you.

NICOLA: I didn't say it had.

MARLOW: I *have* been working, anyway. I've been turning it
into a – into something else.

NICOLA: *What?* (*Control.*) I mean – how? How can you have
   been working?
MARLOW: In my head.
NICOLA: (*With an edge*) Oh. Your head. Yes.
Nurse Mills arrives with a little cup or egg cup containing
Marlow's retinoid drug.
NURSE MILLS: Sorry. But your drug, Mr Marlow –
NICOLA: (*To* NURSE MILLS) Good afternoon.
Nurse Mills pours some water from his carafe, then –
NURSE MILLS: Ope–y tongue–y.
Marlow looks covertly sideways at Nicola, puts out his tongue.
Nurse Mills puts the yellow capsule on his tongue, holds the
glass for him to drink.
   There. All gone.
And she sweeps away, prettily. Nicola looks at him with a glint.
NICOLA: Who's a good boy, then?
Marlow looks embarrassed.

The old woman stands in front of a dead silent, frightened class,
almost choking with rage and disgust. She has a cane in her
hand.
OLD WOMAN: *One* of you, *one* nasty dirty wicked little boy – for
   I cannot believe it was one of the girls, no, not for a
   moment! – One of *you boys* waited until the end of school,
   waited, then sneaked back in and did this horrible–
   horrible–filthy–disgusting thing! Right in the middle of this
   table. My table! And I will tell you this. I will tell you here
   and now, he won't get away with it, whoever it is! I'll make
   sure of that! Ab–so–lute–ly sure!
She stares fiercely all around the class, at boy after boy. And as
is the manner of children faced with some dark accusation, their
faces find it difficult to take the fierce, searching, threatening
nature of an adult gaze. Especially now, as, holding the cane
aggressively, she begins to walk up and down the narrow aisle
between the little desks, towering menacingly over the
occupants.
   Who? Who was it? Who? Who is the dirty–nasty–
   shameless–little *beast* – !
And on the 'beast' thwack! comes the cane, hard down, across

the lid of one particular desk. The boy, Harold, looks tough, almost jumps out of his skin.

Harold.

HAROLD: M–miss?

OLD WOMAN: Was it you!

HAROLD: (*Shocked*) No, miss!

OLD WOMAN: You! Was it!

HAROLD: (*Scared*) No, miss.

OLD WOMAN: Did you come back after school yesterday?

HAROLD: (*Very scared*) Me, miss?

OLD WOMAN: Yes! You!

HAROLD: N–no, miss – !

OLD WOMAN: Are you sure? Are you quite sure?

His eyes are darting about in panic, looking for support.

HAROLD: (*Rising panic*) I didn't, miss, no, I did–unt!

OLD WOMAN: Did you come back into this classroom and climb up on my table? Did you let down your trousers and do that – that – disgusting *thing* – ?

HAROLD: (*Starting to cry*) No, miss – chunt me, miss – honest, miss! No–o–o!

OLD WOMAN: (*Relentless*) Do you know who did?

HAROLD: No, miss!

She pinions him with a long stare, and he cowers. But something tells her, correctly, that he is not the culprit. She moves on, down the row, eyes pouncing from one cringing boy to another, reaches the front again, whirls round, spitting a venomous (and genuine) anger.

OLD WOMAN: Cows do it in the fields, and know no better. Dogs do it on the road, and know no better. Pigs do it in their sties, and no know no better. They can't speak. They can't reason. They know not the difference between right and wrong. They are animals! But – !

Her eyes rake the classroom again, as she lets the word hang for a moment in the air.

But *we* are not animals. God has given us all a sense of good and of bad. *God* has allowed us to tell the difference between the clean and the dirty. And *God* is going to help me now find out who did this thing!

Silence. The children are crunching up inside with tension and

fear. They can hardly bear it. She waits. She waits. Then –
  All of you. In a moment you are going to close your eyes
  and place your hands together. We are going to say a
  prayer. (*In an awful voice*) We are going to ask Almighty
  God Himself. We are going to beseech Almighty God
  Himself. He is going to point His Holy Finger. Almighty
  God will tell us who did this wicked deed. And then we
  shall know. (*A beat.*) Let us pray.
In mortal terror, they close their eyes, and put their hands
together, in absolute unison. Absolute, that is, except for Philip.
He is half a beat too late. Just enough for her to notice, and to
frown speculatively as she looks at him.

In the hospital ward, Marlow is explaining something to his
bedside visitor.
MARLOW: In my head. Yes. In my head. The worst thing about
  a detective story is the plot. The best thing too. What am I
  saying? It's the *only* thing. You have to work it all out in
  your head. And that's what I've been trying to do. Like a
  rat in a maze.
NICOLA: But not with a story you've already written, surely – ?
  How can you work out what you already *know* is going to
  happen?
She seems troubled – perhaps feeling that he is a little loopy.
MARLOW: (*With a glint*) Think I'm cuckoo. Is that it?
NICOLA: No, but –
MARLOW: (*With great satisfaction*) Bananas. You think I'm
  bananas.
NICOLA: It just seems a –
MARLOW: (*Sharply cutting in*) What happened to that
  screenplay? Where is it?
NICOLA: What screenplay?
MARLOW: What do you mean, 'what screenplay'? The one I
  wrote years ago. The one I put in the – Those shoe-boxes.
NICOLA: Shoe-boxes?
MARLOW: Yes! Shoe-boxes!
Silence. They look at each other.
NICOLA: (*Gently*) Philip.
MARLOW: (*Sigh*) I know. I know.

Silence. He seems sad. She speaks again, with vigour.

NICOLA: Write something new, Philip. You should write
something else.

MARLOW: Oh? like what?

NICOLA: Like *this* – what has happened to you. Like real things.

MARLOW: Pooh.

NICOLA: *Use* your talent, Philip.

MARLOW: Bugger that!

NICOLA: Write about real things in a realistic way – real people,
real joys, real pains – Not these silly detective stories.
Something more relevant.

MARLOW: (*With contempt*) Solutions.

NICOLA: What – ?

MARLOW: All solutions, and no clues. That's what the
dumb-heads want. That's the bloody Novel – He said, she
said, and descriptions of the sky – I'd rather it was the
other way around. All clues. No solutions. That's the way
things are. Plenty of clues. No solutions. (*Suddenly*) What
about this option?

NICOLA: It's not grand, or – But, Philip, it would be a way for
you to earn some money again and I think –

MARLOW: *How much?*

NICOLA: Well, it's not huge – I think it's two thousand dollars
for a – for twelve months.

MARLOW: (*Disappointed*) Two cents a dance.

NICOLA: (*Quickly*) But of course if they take it on after that – I
mean, if they actually make a film of it – you would get 2
per cent of the budget, Philip.

MARLOW: So a 10 million dollar film, that would be –

NICOLA: (*Quickly*) Up to a ceiling of one hundred thousand
dollars.

He stares at her. His expression hardens – enough to make her
shift uncomfortably in her chair.

MARLOW: How come you know all this? How do *you* know the
figures? What is it to do with *you*?

NICOLA: The point is, Philip –

MARLOW: (*Cutting in*) The point is that you have these details
and I don't. I'm in the dark. Now – either you've been
reading my mail – getting into my flat! – *or* –

140

NICOLA: *That* stinking hole!

MARLOW: (*Sweeping on*) *Or* you've been party to the offer in the first place. Which is it? What's going on here!

NICOLA: Still the same, aren't you? The same paranoid old Philip. Do you want my help, or don't you?

MARLOW: (*Evenly*) Do I want *you* to help *me* – ?

She stands, cold, brisk.

NICOLA: Think about it.

MARLOW: Piss off.

She looks down at him, steadily.

NICOLA: Philip. You are a barbarian. You will always bite the hand that tries to feed you.

And she turns abruptly away, leaving him.

MARLOW: (*Yell*) Answer the question! Answer me, you interfering cow!

At the far end of the ward, an observer is offended.

MR HALL: The noise that fellow makes. The shouting. The total lack of consideration –

MARLOW: Nicola – !

MR HALL: It beggars description. And I choose my words more carefully than most, Reginald. I mean, *listen* to him – Reginald?

Reginald has his nose buried in the later pages of the same battered and folded-over paperback he has been laboriously reading throughout.

REGINALD: What – ?

MR HALL: (*Disgusted*) Are you company, Reginald? Would you in all honesty say you were good company? Could you put your hand on your heart and say it?

REGINALD: (*Irritated*) What?

MR HALL: See! See what I mean!

Reginald offers an explanation.

REGINALD: Well. It's a good story, ennit?

MR HALL: Is it? What's it about?

REGINALD: You already asked me that.

MR HALL: Well, I'm asking again!

REGINALD: I don't know yet, do I?

MR HALL: What you mean – ?

REGINALD: I haven't finished it yet.

And he returns avidly to the book. A few yards away, Marlow is
simmering about Nicola's visit. He lights a cigarette,
two-handed, to calm himself. He blows smoke. His expression
changes.

MARLOW: (*Thinks*) No luck full stop No good full stop Talk
about difficult exclamation mark I had to give it up because
he was getting very suspicious full stop

Pause. He blows more smoke. His eyes narrow. He speaks out
loud, to himself.

(*Hiss*) Binney. *That* bastard. She says it to Binney.

Meanwhile, it seems, Nicola comes storming out of the ward to
a wide vestibule where the lifts are. There is much movement in
this area, momentarily obscuring the man waiting on the
padded, bench-like seats, as she strides up to him, angry,
disappointed, shaking her head –

NICOLA: No luck. No good. Talk about difficult! I had to give it
up because he was getting very suspicious.

The man now fully revealed on the bench is Binney: a real life,
1986 Binney, so to speak.

BINNEY: (*Anxious*) But you'll try again? He'll see you again?

NICOLA: (*Exasperated*) I don't know whether he will or not.

BINNEY: The thing is, Nicola – I can't wait for too long, can I?

NICOLA: You've no idea how sharp and nasty he can be!

BINNEY: (*Rueful*) Oh, haven't I just! But – Nicola. I don't want
us to be – I mean, we could be sued for misrepresentation,
or –

NICOLA: (*Urgent*) Don't worry. Don't worry. I'll think of
something.

They begin to move towards the lifts. He is morose, worried.

BINNEY: Jesus. I'd wish we'd –

NICOLA: Stop it! I'll deliver. I said I would. And I will. (*Then* –)
He still looks terrible.

BINNEY: Don't start feeling sorry for him! Think about the
half-million dollars!

NICOLA: (*Fiercely*) Oh, I don't feel a bit sorry for him. I hope it
gets right down into his bones.

She jabs the call button by the lift doors with such a beautiful
venom that spirits miraculously revive.

BINNEY: Phew – ! You look *terrific* when you're angry. Like a wasp caught in the tabasco.

Her eyes settle on him, steadily, almost suspiciously.

NICOLA: That's what Marlow used to say. You sound like
  Marlow, you know that?

The lift doors clatter open. Poor old Noddy has been down for
X-ray, and is pushed out of the very wide lift by the familiar
porter. Nod–nod–nod, goes the old head. Nicola and Binney
step a little aside to give them room, and then they get into the
lift. The doors Whoosh! shut on them, and the beginnings of
their nervous laughter.

'It's a Lovely Day Tomorrow' in the 1940 Jack Payne
recording begins to play. A merry little journey, so to speak,
with the sagging-mouthed, vacant-eyed, apparently gaga Noddy
as he is pushed back to the ward in his wheelchair. The old·man
is wheeled to his new position, at the side of the unlucky bed
next to Marlow in which Ali and George have already died.

The porter has a difficult job to get the frail, shaking arms out
of the X-ray smock, to lift him up out of the chair (nod, nod,
shake, shake) and lay him down on the fatal bed as the
helplessly mocking song winds to its conclusion. Marlow is
watching all this with a sort of fascinated repulsion, in which he
finds he has to light another cigarette. Then, eventually –

MARLOW: (*Thinks*) The thing is – It's always the least likely
  character who turns out to be the killer. Got to obey the
  rules. (*Blows smoke.*) The least likely. (*A twisted grin, a
  sidelong look.*) This must be him. This *must* be the one. Old
  Noddy here. Defin–ite–ly. Noddy did it. You hear that,
  Nicola? You get that?

Silence. He smiles, in a private, twist-of-mouth fashion. Then
stops smiling, and broods.

  Well – it can't be *me*, that's for sure. It can't be me. *I* didn't
  do it.

His younger self, similarly disposed, is again perched like a bird
in the top cleft of branches of the old oak. He turns to us, and
speaks in a scared, near whisper.

PHILIP: They won't find out who it was. Na! Thoy'll never
  ever-ever find out. Na!

He thinks about it, as the birds sing loudly.

Thoy can give I the worst Chinese burn ever. The worst in
the history of the world.

Thinks about it, and the birds rhapsodize.

Thoy can tie I down on a hill of cruel, poisonous black ants,
with my shirt off my back –

In the classroom, the boys and girls have their hands clasped
and their eyelids clenched, absolutely still, in terrorized prayer.

OLD WOMAN: O Lord God who loves and cares and watches and
admonishes all of us miserable and unworthy sinners. O
Lord God look down on us now in Thy Awful Majesty and
search out our hearts, look into our heads, seize hold of our
innermost thoughts.

Her eyes are fiercely studying every one of the boys' faces in
turn as they submit to her dreadful prayer, looking at every
small tic or twitch for any signs of a stress greater than the one
she herself is inducing.

Dear Lord. *You* can see *You* know. (*Deadly pause.*) You are
looking down now upon one boy, one particular boy, one
boy in this room. (*Little pause.*) You are entering the bones.
You are peering into the space between the bones. (*Eyes still
darting, settling, moving on*) Dear God. Almighty God.
Terrible in Wrath. With the stars to guide, with the whole
earth to turn, with the flowers to grow, with the rain to
make fall, the sun to make shine, with all this, all of these
things, you stop, you look, you watch. Because all of these
things – the weight of the mountains and the deeps of the
ocean, the day and the night, the cares and troubles of the
whole slow spin of the whole big world – All. All of these
things you, O God, Thee O God, Almighty and Awful
Creator, you leave for the moment to – *point down at the
one! Who? Who? Which one? Who is it?*

Marlow the Singing Detective lurks at the dead of night in an
elegant Mayfair or St James's doorway, up a wide flight of stone
steps that allows him to look down on the dark but lamplit street
– and, in particular, the entrance to the basement where, just
visible at near-pavement level, the small red sign of SKINSCAPE'S
glows neonly.

Marlow is wearing his snap-brim hat, and smoking, looking the complete 1940s private eye on a stake-out. His eyes are clamped on the Skinscape's basement entrance, watching for any comings and goings. He looks at his wrist-watch, using the glow of his cigarette, or his lighter. 3.10 a.m. The small red neon sign flicks off. Marlow's eyes narrow. He throws down and treads out his cigarette, allowing us to see that around his feet cigarette ends are duly littered.

MARLOW: (*Thinks*) That *is* the question. Always the question – Which one? Who is it?

He watches, tensing, ready to move. A few girls come out of Skinscape's, well-wrapped, arm in arm in a mildly alcoholic sistership. One of the girls laughs, loud and long, and the sound seems to hang in the small-hours night air. Marlow suddenly darts out, just a little, and calls out to the girls, immediately darting back to cover, and watching.

(*Calls*) *Achtung*! Amanda – *Achtung*!

The few arm-in-arm girls have reached the soft blue glow of a 1945 street lamp. They peer back along the street into the darkness beyond the lamp's glow.

A GIRL: 'S all right – some loony –

SECOND GIRL: That's what they all are, if you ask me.

The girl who laughed before laughs again, and they go on their way, heels clacking. Marlow, in shadow, lets out his breath. Then he is still. And watching – A splash of light showing an opening door.

WOMAN'S VOICE: (*Off*) Right, then. Tomorrow! Keep yer nose clean!

And into view up the basement steps on to the pavement comes Amanda. Marlow, of course, has not seen her before. She walks up the street, alone, when –

MARLOW: *Achtung*! Amanda – *Achtung*!

She stops. She hesitates, puzzled. Shadowy Marlow pulls back even deeper into the dark of the big doorway. Her face shows doubt, or even a little fear. She looks from side to side. Amanda begins to walk back, towards where Marlow's seemingly warning shout had come from. But after a few paces, she stops, suspicious. She looks, and can see nothing, and no one. She decides that something is wrong. She turns again then suddenly runs click–clack–click along the empty pavement. Her run takes her past the bluish glow of the old street lamp, so that her shadow is first behind her, then diminished, and then in front of her.

(*Voice over*) You can throw a long shadow. You can cast a short one. And you know the mistake people make? They think the size has something to do with what's inside them. Am I right? Or am I right?

In the nighttime ward, the real Marlow's small lamp is on, a circle of light in the surrounding darkness. He is propped up in his same old position, still chewing on things.

MARLOW: Shadows.

Binney is as he was earlier, at the window of his house looking down on to the Mall and the river. He stares, broodingly. And then speaks with a small, rueful, almost shame-faced twist of a smile.

BINNEY: Doesn't *any* of it seem peculiar to you?

But, this time, deeper in the room, Nicola breaks up his speech. A table lamp throws her shadow.

NICOLA: No.

BINNEY: I tell you, it gives me the creeps. I mean, I half expect him to be out there somewhere, looking at me.

Bored or disdainful Nicola, lying back on a chaise-longue or similar, is using the lamp in this now distinctly *film-noir*-lit room to make strange shadow shapes on the wall with her hand.

NICOLA: Shadows.

Binney turns from the window, strangely agitated.

BINNEY: And I'll tell you another thing. He seems to *know* too much. He's got hold of too many details. Where's it coming from? How does he get it? What's his game?

NICOLA: Parrot.

BINNEY: What – ?

NICOLA: I just made a parrot.

She means the hand shadow she has made on the wall.

BINNEY: (*Angry*) Are you listening to me? Am I talking to myself here?

She lowers her shadow-making hand, and gives him a steady look.

146

NICOLA: I like moody men. I simply a—dore moody men.

BINNEY: What I'm trying to get you to —

NICOLA: (*Cutting in*) Two years and more I had of that with that
shit Philip Marlow. Black looks. Mysterious glances. Sulks
that came up out of nothing – and you know what else?
Paranoia. Think about it, will you?

BINNEY: (*Grimly*) It's Marlow I'm thinking about.

NICOLA: Then don't!

BINNEY: He's on to me. He *knows*.

NICOLA: (*Not pleased*) What do you mean? How can he?

BINNEY: I feel it, that's all. I *sense* it.

NICOLA: Oh, no! Not again! What is it with you?

BINNEY: Nicola. He's never been here. He's not set foot inside
this house, ever. Has he?

NICOLA: Of course he hasn't!

BINNEY: But that script of his –

NICOLA: You mean, that script of *yours*.

BINNEY: Let's be accurate, Nicola –

NICOLA: Let's be *consistent*.

BINNEY: (*Irritated*) Yes, so far as anyone else and the outside
world is concerned –

NICOLA: (*Cutting in*) Half a million says you'd better believe it!

BINNEY: But I'm not talking about that, am I? *We* know. I'm
talking about that dog-eared, messy, food-stained script
that we *hope* he's forgotten –

NICOLA: It still stinks of tobacco and something that –
well, smells to me like old cabbage stumps. (*Sniff.*)
Typical!

BINNEY: It smells of something worse than that. It – (*Stares at
her.*) It smells sulphur.

NICOLA: *What?*

BINNEY: It's as though – as though – (*With difficulty*) Nicola. I
know this sounds crazy. I feel almost as though he has
made all this up. I feel –

But he has to stop, unable to explain, but still working his face.
She stares at him, almost scared, wondering if he is not a little
mad.

NICOLA: My God. I do pick them.

BINNEY: Nicola. Please. Think about it. I'm talking about the

147

actual bloody script he wrote –

NICOLA: Years ago.

BINNEY: Yes. But –

NICOLA: Before I even knew you.

BINNEY: Yes. That's – (*Frown.*) Yes. True.

NICOLA: Well then!

BINNEY: But – but isn't that what's so creepy – ?

NICOLA: (*Patiently*) Now, look – you're working yourself up
about this because what we're doing is criminal. Right? I
mean, we're stealing *his* script and passing it off as *yours*.
Right?

Binney moistens his nervously dry lips.

BINNEY: Right.

In his hospital bed, a maliciously inventive assent –

MARLOW: Right!

In the riverside house, Binney moistens his nervously dry lips,
half aware of something bad, something impossible, at the fringe
of his mind.

BINNEY: Right.

NICOLA: And this is because *I* intercepted the offer to him.
They don't know him from Adam. *They* don't know he's
sick, do they? But *you've* gone and got cold feet –

BINNEY: No, no.

NICOLA: Then what else? Why are you crackling your nerves
like this? You *do* know you're talking about coincidence,
don't you? (*Looks hard at him.*) Mark. Don't you?

He looks at her. He does not want to appear ridiculous. But –

BINNEY: I'm –

NICOLA: (*Insistent*) You *are*. Aren't you?

BINNEY: (*Reluctantly*) I suppose so.

NICOLA: What–else–could–it–be? Come on! Use your head. If
he didn't know of your existence when he wrote that thing.
If *I* didn't know you, even. If he had never been here,
never seen you – Oh, what the hell! This is all so – What's
the *matter* with you?

Binney stalks to one of the side tables in this large room, a room
which is so very similar to the one in which the fictional Binney

lives. He brandishes an old paperback, from the table. It is *The Singing Detective* – of the same edition as was on Gibbon's table.

BINNEY: It's *this* that's the matter! In here – Nicola, listen – in the *book* the story is the same, of course –

NICOLA: (*Sardonic*) It had better be. That's what is being sold, hon–ey.

BINNEY: The *story* is the same, but the *settings* are different!

NICOLA: Oh, for Christ's sake.

BINNEY: And the *names* are different!

NICOLA: So he changed his mind. He gets bored easily.

BINNEY: He's changed the setting of the client, his house I mean, from New Cavendish Street to *this* Mall, overlooking the river at Hammersmith – he's even got the murdered girl floating in the water underneath Hammersmith Bridge –

NICOLA: (*Scornful laugh.*) It's public property –

BINNEY: And he's changed the client's *name* from Haynes to Finney. Look how close that is to my name. One letter!

NICOLA: (*Still scornful*) One letter's all there is between trick and prick, so what –

BINNEY: Finney to Binney is too close! If he'd changed the original name from Haynes to almost anything else, any name you can think of –

NICOLA: How about Walley? Changing it to Walley.

And she laughs again, still with scorn.

BINNEY: And the same first name! Oh, stop being so bloody smart a minute, will you, *will* you – !

NICOLA: Mark is not an unusual name.

He slaps at his chest, getting angrier and angrier.

BINNEY: Mark Finney! Me! Right!

NICOLA: How do you do.

BINNEY: Mark Binney! In the script! Right! In his bloody script that we've purloined! Mark Finney to Mark Binney is as close as – as close as –

He stops suddenly, then his tone changes.

I have this awful – I have this awful dash he stops himself comma and all but shudders full stop

NICOLA: Darling dash question mark

They look at each other. Weirdly, almost frighteningly, they seem to have no idea of what they have just said, which is delivered in a totally straightforward manner. Then –

BINNEY: Mark Finney to Mark Binney is as close as – as close as – (*Stops.*) I have this awful –

He stops himself, and all but shudders.

NICOLA: Darling – ?

He tries to smile at her, would-be-rueful, but fear springs in him again.

BINNEY: Premonition. This awful premonition. (*Then, incredulous*) Nicola? Why are you doing that?

NICOLA: (*Distracted*) What?

She is making a shadow with her hand again.

BINNEY: (*Angry*) Nicola!

NICOLA: See. A rabbit. Don't you think that looks like a rabbit, Mark? And I thought I could only do parrots.

A gleaming wet street and pavement in which the neon sign of a dance hall skeeters in the puddles, reflected. A 1940s car arrives, tyres hush–slushing to a halt in the wet. There are blobs of rain on windscreen, and a bright blur of rainy-pavement reflections beyond. Hunched in the car, the two mysterious men.

FIRST MYSTERIOUS MAN: He followed the stupid cow. He bloody well followed her.

SECOND MYSTERIOUS MAN: Oh, it happens.

FIRST MYSTERIOUS MAN: Called out some kraut word, apparently.

SECOND MYSTERIOUS MAN: Oh, yeh?

FIRST MYSTERIOUS MAN: Yeh. And *she* had to go and react. I mean, she's not even a bloody Hun to begin with, is she?

SECOND MYSTERIOUS MAN: There you are.

FIRST MYSTERIOUS MAN: These tarts. Brains in their bleed'n nipples.

SECOND MYSTERIOUS MAN: Clever, though. Him, I mean.

FIRST MYSTERIOUS MAN: Not once she'd shown herself like that. It was in the manual then, wasn't it? Easy as pie. Watched her arse all the way home.

SECOND MYSTERIOUS MAN: But clever. The way she never saw him. Had no idea.

FIRST MYSTERIOUS MAN: A tail is a tail. Follow the wiggle.

SECOND MYSTERIOUS MAN: But he's clever. Go on. Admit it.

FIRST MYSTERIOUS MAN: (*Reluctantly*) Yeh. Well. (*Disdainful sniff.*) Who'd have thought it, eh? I mean – a *warbler*. Thought they were all poofs.

SECOND MYSTERIOUS MAN: There you are!

FIRST MYSTERIOUS MAN: Shut up!

SECOND MYSTERIOUS MAN: Right you are.

The second mysterious man looks sidelong at him, with a dislike that is tinged with nervousness.

FIRST MYSTERIOUS MAN: Who'd go dancing? Christ.

SECOND MYSTERIOUS MAN: Oh, people. Couples. You know.

FIRST MYSTERIOUS MAN: On a night like this.

SECOND MYSTERIOUS MAN: There you are.

FIRST MYSTERIOUS MAN: We'll have to go in there. Eventually. But not together. I don't want to go to a dance with another bloke. What'd people think?

SECOND MYSTERIOUS MAN: Nor me. No fear. (*Hesitates.*) Got the gun?

FIRST MYSTERIOUS MAN: What do you think! I had to kill the silly tart with it, didn't I? Amanda.

SECOND MYSTERIOUS MAN: Yeh. (*Ponders.*) Pity, that. A pity, really.

Inside the dance hall Marlow steps forward, eyes flicking over the dancers, to 'sing' 'I Get Along Without You Very Well'.

The two mysterious men are separated from each other by half the length of the bar, each drinking Scotch and water.

The song comes with that especial dance-hall resonance when heard from the balcony and bar above. Marlow's eyes are alertly surveying everything as he 'sings' in front of the band.

The dance-hall tune continues to syncopate over the constantly nodding and shaking, apparently near gaga old man, in the next bed to Marlow. Cruelly, it is almost as though the helpless nod– nod–nod of the head is in rhythm with the remainder of the song.

The dance-band music takes over, in sweet deceit, as the faces of the patients are examined, in their various degrees of illness, exhaustion, boredom, sleepiness . . . a Sunday afternoon, long, dolorous, empty of incident.

Reginald is reading, as usual, from his folded-over paperback, his lips moving a little, silently, as he labours slowly through the lines on the page. He is obviously not one of the compulsory bed-bound patients, and is again sitting in his chair, between his bed and Mr Hall's. Mr Hall is utterly bored and fed up. He spits out some grape pips into his hand, and pulls a discontented face.

MR HALL: Grapes.

Reginald, avidly reading, does not look up. Mr Hall glares at him, comically.

> Why people insist on bringing them into *hospitals* I never know. The grape, Reginald, is a very irritating fruit. Especially if you should have the misfortune to wear dentures, my boy.

He waits, but there is no response.

> The skin – which on the whole is more *bitter* than it should be – the skin, the bloody skin, sticks on your teeth – And the *pips*, Reginald. As for the pips – That's what you do! You know that?

REGINALD: (*Distractedly, at last*) What?

MR HALL: Give me the pip! You – that's what *you* do!

REGINALD: (*Amiable*) What's the matter now, Mr Hall? What's wrong?

MR HALL: Wrong? Wrong? What's *wrong*?

REGINALD: That's what I asked.

MR HALL: Sundays!

REGINALD: What? Well –

MR HALL: That's what's wrong. Sundays. How I loathe and detest this day of rest, this sabbath, this – Even outside, Reginald, at the best of times. But in *here* – well! It is the longest two days of the week rolled into one.

REGINALD: Quieter, though. A bit of peace.

And he returns to his book, without any ado. Mr Hall looks at him with total disgust. He opens and closes his mouth to speak, but it seems he has run out of words. But only for a moment, for, inevitably –

MR HALL: Talk about the Sahara. The desert's got nothing on –

He stops, diverted. At last, something seems about to happen in Sunday's empty cavern. Coming through the double doors into the ward is a sudden surge of newcomers. About eight or nine people, in 'ordinary' clothes, though they are all on the hospital staff, either as nurses or junior doctors or auxiliaries. Something about the glow on their faces, and the way they stride, even their haircuts, and the manner of their dress indicates what they are: Evangelists. Not just Christians, but eagerly buttonholing, chapel-orientated, what–think–ye–of–Christ, good-cheer, good-news fanatics. One of them has a case, which looks as though it holds some kind of instrument. An earnest girl starts going from bed to bed, handing out hymn sheets, with an insistent smile.

GIRL EVANGELIST: Please take one. You'll be able to follow the words. (*And on –*) Please take one. You'll be able to follow the words. (*And on –*) Please take one. You'll be able to follow. Please take one!

But some are too weak or too far gone to respond. Meanwhile, the others have clustered in the centre of the ward. Dr Finlay, a houseman in his worldly life, begins to address everyone.

DR FINLAY: If I could have your kind attention, please. Everyone. *Good* afternoon! My name is Dr Finlay. And may the Lord Jesus Christ be with you!

Marlow's eyes roll in incredulity and disdain.

MARLOW: Oh, no–o–o!

The earnest girl tries to hand out a hymn sheet to the next bed she has reached, that of the nod–nod–nodding old man.

GIRL EVANGLIST: (*Quieter now*) Please take one. You'll be able to follow the words –

Nod–nod–nod.

Or perhaps you'd prefer just to listen –

Nod–nod–nod. She withdraws.

Yes. Well. Jesus loves you.

DR FINLAY: Let me introduce ourselves to you. (*Simper*) If introductions are necessary. We, all of us, we all work here in this hospital, as doctors, as nurses, administrators, or whatever. And we, who have ourselves experienced the direct and personal love of our Saviour, the Lord Jesus Christ, wish to share this love, this grace, this *joy* with you, today, on the Sabbath Day –

GIRL EVANGELIST: (*To* MARLOW) Please take one. You'll be able to follow the words –

MARLOW: (*Loudly*) No.

GIRL EVANGELIST: (*Startled*) It's a hymn sheet, and –

MARLOW: (*Violently*) Stuff it!

Hearing the one and only objection, Dr Finlay momentarily falters –

DR FINLAY: We – ah – We ask you only that – Yes. Today, this afternoon, we go from ward to ward, to invite you to share with us the infinite joy and comfort we have ourselves received –

MARLOW: (*Loudly*) Leave us alone! Why don't you bugger off and leave us in peace, Finlay.

DR FINLAY: Nurse Godfrey has given out the – If I could just have your attention –

Noddy, too, is surprisingly envenomed. He cannot stop his head shake–shake–shaking, nor properly control his slack mouth, or any words which might issue from it, but –

NODDY: F–fuf–fuf–fuf–F– !

With no doubt about the meaning: 'Fuck off.' The great majority in the ward, however, appear to be properly attentive.

DR FINLAY: – We ask you to join with us in fellowship, and in the love of Jesus, to celebrate what is good in our lives, and to ask for help in alleviating or in understanding what seems to us to be less than happy in the world and our place in it. Now – you have each been given, or should have been given, a printed sheet with the words of the two or three hymns that we are going to sing this Sunday afternoon with you, and we hope that you –

MARLOW: (*Shouts*) Hoy! Hey! You! Finlay!

DR FINLAY: (*Faltering*) We hope that you, too, will feel able to come into the –

MARLOW: (*Yell*) Hey! You!

DR FINLAY: Yes? What is it, my rather loud friend? Do you wish to say –

MARLOW: (*Call*) What about those of us who *don't* 'feel able' – ?

Dr Finlay is not at all used to this, nor are his companions, to judge by their mixed consternation, and indignation.

DR FINLAY: You deliberately misunderstand our purpose. I am sure that if you will suspend your prejudice and join with us in –

MARLOW: (*Shout*) There's no misunderstanding! This is a
     principle not a prejudice!
There is a comical conflict going on in Finlay. He wants to show
Love Sweet Love but he would also like to tape up Marlow's
mouth. He grits his teeth. He is the sort who is on a very tight
rein.
DR FINLAY: (*Fairly controlled*) If you would *kindly* spare a
     moment to *listen* to –
MARLOW: We don't want this crap! Leave us alone!
Finlay snaps.
DR FINLAY: (*Yell*) Shut your mouth!
Consternation amongst his colleagues. Finlay, face twitching,
pulls himself back from the brink, but only just.
     Those who do not want to take part in (*Gritting teeth*)
     celebrating Our Lord Jesus Christ do not have to take part.
     Those who are not with us are against us. Those who
     (*Near yell*) lack the good manners (*Yell*) and who lack
     the grace – (*Controls himself again.*) They should remain
     quiet so that – so that – others can enjoy the service – (*Gasp
     of suppressed rage*) and partake in the peace which comes
     from the Personal Love of Our Saviour, the Lord Jesus
     Christ.
MARLOW: (*Yell*) And afterwards we can all pick up our beds
     and walk out of here!
Head still helplessly nod–nod–nodding, mouth still
uncontrollably slack, Noddy is nevertheless laughing with
malicious, cackling delight. Dr Finlay, quivering with a
comically ill-suppressed rage, reflecting whatever inner torment
has oddly led him to primitive Evangelism and authoritarian
versions of Medicine, flaps his hand urgently –
DR FINLAY: Plug in the organ! Let us begin! Let us begin!
The instrument case, it is now clear, contains a slim,
computerized, electronic 'organ' of Japanese manufacture,
capable of making as much noise as a proper Church monster. It
now belches out a sombre, loud, unmistakably low-church sort
of chord, for attention, and – Finlay visibly simmers down, into
unction.
     My dear fellows. We ask you now to spend these few
     moments with us in praise and reflection and comfort –

He glares across the ward, expecting a shout of protest from Marlow, but none comes.

> Thank you! On your sheets – I mean, your word sheets – you will see the words of the hymn 'Be in Time!' Good and urgent advice! Expressing in honest, plain and direct terms our personal hope in Jesus, and our wish to tell you, too, the good news. (*Glares at* MARLOW.) Join with us! Do not hesitate!

A downward beat of his arm, and the electronic chords become decidedly jaunty. The Evangelists, clustered together in the middle of the ward, dive into the hymn, with bold, shining faces, and impregnable gusto.

THE EVANGELISTS: (*Sing*)
> Life at best
> Is very brief
> Like the falling
> Of a leaf
> Like the binding
> Of a sheaf
> *Be in time!*
> Fleeting days
> Are telling fast
> That the die will soon be cast
> And the fatal line be passed
> *Be in time!*

The patients sometimes offer a mordant contrast to the bounce of the tune, or an apt simulacrum of the lack–of–time–here–on–earth message. Some are trying to sing along, a few are puzzled, and one or two too far gone to care anything about what's going on in front of them.

> Marlow is ostentatiously trying out a yawn, a snigger, and a contemptuous glare. But as the Evangelists bounce themselves into the urgencies of the chorus, it is almost as though his face is hit by a sudden blast of ice-cold air, freezing his expression into a sort of rigid or mortified (and reluctant) attention.

> *Be in time! Be in time!*
> While the voice of Jesus calls you,
> *Be in time!*
> If in sin you longer wait

> You may find no open gate
> And your cry be just too late
> *Be in time!*

Organ, Evangelists and, now, rather more of the patients,
affected by the music and the words, attack the second verse.

EVANGELISTS and PATIENTS: (*Sing*)

> Fairest flowers
> Soon decay
> Youth and beauty
> Pass away
> Oh, you have not long
> To stay
> *Be in time!*
> While God's Spirit
> Bids you come
> Sinner, do not longer roam
> Lest you seal
> Your hopeless doom
> *Be in time!*

And once again, ever more emphatic with admonition, they
charge into the chorus.

> *Be in time! Be in time!*
> While the voice of Jesus calls you
> *Be in time!*
> If in sin you longer wait
> You may find no open gate
> And your cry be just too late
> *Be in time!*

Marlow is showing a ferocious sort of concentration.

The village school of long ago is resurfacing in his mind.

THE EVANGELISTS: (*Voices over*)

> Time is gliding
> Swiftly by
> Death and judgement
> Draweth nigh
> To the arms of Jesus fly
> *Be in time!*

All the children are as when last seen: their eyelids crinkled

157

tightly shut, their hands prayerfully clasped.
> (*Voices over*)
> Oh, I pray you
> Count the cost
> 'Ere the fatal line
> Be crossed
> And your soul in hell
> Be lost
> *Be in time!*

As the 'Be in Time' thunders to a stop, it is instantly taken up
by the old woman's prayer –

OLD WOMAN: – the weight of the mountains and the deeps of
the oceans, the day and the night, the cares and troubles of
the whole slow spin of the whole big world –

And there are signs of fatal stress on Philip's prayer-clenched
face.

In the ward, they are bouncing and thumping into the chorus
again.

THE EVANGELISTS: (*Sing*)
> *Be in time! Be in time!*
> While the voice of Jesus calls you
> *Be in time!*

Marlow stays completely still, and very tense. Memory crashes
into him again.

The old woman's eyes have fixed now upon the evident stress on
Philip's face as she finishes her awful prayer.

OLD WOMAN: – You, O God, Thee O God, Almighty and Awful
Creator, you leave for the moment to – point down at the
one! Who? Who? Which one? Who is it?

A tiny but terrible pause. Philip twitches, and tears press at the
edge of his closed eyelids, in slow globules. He opens his eyes,
he alone in the class opens his eyes, and looks at the old woman,
to find that she is staring hard, straight at him. Then –

> Philip Marlow.

PHILIP: Y–yes, miss?

And everyone opens their eyes. Every head turns and looks at
him.

OLD WOMAN: Come out to the front.

A just barely suppressed murmur of tension and excitement all around the class. Philip remains at his desk, limbs and tongue locked, unable to move for fear and shame.

Come out to the front! Do you hear what I say! Come here! Slowly, like one whose body will scarcely let him, the–flight–is–not–possible nightmare, Philip somehow leaves his seat and comes down the aisle between the desks to the front, where he stands in front of the staring yet incredulous old woman. The class has once again fallen totally silent.

Philip.

PHILIP: (*Barely audible*) M–miss – ?

She is looking at him intently. Then she puts her hand on his shoulder, almost gently, though he flinches as she does so. Her tactics change.

OLD WOMAN: I want you to look at something, Philip.

It could be something nice, by the changed tone. Her hand firmly on his shoulder, she steers him to her table.

Now. You see that? You see that – that *thing* in the middle of the table?

No answer.

Well? Do you see it?

PHILIP: (*Barely audible*) Yes, miss.

OLD WOMAN: Did *you* do it?

No answer. She takes her hand from his shoulder. She stares hard at him. He has dropped his head. Then –

(*Much harsher*) *You* did it. Didn't you? *Didn't you?*

His head is now as low as it can be, and a barely muffled sob of total despair rises in him.

PHILIP: No–o–o.

She takes hold of his ear between her fingers, with a strangely meticulous precision, as a doctor might.

OLD WOMAN: If you didn't do it, my lad, then you know a great deal more about it than is good for you.

He lifts his head at last, and looks at her. It is as though he has suddenly realized that all is not necessarily lost.

PHILIP: Miss?

She catches the change.

OLD WOMAN: You *didn't* do it?

PHILIP: (*Whisper*) No, miss.

She keeps staring at him, not so sure now. His previous performances in class now stand him in good service.

OLD WOMAN: I would have been very surprised if a boy like you – (*Stops herself.*) So you know, do you? You know who did this filthy thing?

He manages to keep his eyes on her face.

PHILIP: (*Whisper*) Yes, miss.

She expels her breath in an audible hiss, and leans in to him, a gleam of excitement in her.

OLD WOMAN: Then you had better tell me, my boy! You had better tell me, hadn't you?

PHILIP: (*Mumble*) Dontliketo –

OLD WOMAN: (*Sharply*) What?

PHILIP: I don't like to, miss.

OLD WOMAN: Oh, you don't like to. What a pity. What a terrible shame. That means that first of all you will have to stand here for the rest of the day, absolutely still, not moving a single muscle, looking at *that thing* on the table, until you decide to be sensible. And then, when the bell is rung at the end of the day, and you *still* have not told me what I want to know, do you know what will happen then?

Lips pressed tightly together, fists clenched tightly together, he looks at her, and says nothing.

You don't want to know? Well. I'll tell you. I shall take hold of your ear, little boy, and I shall lead you through to Mr Hopper in the big room, where he will take the big cane out of the big cupboard and give you the biggest thrashing you or anybody else in this school has ever had. And he will keep on doing it, little boy, until you *do* decide to tell us what you know. Understand?

No reply.

Do you understand?

PHILIP: Yesmiss.

OLD WOMAN: Very well. Now, then. Think about all that I have said. Think about the *stick*, my lad. And tell me. Who did it? Mmmm? Who?

Philip looks slowly around the class, making the boys cringe. Then lowers his eyes.

PHILIP: (Mumble) Don't like to say, Miss.

At the dance hall, the two mysterious men have positioned themselves at opposite ends of the bar, which is so shaped that they can look directly across at each other, past a lugubrious barman in the middle who is cleaning glasses with a cloth.

The first mysterious man is swallowing a drink in the mannered style of a B-movie hood, and nods at his companion in some kind of signal. The second mysterious man swallows his drink in an identical style, and nods back his reception of the message.

MARLOW: (*Voice over, during this*) Some Duke or other with a name like a boot said Never Explain, Never Apologize. They should write that over the gates at Wormwood Scrubs. Am I right? But the way things were looking for yours truly, me with the snappy hat, they were about to write it on my gravestone –

During which, too, from below, over the lip of the balcony, the dance band is driving into 'Accentuate the Positive', with dance-band resonance –

The hymn in the Sunday ward has become 'Accentuate the Positive', and the Evangelists suitably transformed. The patients in or at their beds, clutching their handed-out hymn sheets, are listening and watching with exactly the same manner and expressions as they would to the hymn – that is, with uncomfortably false piety, sickly grins, due embarrassment.

But Dr Finlay and his companions are using their hands (shaking the palms from the wrist) in the alleged manner of the black Evangelicals the song purports to imitate. They also roll their eyes and flash their teeth. Gradually, they bear down on Marlow, who has his slightly far–away–and–over–the–hills look.

During the original record – to which their lips are synchronized – there is a boogie roll on the piano – alleged, here, to come from the portable electronic organ, then a solo female voice takes over. Here, it is the Girl Evangelist who had distributed the hymn sheets.

The Evangelists have reached and now spread themselves on either side, and at the foot, of Marlow's bed, still singing the

1940s dance-band number, with its like-message to the hymn. The 'singing' Dr Finlay, at his fiercest, jabs an admonitory forefinger at the apparently impassive Marlow. The others do the same, jabbing out their arms and forefingers at the now surrounded Marlow.

Back in the dance hall, at the bar, the second mysterious man has come up close to the first mysterious man as, below, 'Accentuate the Positive' reaches towards its end. The second mysterious man seems nervous. His tongue has to moisten his lips before he can lean in and speak, conspiratorially.

SECOND MYSTERIOUS MAN: Are you – um – are you going to wait for the number to finish, or what?

FIRST MYSTERIOUS MAN: That is so.

SECOND MYSTERIOUS MAN: Only – he's a good target now, a sitting duck –

FIRST MYSTERIOUS MAN: My glass. Look at it. I'd say it was empty. What would you say?

SECOND MYSTERIOUS MAN: The same.

FIRST MYSTERIOUS MAN: What?

SECOND MYSTERIOUS MAN: I'd say it was empty too.

Pause. The first mysterious man keeps rigidly still. The second mysterious man wilts, and sighs.

All right. All right.

FIRST MYSTERIOUS MAN: The same. The same again. Thank you.

SECOND MYSTERIOUS MAN: (*Upset*) We draw the same expenses, you know. Me and you.

FIRST MYSTERIOUS MAN: Who does the shooting? Who's got the shooter? A Teacher's, please. That'd go down very nicely, ta. And you go and see what Marlow does when this bleed'n toon is over. Ta. *Then he's had it!*

Philip in the village school is standing alone, face clenched, fists clenched, at the foot of the class.

The sounds of the real hospital Evangelists begin again –

And here they are, safely back in the middle of the ward, hitting the stuffing out of their last chorus.

THE EVANGELISTS: (*Sing, genuinely*)
> *Be in time! Be in time!*
> While the voice of Jesus calls you
> *Be in time!*
> If in sin you longer wait
> You may find no open gate
> And your cry –

Once again, Marlow is fully registering what is in front of him –
and his face is full of hard hatred, as –

> – be just too late
> *Be in time!*

The boy Philip is standing in front of the class, by the old
woman's table, in the same clenched and worried and shamed
manner. All the other children's eyes are upon him when they
think they are not under the direct gaze of the old woman. The
old woman, in the middle of a lesson, occasionally darts Philip a
sharp look, to see if he is ready to speak, or to keep up pressure
on him. She has drawn a giant leaf in outline on the blackboard.

OLD WOMAN: A leaf, boys and girls, a leaf may not seem all that
much to you. Just a leaf. Only a leaf, you might say. Green
in the summer, and then going brown, and dry, falling off
the tree, and rotting away to nothing. That's all. (*A swift,
sharp glance at* PHILIP.) But look again! And you will be
surprised! A leaf, like you, has a rib. A leaf, like you, has
veins. A leaf, like you, *breathes.*

As she turns back to the blackboard, chalk in hand, to
demonstrate what she means, the eyes automatically, it seems,
switch to Philip. And one of the boys in the front pulls a quick
face at him, thumb to nose, tongue lolling. Philip clenches his
lips, his fists, even more tightly.

(*Meanwhile*) If you look at a leaf, if you hold it up to the
light, you will see the rib running through the middle of it –
like this – (*Squeak of chalk.*) From the bottom of the leaf at
the stem right through to the tip of the leaf. (*Sharply,
suddenly*) Keep still! Don't move an inch!

Startled, the jeering boy stops immediately, having momentarily
forgotten that the old woman does indeed have eyes in the back
of her head.

163

(*Continuing as before*) And if you look even more closely, you will see that coming out from this rib, like this – (*Squeak, squeak.*) There are *veins*. You see? Like this. Now – (*Turns back to the class.*) If you were to shine a very strong, a very powerful torch through the leaf, you would see that there is a very fine pattern in between these veins. Some of this pattern – which is just like a net, a small net – some of this pattern shows up as *green* and some of the pattern shows up under the bright light of the torch as *white*. The white stuff is tougher than the green. It is like the *bones* of the leaf.
They are all very quiet, but they are also all very bored.
    (*Suddenly*) George.
George, a boy near the front, jerks as though he has been shot.
GEORGE: Miss!
OLD WOMAN: I said there were two colours in the – what?
GEORGE: (*Anxiously*) The leaf, miss.
OLD WOMAN: Yes, but in *what* in the leaf?
George looks everywhere to see if the answer will fly at him. It doesn't.
GEORGE: Um.
OLD WOMAN: In the *pattern* of the leaf. Two colours, I said. Two. What are they? George?
GEORGE: (*Tentative*) Green – miss?
OLD WOMAN: (*Menacingly*) Yes! *Green*, I said. *And*?
GEORGE: (*Scared*) Um –
OLD WOMAN: Come here.
GEORGE: (*Panic*) Black, miss – ?
Some titters.
OLD WOMAN: Quiet! George. Here. At once.
George slouches forward, with great reluctance.
    I saw you picking at the wood on your desk – I *knew* you were not paying attention! – Fetch me the stick.
GEORGE: Oh, miss –
OLD WOMAN: Fetch me the stick!
GEORGE: Yes, miss.
He passes in front of Philip, standing stock-still, to the soiled table, gathers up the cane, crosses again in front of Philip, gives her the stick.

OLD WOMAN: Hold out your hand!

GEORGE: Yes, miss.

At the swish! of the rise and fall of the cane, and the whap! of it across the other boy's hand – once, twice –

PHILIP: (*Voice over, intense gabble*) Ourfatherwhichartinheaven –

As George, half grinning and half snivelling, but the pain winning, goes back to his desk –

OLD WOMAN: Pay attention next time. Pay attention all of you. Green, I said, Green and *white*. And count yourself lucky, George, that you only had two strokes and only across the hand. In – let me see – in just over ten minutes' time all of you in Standard Three will join up in the Big Room with Standard One, Standard Two and Standard Four to see a caning that not one of you will ever forget! (*Suddenly*) *Philip*.

PHILIP: M–miss?

OLD WOMAN: You *do* know this. You *do* know that you will have to have the Big Stick. You *do* know that you will have to have it across your behind, and in front of the whole school.

She waits. His terror is now total.

PHILIP: (*Faintly*) Yes, Miss –

OLD WOMAN: *Unless*. You understand? *Unless*.

PHILIP: (*Faintly*) Miss.

The old woman examines him a moment, noting that he is near breaking point, and then briskly continues her lesson – with an *exceptionally* attentive class now.

OLD WOMAN: The leaf! When you are in the woods, and the leaves have fallen from the trees, then if you pick up a leaf from the ground –

There is a disturbing sound, which she ignores.

– you will soon see that it is the *green* part, the *green* pattern, which is the first bit of the leaf that rots away, that dies.

The disturbing sound is that of weeping. It is Philip. He is losing control, for the weeping is that of the deepest grief and fear. The old woman darts him one swift glance, but then –

But if you look at this leaf, the leaf you have picked up

165

from the soft floor of the forest, you will also see –
She stops. The only sound is that of Philip weeping. She goes across to him. She puts her hand on his juddering shoulder. Her voice sounds, now, kindly, concerned: it is an old technique.

> There. There. You have been very brave in sticking up for the wicked boy who did it. I am sorry you will have to be punished. And punished so very, very hard. I think we've had enough of this, don't you?

PHILIP: (*Sob*) Yu–yu–yes, miss –

OLD WOMAN: (*Soothingly*) I think the time has come to tell me what you know, hasn't it?

PHILIP: (*Sob*) Y–yes, miss –

She pats his shoulder. Then –

OLD WOMAN: (*Softly*) Who was it? Tell me. There's a good boy.

He looks up, face wet, hesitates desperately, then looks around the class. Various boys flinch. But, with a sort of dreadful inevitability, Philip's eyes fall upon the boy at the front of the class who had pulled the jeering face at him, thumb to nose. A moment too late, the boy realizes his plight, and – Philip points straight at him.

PHILIP: Mark Binney, Miss. It was *Mark Binney*!

5

Outside the 1945 dance hall, there is an extravagance of rain.
Rolls of thunder overhead. The rain smacks and hisses and
puddles, and the street lights make everything gleamy, wavery,
ill-defined, dramatic. It bounces ping–pong–pong on the roof
and bonnet of the parked car belonging to the two mysterious
men. They are not in it. A voice is heard, from another time and
another place.

MR HALL: (*Voice over*) Look at it. Just look at the bloody stuff.
     Look at the window, Reginald. Rain, rain, rain.

Inside the dance hall, Marlow, the Singing Detective, steps in
front of the band on the stage, with the wry grin of a showman
about to pull a trick. The band is about to play 'The Umbrella
Man' in the version originally recorded by the Sammy Kaye
Orchestra, The Three Barons and chorus.

MARLOW: (*Drawl*) The old Umbrella Man.

And he suddenly opens a big bright umbrella as the music takes
over. Wet streets are gleaming outside as before, and the rain
bouncing, as before, but now the music is bouncing too.

'The Umbrella Man' bounces as strongly in the head of
Reginald, in the hospital, clutching his battered paperback, his
lips moving slightly as he labours along the line.

REGINALD: (*Very slowly*) Toodle–lum–a–lum–a . . .

The line yields up the dance hall, where Marlow, wielding the
bright umbrella, flicks his eyes about the floor, and then begins
to sing with a sardonic expression, the band providing the *Oo–
ooo–oooh* chorus, behind him.

In the hospital, the slow reader has difficulty with a phrase on
the page.

     A thing–a–me–jig –

An irritated Mr Hall stares at him.

MR HALL: You move your lips, did you know that? When you
     read. You move your lips.

Reginald does not look up, but his attention flickers.

REGINALD: What?

MR HALL: That's the sign of a slow reader. A backward reader. You could go so far as to say that anyone who moves their lips when they read is mentally retarded.

REGINALD: What?

MR HALL: Are you aware of that?

Reginald slowly lowers the book, and looks at Mr Hall. His face is suddenly not so amiable.

REGINALD: What did you say?

MR HALL: (*Quick retreat*) Raining. I said it's raining. Look at the windows.

REGINALD: Yeh.

And he puts his eyes back on the page. Mr Hall covertly, comically, glares at him. Reginald moves his lips.

MR HALL: What's it about? Reginald – ? I said – What's so special? What's it about?

REGINALD: You asked me that. 'Undreds of times.

MR HALL: Well, I'm asking again! Ent I?

Reginald sighs heavily, drags his eyes off the page.

REGINALD: (*Slowly*) Well –

And then a comically lengthening pause.

MR HALL: My God.

REGINALD: It's hard to say.

MR HALL: (*Snort*) Well, if you don't know *now* –

REGINALD: Murder.

MR HALL: Good!

REGINALD: Killing, and that.

MR HALL: Let's bloody hope so.

REGINALD: And women. *Loose* women.

MR HALL: There you are.

REGINALD: We could do with a few of them in here, eh? Plenty of beds.

MR HALL: Now, now.

But they both simper a little.

REGINALD: (*Slowly*) Except –

And he stops again, Mr Hall rolls his eyes. Beyond them, the drug trolley comes into the ward.

MR HALL: Except. Except. Except what?

REGINALD: Except they're not really. Well, not all of them. Some of them are spies. Even though they have to go to bed with the customers –

MR HALL: What sort of shop is this? A knocking shop?

REGINALD: Club.

MR HALL: Go on. I grasp that.

REGINALD: And some of them are whatchacallits – Nazis. And some of them are – Oh, I don't know.

MR HALL: Footballers?

REGINALD: Get off.

He goes back to his book, leaving Mr Hall to ruminate nastily.

MR HALL: Well, I think that's clear. I think you've got the plot in a nutshell, my boy. Very succ–int. Totally understandable. You will always be able to get a job on *Reader's Digest*.

REGINALD: What?

MR HALL: With a mind like yours.

Reginald looks at him evenly, conscious now of the need to hit back. He waits, then lobs his response, knowing it to be a grenade.

REGINALD: Don't you feel the need to do something? Shall I call for the bedpan for you, Mr Hall?

MR HALL: (*Immediately embarrassed*) Hey, now –

REGINALD: It's a good many hours since you had a shit behind your curtains.

MR HALL: (*Agitated*) Stop! Stop it, now – Reginald. This is not a proper subject –

REGINALD: Here's the nurses coming with the pills. Ask the pretty one. Tell her you got to have the bedpan.

MR HALL: (*Hiss*) Reginald – !

REGINALD: Well, you got to shit *sometimes*, Mr 'All, aintcha? I mean, your arse ain't sewed up, is it? Though the grunts and groans you make – Shall I shout for you – ?

Pretty Nurse Mills and tough Staff Nurse White are getting nearer with the trolley, dispensing to each bed in turn, and Mr Hall is very aware of their approach.

MR HALL: (*Agitated*) Shut your chops, Reginald. This is uncalled for. This is very offensive –

REGINALD: This is not chops, Mr Hall. This is a mouth.

169

MR HALL: And a very dirty one –

He breaks off in a paroxysm of embarrassment as the trolley suddenly accelerates.

> Shh! Shhhh! No more. Say no more.

REGINALD: (*Triumphant*) Carry on reading, then, is it? Go back to my story, can I?

NURSE MILLS: (*Arriving*) You must be enjoying it.

REGINALD: When I get the chance. It's very busy in here.

STAFF NURSE WHITE: It's not the *same* book, surely?

MR HALL: He's a slow reader is our –

REGINALD: (*Threateningly*) I think Mr Hall wants the –

MR HALL: (*Quickly*) But of course I keep on interrupting him, with my love of conversation. It's only fair to say that – I *do* divert him, oh yes –

He is given two tablets and a capsule, on a spoon.

STAFF NURSE WHITE: (*Brisk*) Open.

And Mr Hall is glad to do so, and swallow them down with his glass of water.

NURSE MILLS: (*Meanwhile*) What is it, Reginald? What's it called?

Reginald has to unfold it to look at the cover.

REGINALD: *The Singing Detective.*

NURSE MILLS: By P. E. Marlow?

Reginald has to look again.

REGINALD: That's the geezer.

STAFF NURSE WHITE: Open!

Reginald has to take four different kinds of pill. Nurse Mills hands him his water glass –

NURSE MILLS: You know he's in here, do you? The man who wrote the book you're reading. In this ward.

In the act of swallowing, Reginald has to give an extra gulp, of astonishment.

STAFF NURSE WHITE: (*Severely*) All gone? Have you swallowed them?

Reginald gulps again, wide-eyed.

REGINALD: Fanks, nurse, yeh – (*To* NURSE MILLS) What? *Oo* is?

Nurse Mills nods in the general direction of the top half of the ward.

NURSE MILLS: Mr Marlow, down there – P. E. Marlow. He
wrote it. That book.

Astounded, greatly over-impressed, Reginald goggles along the
ward.

REGINALD: What? *'Im? He* did? That poor old sod who can't
stop nodding his bonce?

STAFF NURSE WHITE: That's not the right way to talk!

NURSE MILLS: No. In the next bed this side down – Mr
Marlow –

MR HALL: (*With relish*) Nobody there. The Invisible Man. He
wrote that?

NURSE MILLS: He's out of the ward at the moment, having
treatment – But that bed, yes.

Which, to Reginald, is almost equally incredible.

REGINALD: What? *'Im?*

MR HALL: The loudmouth. With the skin.

STAFF NURSE WHITE: (*Nastily*) The very one.

NURSE MILLS: Oh, I wouldn't say –

But she stops, interestingly. Staff Nurse White looks at her.

MR HALL: Well, you'll be able to ask him how it finishes now,
Reginald. That story of yours.

The drugs trolley is being pushed onward to the next bed, but
Staff Nurse White gets in a contemptuous remark over her
shoulder as she goes.

STAFF NURSE WHITE: *He* won't know, I'll guarantee you
that.

But Reginald is still astounded.

REGINALD: I'd like to talk to him, though. Fancy that, eh?
What a turn up!

The rain is also splattering upon the window of Dr Gibbon's
room, where Marlow sits in his wheelchair.

MARLOW: The rain, it falls. The sun, it shines. The wind blows.
And that's what it's like. You're buffeted by this, by that,
and it is nothing to do with you. Someone you love dies, or
leaves. You get ill or you get better. You grow old and you
remember, or you forget. And all the time, everywhere,
there is this canopy stretching over you –

GIBBON: (*Determined to interrupt*) What canopy?

Marlow stops. Glares. Seems about to speak, doesn't. Then does.

MARLOW: Things–as–they–are. (*Almost laughs in scorn*) Fate.
Fate. Impersonal. Irrational. Disinterested. The rain falls.
The suns shines. The wind blows. A bus mounts a
pavement and kills a child. And –

Then, suddenly, with a savagery which implies the opposite of
what he is saying.

– I believe in no systems, no ideologies, no religion, nothing
like that. I simply think – Oh, it's very very boring, this.
Very – I just think that from time to time, and at random,
you are visited by what you cannot know cannot predict
cannot control cannot change cannot understand and cannot
cannot cannot escape – Fate. (*Little shrug.*) Why not? 'S
good old word.

GIBBON: Accident.

MARLOW: What?

GIBBON: You say Fate. I say Accident.

MARLOW: (*Unimpressed*) You can call it what you like. Either
way, there's sod all you can do about it. Right?

Gibbon smiles at him, noticing the way Marlow uses his head
and torso in the wheelchair as he speaks.

GIBBON: Progress.

MARLOW: That depends on where you are standing when the
bomb falls –

GIBBON: No. You.

MARLOW: Me?

GIBBON: The way you move your head and body when you talk
some particularly urgent gibberish –

MARLOW: Ta.

GIBBON: And the skin patches. Your skin is genuinely
responding.

Marlow unaccountably glares.

MARLOW: Yes?

GIBBON: Yes!

MARLOW: (*Without grace*) You see. Some biochemical or other.
Nothing to do with me at all – Nothing to do with my *mind*.

GIBBON: Have you tried to stand?

MARLOW: Who'd vote for me?

DR GIBBON: (*Sigh*) Have you tried to stand up?

MARLOW: Yes.

GIBBON: And?

MARLOW: I fall down.

GIBBON: Have you tried to hold a pen?

MARLOW: Yes.

GIBBON: And?

Marlow measures him. Then –

MARLOW: I wrote a whole word.

GIBBON: (*Pleased*) Oh, well done!

MARLOW: Yep. A whole word. Four whole letters.

GIBBON: That may not seem much, four lett–

He catches himself, too late.

Oh. I see. A four-letter word.

MARLOW: (*Derisive hoot*) You got to be sharper, doc. I had you down for a man who could strike matches on his thumbnail.

GIBBON: Then I'm sorry to disappoint you. If I smoked, I would use a lighter, I think.

MARLOW: (*Delighted*) Ooh, look! *Hurt*, are we?

Gibbon sits back, like one genuinely considering the matter.

GIBBON: You might conceivably have a point – a very small one –

MARLOW: Don't be ashamed. You're only human.

GIBBON: – but what interests me is the surely disproportionate pleasure you get out of it.

MARLOW: (*Indifferent*) Well, there you go. Different strokes for different folks.

GIBBON: You are making physical progress. Indisputably.

MARLOW: Even a doctor can see that.

GIBBON: But – do you still feel so – (*Carefully choosing a word*) disappointed? In things as they are.

MARLOW: Not a bit. *Things* as they are, are no concern of mine.

GIBBON: You object to the word 'things'?

MARLOW: Oh, there are lots and lots of words I object to.

GIBBON: Such as?

Marlow is suddenly aware that Gibbon has fallen into his strange old habit of walking up and down behind him on the wooden floor.

MARLOW: Such as – loitering.

GIBBON: Another.

MARLOW: (*Frown*) What?

GIBBON: Another word you dislike.

MARLOW: Oh, goody. Games.

Gibbon comes round in front of him again, and folds his arms, looking at Marlow with a new glint.

GIBBON: If you like, Mr Marlow.

It is said like a challenge. A small moment of tension. Marlow glowers, but then, too, takes on the same choose-your-weapons glint.

MARLOW: Word games.

GIBBON: If you like.

Again, the sense of challenge, the slight tension.

MARLOW: (*Jeer*) Like Scrabble.

GIBBON: No. Like, I say a word, any word, and –

MARLOW: And I throw up the word *I* associate with it.

GIBBON: Instantly.

MARLOW: (*Rapid fire*) Nescafé.

GIBBON: (*Laugh.*) We haven't started yet. I meant – you have to respond instantly, without hesitation.

MARLOW: Ah. But I did.

Gibbon smiles faintly. He walks away. Click–clock–clack.

Marlow seems to tense. Then, suddenly –

GIBBON: Doctor –

MARLOW: (*Rapid fire*) Charlatan.

Gibbon smiles. Click–clock–clack. Then –

GIBBON: If we're going to do this –

MARLOW: – We have to agree *in advance* that it is meaningless.

GIBBON: Oh, quite.

MARLOW: Has no diagnostic value.

GIBBON: Fine.

MARLOW: (*Rapid fire*) Judge.

Gibbon blinks, then nods. Click–clock–clack. He moves around a little. It is like someone about to start a serve at tennis.

GIBBON: (*Snap*) Wall.

MARLOW: (*Rapid*) Blank.

GIBBON: (*Snap*) Will.

MARLOW: (*Rapid*) Bard.

GIBBON: Black.

MARLOW: Magic.

A small pause. Marlow's responses are ultra-fast.
Click–clock–clack go Gibbon's shoes. Marlow's eyes dart and
gleam, at the ready.

GIBBON: (*Suddenly*) Comb.

MARLOW: (*Rapid*) Honey.

GIBBON: Blonde.

MARLOW: Honey.

GIBBON: Money!

MARLOW: Shit!

GIBBON: Fish.

MARLOW: Jesus.

GIBBON: God.

MARLOW: Doctor.

They pause fractionally, almost as though for a breath. Marlow
seems to relax a little, underestimating his 'opponent'.
Click–clack–clock.

GIBBON: (*Suddenly*) Guardian.

MARLOW: Misprint.

GIBBON: Sun.

MARLOW: Trash!

GIBBON: You.

MARLOW: Me.

GIBBON: Me.

MARLOW: Tarzan.

GIBBON: Legs.

MARLOW: Eleven.

GIBBON: Arms.

MARLOW: Bombs.

GIBBON: Hands.

MARLOW: Clap.

GIBBON: Clap.

MARLOW: Promiscuity.

GIBBON: Loose.

MARLOW: Tight.

GIBBON: Free.

MARLOW: Gift.

GIBBON: Fair.

MARLOW: Bus.

GIBBON: Train.

MARLOW: Puff.
GIBBON: Queen.
MARLOW: Poof.
GIBBON: King.
MARLOW: Check!
Marlow glints with triumph, thinking he is 'winning', but he is in fact being led into various sorts of trap.
GIBBON: Young.
MARLOW: Green.
GIBBON: Old.
MARLOW: Cliff Richard.
And Gibbon almost falters. But then –
GIBBON: (*Snap*) Fly!
MARLOW: Crash!
GIBBON: Float.
MARLOW: Hook.
GIBBON: Dream.
MARLOW: Wake.
GIBBON: Sleep.
MARLOW: Lie.
GIBBON: (*Deliberate temptation*) Politician.
MARLOW: (*Smirk*) Lie.
GIBBON: Tale.
MARLOW: Lie.
GIBBON: Writer.
MARLOW: Liar.
GIBBON: Sentence.
MARLOW: Prison.
GIBBON: Cage.
MARLOW: School.
And he blinks, self-surprised, but he has no time. Another word comes whipping at him.
GIBBON: Light.
MARLOW: Cigarette.
GIBBON: Lung!
MARLOW: Fish!
GIBBON: Evasion!
MARLOW: Taxi!
GIBBON: Duty.

MARLOW: Humbug.

GIBBON: Cant.

MARLOW: Can!

GIBBON: Tin.

MARLOW: Tack.

GIBBON: Nail.

MARLOW: Cross.

GIBBON: Passion.

MARLOW: Pretence.

GIBBON: Woman.

MARLOW: Fuck.

GIBBON: Fuck.

MARLOW: Dirt.

GIBBON: Dirt.

MARLOW: Death.

Marlow jerks suddenly, and knows it is no longer a game: and never was. Gibbon, alertly watching him, gives Marlow a chance to get out or get off.

GIBBON: Start.

MARLOW: (*Shout*) Stop!

A little pause. They look at each other. Then –

    A game.

GIBBON: Do you think so?

Marlow slides his eyes away, oddly furtive.

MARLOW: That's what you called it. And we agreed – No diagnostic value.

GIBBON: Oh, none at all. None whatsoever.

MARLOW: I mean – it's words. Just –

GIBBON: Just words.

A tiny pause. Marlow sucks in his breath. Then –

MARLOW: I don't think I'll come here any more.

GIBBON: No?

MARLOW: No.

GIBBON: (*Gently*) Why is that?

Marlow is looking steadily at the rain on the big window, which is heavier than ever.

MARLOW: (*Steadily*) Toodle–lum–a–lum–a Toodle–lum–a– Too–ray–ay–aye.

177

Words blip their faintly glowing track across the screen of the word processor.

Over now. Finished. He's dead. Out of it.

A pause in the progression. And then, underneath, in capitals –
THE EN

Before the 'D' comes up, Nicola at the keyboard laughs in relief and triumph.

NICOLA: That's it! All done.

BINNEY: (*Pleased*) And about time, too.

In Gibbon's room, Marlow is looking at the heavy rain on the big window.

MARLOW: (*Steadily*) Toodle–lum–a–lum–

Nicola is talking, at the word processor, in Binney's (or Finney's) house by the river.

(*Voice over*) – Toodle–lum–a– Too–ray–ay–aye.

NICOLA: – since I did any typing. And this gadget of yours. My
     God. You'd think it could pour a drink. Or answer back.

BINNEY: U–uh. That's my job. You want a drink?

NICOLA: Why not?

BINNEY: (*Attending to drinks*) Now that script is in the machine,
     we can run off as many copies as we need. Ice?

NICOLA: Ice.

BINNEY: And now we deliver.

NICOLA: And collect!

They look at each other, and start to laugh, but his anxiety intervenes.

BINNEY: But you must, *must* get Marlow to sign the option with
     my company. That's an absolute essential. First things first.
     One – he signs with me. Two – I sell it on to Medro Films.
     Three – net profit, half a million plus all the points. Not
     bad, eh?

NICOLA: (*Raising her glass*) Cheers!

BINNEY: He's got to sign, though.

NICOLA: I know, I know.

BINNEY: Can't you be *nicer* to him? Nicola – sweeter. Promise
     more. All that stuff.

NICOLA: Hitch up my skirt, do you mean?

BINNEY: Nicola.

NICOLA: All right. All right. But if you had any idea how difficult he can be –

BINNEY: See him this evening. And be nice, be –

He stops at a loud rat–a–tat on the front door, below. And some unconscious, nervous gesture, like a tic, makes his hand go to his throat. She stares.

NICOLA: (*Frown*) What's the matter?

Rat–a–tat again, insistent.

In the hospital, the big lift doors open to let out Marlow in his chair, pushed by the porter, who is wearing his Sony Walkman. They traverse the busy lobby-like area which leads to Marlow's ward. Marlow is looking neither to the left nor to the right, unhappily self-absorbed. He is brooding on his encounter with Gibbon, from which he is returning, but the voices in his head are currently displaced, with a door being banged rat–a–tat.

(*Voice over, rapid*) Passion.

BINNEY: (*Voice over, rapid*) Pretence.

NICOLA: (*Voice over, rapid*) Woman.

BINNEY: (*Voice over*) Fuck.

NICOLA: (*Voice over*) Fuck.

BINNEY: (*Voice over*) Dirt.

Marlow's thoughts take flesh.

NICOLA: (*Laugh*) Dirt.

BINNEY: (*Laugh*) Death.

They hoot, and embrace, passionately. The front door is still being banged.

In the hospital, the earphoned and abstracted porter pushes the self-absorbed patient on through doors into the corridor to Marlow's ward. The imagined sound of a door being banged gradually ebbs.

In the lobby, out of their proper realm, are the two mysterious men, one sitting, one standing, in seemingly earnest conversation. They stop talking, and look at the wheelchair as it passes. Then –

SECOND MYSTERIOUS MAN: Do you think that's him?

FIRST MYSTERIOUS MAN: Could be.

SECOND MYSTERIOUS MAN: Do we go in – or what?

FIRST MYSTERIOUS MAN: Perhaps. But we got to be bloody careful!

Marlow is pushed on into the ward and to the side of his bed. The porter flips up his little headphones.

PORTER: Still needing the assistance?

MARLOW: (*Morose*) 'Fraid so.

PORTER: Aah. Tomatoes.

MARLOW: What – ?

PORTER: Still eating them tomatoes.

MARLOW: No, no.

PORTER: Stay off them, man. It's the pips.

MARLOW: (*Flat*) I hear you.

Down the ward, Reginald is still reading, and still moving his lips a little as his mind crawls slowly along the page. He has not noticed that Marlow is back in his bed. But Mr Hall has: he sees everything, in his boredom.

MR HALL: He's back, then, Reginald. The scribe. He has returned to his little paradise, and the oasis of his pit. The loudmouth. Your bloody so-called author, Reginald.

Reginald looks up, with great interest, and disproportionate awe.

REGINALD: You wouldn't think it, would you? You'd never think it. Not in a million years.

MR HALL: Oh, there's lots of things *I'd* never think, my boy. Like – when will I ever again have an intelligent conversation?

But Reginald is too fascinated to register sarcasm.

REGINALD: He don't *look* like a bloke as writes a book like this –

MR HALL: (*With an edge*) No. He don't.

REGINALD: Just shows.

MR HALL: What does it show?

REGINALD: Shall I go over and have a word? Talk to him.

MR HALL: Like you talk to me, do you mean?

REGINALD: No –

MR HALL: *Dazzle* him, do you mean?

REGINALD: No – tell him – you know – how I like his story,

and that – Why this happens and this don't –

MR HALL: And ask him how it ends, for God's sake. And how soon!

Back in his bed, Marlow reaches for the inevitable packet of cigarettes on his locker. He takes out one and lights it yet more easily than before – virtually one-handed this time. He blows out a column of smoke: understood, now, as one means of entry to his thoughts.

GIBBON: (*Voice over*) Dirt.

MARLOW: (*Voice over*) Death.

Pause. Then, out loud, to himself.

    Knock. Knock. Knock.

The front door to Binney's house opens, from inside. Binney looks puzzled. He comes out a few feet, and looks up and down. There is no one knocking at the door – and it upsets him. He looks across to the river. It happens that a River-Police launch is passing – of the kind which fished a naked woman out of the water. His eyes narrow in unreasonable and oddly fearful speculation (if indeed this is the 'real' Binney), then he forces his thoughts away, turns back into the house, and goes up the elegant stairs pensive.

He is about to pass the place on the wall where, in the script of *The Singing Detective*, the nude portrait hangs. Now, there is just a blank space, a painted wall. Yet, about to pass, Binney suddenly stops, and looks at it, as though trying to work something out, something that does not make sense. As he stares, the nude portrait forms itself, so to speak, on the blank wall of the stair. It is indisputably Nicola.

GIBBON: (*Voice over*) 'Mouth sucking wet and slack at mouth, tongue chafing against tongue, limb thrusting upon limb, skin rubbing at skin. Faces contort and stretch in a helpless leer –

Back in the riverside house, oddly, in a dislocation of the narrative, Sonia's fur coat and underwear are on the floor, and Sonia is in the bed, lying still, and expressionless, the sheet around her, eyes fixed on – *not* Binney as before (much earlier) but Marlow, who is turning from the curtained window.

Marlow, oddly, has his shirt on, buttoned down, and pyjama trousers tucked into long socks, as though hiding his skin. The way he now suddenly sucks in his breath, in a half-shudder, shows that he has not succeeded in hiding his soul.

MARLOW: I'm sorry I – Look. It wasn't really *me* calling you names. I don't mean them. I don't want to do it. It's just that – afterwards – I always feel – (*Gives up.*) It's nothing personal.

'Sonia' in or on the rumpled bed looks at him with blank incomprehension – or disdain. Her speech is not a bit like her previous Russian-accented incarnation. She is unambiguously a prostitute.

SONIA: Takes all sorts.

Then –

What you covered up for? Something wrong with you?

Marlow stares at her, twitches, then, rather than answer, turns back to the window, to twitch the curtain a little aside, showing only darkness. 'Sonia' watches him, with a small curl of the mouth.

MARLOW: (*Strained mouth*) The river looks as – (*Turns, looks at her.*) The river.

SONIA: What about it?

MARLOW: (*Dully*) The river looks as though it's made of tar, sludging along. Full of filth.

The 'filth' sounds too pointed.

SONIA: What do you expect? Badedas?

Marlow glares, dark-minded, envenomed.

MARLOW: Doesn't it disgust you, what you do?

SONIA: (*Cool*) Depends on who I do it with, don't it?

MARLOW: Being *paid* to stretch yourself out and let a stranger enter you.

SONIA: You expect me to do it for nothing?

Marlow looks at her.

MARLOW: Of course not.

SONIA: I mean, how long does it take? What does it matter?

MARLOW: You really think that?

And it sounds more like a plea than a question.

SONIA: Christ! That's what you wanted, ennit?

In his hospital bed, Marlow seems to absorb his remark. Then –
MARLOW: Yeh.
But something makes him look sideways towards the next bed –
Here, Noddy's wet old mouth slack and almost drooling, and his
cadaverous head ceaselessly bob–bob–bobbing as it nods without
stop. Marlow is suddenly very interested in Noddy, watching him
intently.
(*Softly*) Roll on, eh, Pop? Roll on.
His expression changes, eyes still fixed on Noddy, but now with a
new gleam as he summons up, in his intemperate imaginations, the
opening chords of 'You Always Hurt the One You Love', in the
1940s recording by the Mills Brothers. As a result, the apparently
gaga old fellow in the next bed has a head that nod–nod–nods in
perfect time to the song, like a bandleader's baton. Better still, his
slack mouth forms the background 'Boom, Boom' of the male
voices as first one and then another of the Mills Brothers sings the
lugubrious melody.

Relaxing into his fantasy, Marlow widens his gaze from Noddy
to the whole ward, as the record thunders out, full blast. It appears
that Mr Hall takes up the solo, and 'sings' with Reginald providing
the *Bom–Om–Oom* 'accompaniment'. Marlow's pleased glance
swivelling to take in Staff Nurse White, who is taking blood
pressures down ward. She, too, becomes a soloist. Delighted now,
Marlow's gaze skids back to nod–nod–nodding, slack-mouthed
Noddy, at the point where the higher-voiced Mills Brother croons
through the same much-parodied verse.

But the unexpected lightness or whimsy of Marlow's thoughts
cannot be maintained. The gleam of pleasure and amusement
leaves him, and he starts to brood again. And yet, the music
continues, almost as though once summoned, it will not now
dismiss itself. Instead, it brings into being –

The crowded and smoke-laden club in the Forest village, with Mrs
Marlow at the piano, and Mr Marlow and Raymond standing
beside her. It is Mr Marlow, now, who sings of breaking hearts,
and Raymond who *bom–om–oms* beside him. Each man has his
hand on the other's shoulder. And then the song, like a mood still
darkening, summons up –

183

Deep down in the gloom of an Underground station, the platform is occupied only by a pacing man talking to himself, a young woman and a boy. The Mills Brothers' recording continues without interruption. The woman and the boy are Mrs Marlow and Philip. They are sitting on the wooden seats near the end of the platform, where the black hole gapes.

Mrs Marlow is silent and absorbed, now carrying a sense of pervasive melancholy. Philip swings his legs a little. He looks at the rails. He looks at his mother. He looks at the rails. He looks at his mother – then, almost furtively, as though his hand is a small burrowing animal, he slides it on to her lap to hold her hand. She looks down at the hand holding hers, like one surprised. Then, coming back from some dark or sad reverie, she squeezes his hand.

MRS MARLOW: There's a good boy.

PHILIP: Mum?

MRS MARLOW: Looking after your Mother, aren't you?

PHILIP: (*Matter of fact*) Ant worked out.

MRS MARLOW: What?

PHILIP: You don't like it here, doost? Not if the truth be told.

She evades the directness.

MRS MARLOW: 'Do you?' You'd better say 'Do you?' now, not 'Doost', Philip. Up here, anyway. People'll think you're funny –

He thinks about it, pressing his lips tightly together.

PHILIP: But you don't like it. Doost?

She smiles, but only a small smile.

MRS MARLOW: You're a very stubborn boy –

PHILIP: (*Grimly interrupting*) Ay. I be!

MRS MARLOW: Well – I don't know where you get it from.

PHILIP: Our Dad.

MRS MARLOW: No.

PHILIP: (*Firmly*) Our Dad.

She looks at him, and then shakes her head.

MRS MARLOW: I wish you did. I wish he had it to give. But he's not made that way, Philip. Don't you know that?

PHILIP: When's him a-coming?

She looks away, pretending to see something.

Mum? When's our Dad going to come?

MRS MARLOW: Stop it.

PHILIP: No! I want to go whum! I want to go back to our Dad. Back to them trees.

MRS MARLOW: (*Violent, sudden*) Sod the trees!

PHILIP: Oh, no. Oh, no. The oak and the beech and the ash and the elm. Oh, no. No, no. (*Like an odd incantation, rocking his body a little*) The oak and the beech and the ash and the elm. The oak and the beech and –

MRS MARLOW: Philip!

PHILIP: – the ash and the elm. The oak –

She jerks at his arm, forcing him to stop.

MRS MARLOW: Do you want a smack! Stop it, I said.

He looks at her, resentful.

PHILIP: My arm d'*hurt*.

MRS MARLOW: Oh, come on –

PHILIP: You caught me on my sore.

MRS MARLOW: Your *what*?

PHILIP: On my arm, mind.

MRS MARLOW: Let me see.

PHILIP: Chunt nothing.

MRS MARLOW: Let me see.

He rolls up his sleeve. On his forearm is a big red and silvery-white patch. She is astonished, not knowing what it is. (In fact, a first psoriatic lesion.)

Philip! When did this come! Did you bump into something?

PHILIP: (*Subdued*) Dunno.

MRS MARLOW: (*Concerned*) Let's get back. I'll put some Zam-Buck on that. Pull your sleeve down.

As he does, face tight, he returns to what concerns him.

PHILIP: Better show our Dad, an' us? We'd better show this here arm to our Dad. That's what we got to do, ant us?

Her voice sounds strange, too near to tears, too strained –

MRS MARLOW: Oh, for God's sake – Philip – Don't keep on – you'll drive me off my – Philip. Once and for all. Shut up about it. *Shut up*.

PHILIP: When's him a-coming, then?

MRS MARLOW: He's not!

Philip is shocked, even though he knew it.

PHILIP: (*Gulp*) Mum? Why? *Why*, Mum?

MRS MARLOW: Philip. Listen to me. I want you to listen
to –

PHILIP: (*Interrupts.*) Is it coz of what thik bloke did to you in
the woods. In thik dell. Is it?

She freezes.

MRS MARLOW: Philip – ?

His legs start to swing.

PHILIP: Doing that stuff. With thik Mr Binney. With Raymond
Binney. Mark's Dad.

She is still holding herself stiff.

MRS MARLOW: What stuff? What do you mean – ?

PHILIP: Him on top of tha! Rolling about on top of tha!

MRS MARLOW: (*Mock incredulity*) *What?*

Philip stops swinging his legs, and works his face a bit. Then,
matter of fact –

PHILIP: Shagging.

Wallop! She instinctively slaps him across the face. Too hard.
He blinks at her, half his face red, eyes welling, and she realizes
what she has done.

MRS MARLOW: (*Tiny sob*) Oh – Philip –

PHILIP: (*Yell*) Shagging!

MRS MARLOW: Philip – !

Too late. He is up and running. Run–run–run, pant–pant–pant,
along the platform, and through the endless, dark tunnels.

　　　Philip! Come back! Philip! Please! Phil– !

Run–run–running. And 'You Always Hurt the One You Love'
starts to strum again, along the tunnels which suggest and then
actually become the corridor into Marlow's ward; and the ward
itself.

The music Marlow had himself triggered, so to speak,
returning, more heavily laden to him in the hospital bed.
Marlow's eyes are staring into Hell. Then an intruding voice
visibly jolts him –

VOICE: *Oo killed 'er, then?*

MARLOW: (*Startled, almost frightened*) *What* – ? Who?

Reginald it is. He has walked up to Marlow's bed, in his
dressing-gown and slippers.

REGINALD: Her in the river. The tart they dragged out of the
    river.
Marlow stares at him, recovering from the shock of the
intrusion.
MARLOW: What are you talking about?
REGINALD: Your book.
Because Marlow still stares at him, and now rather coldly,
Reginald feels it necessary to pull the much battered and folded
paperback from his dressing-gown pocket.
MARLOW: Christ. A reader.
REGINALD: (*Beam*) Yeh!
MARLOW: (*Without warmth*) You come under the Protection of
    Endangered Species legislation, no doubt.
REGINALD: What's that? Wit, is it?
Marlow blinks, but Reginald is looking at him with beaming,
simple admiration.
MARLOW: No. Not that. No fear.
REGINALD: All this time you've been in here and I been in here
    and you wrote it and I been reading it. Funny, ennit?
Marlow is not warm with strangers, if, indeed, to anyone he
knows.
MARLOW: Hilarious.
REGINALD: Good though. It's good.
MARLOW: Thank you.
REGINALD: Very good.
Marlow just looks at him. There seems to be nothing else to say.
But Reginald, over-impressed, keeps beaming at him. So –
MARLOW: Thank you.
Reginald beams wider, and thinks of something more to say.
REGINALD: Tell you're a writer.
MARLOW: Oh?
REGINALD: Not 'alf!
Marlow is finding this difficult.
MARLOW: How?
REGINALD: (*Admiring*) Should have known!
MARLOW: (*Colder*) How?
REGINALD: All that effin' and blindin'. Cor! You didn't half let
    rip, eh?
Marlow looks at him. Then –

MARLOW: 'Good writers who once knew far better words now use only four-letter words.'
REGINALD: Do they?
Marlow can see that Reginald does not know the words of the particular song.
MARLOW: The song.
REGINALD: Yeh?
MARLOW: 'Anything Goes'.
REGINALD: Not 'alf!
Marlow visibly gives up.
MARLOW: Yes. Well. It's the day and age.
REGINALD: You're not going to tell me, are you?
MARLOW: Tell you?
REGINALD: Who killed her. Who put her in the river. That girl.
MARLOW: A swine.
Said with just a little too much feeling.
REGINALD: Yeh. But which one, do you reckon? I mean, there's a lot of 'em in your book. Ent there?
The sudden hint of anger leaves Marlow, as quickly as it had flashed.
MARLOW: Oh, you'll find out. But only by reading it.
Even Reginald can see that he has been dismissed.
REGINALD: Yeh. Well – all the best, then.
MARLOW: And to you.
REGINALD: We'll have another little chat sometime.
MARLOW: Yes. I like these literary discussions.
REGINALD: Right, then.
MARLOW: Thank you.
REGINALD: (*Departing*) I'll bet you lie there all day long thinking of *murdering* people – eh?
And he continues on his way down the ward, chuckling, pleased with himself. Marlow watches him go, with a slightly superior half-smile. But then the small smile disappears.
MARLOW: (*Quietly*) Yes. Yes. I do.

And in the village school, the old woman pats Philip's shoulder.
OLD WOMAN: (*Softly*) Who was it? Tell me. There's a good boy.
He looks up, face wet, hesitates, looks around the flinching

class. A moment too late a boy (Mark) at the front of the class realizes his plight – and Philip points straight at him.

PHILIP: Mark Binney, miss. It was Mark Binney!

Mark jerks in his desk like someone who has been shot in the heart.

MARK: No! No–o–o miss – !

Philip stares at him, relentlessly blank, and speaks in flat, slow tones.

PHILIP: Mark Binney. It was Mark Binney. I saw him.

Mark opens and closes his mouth for a moment, like a landed fish, and then, in near-howl.

MARK: No–o–o! Miss! No! Chunt true! Chunt me! Chunt!

The old woman looks at him steadily as he quakes. And then at Philip.

OLD WOMAN: Are you sure you saw him?

PHILIP: Yes, miss.

MARK: No!

OLD WOMAN: Quite, quite sure?

MARK: I didunt! No–o!

PHILIP: Yes, miss.

The class is holding its collective breath, alive with real pleasure and excitement.

OLD WOMAN: *How* did you see him? Where were you? What were you doing?

Philip senses danger, and swallows his diction.

PHILIP: Door.

OLD WOMAN: (*Sharply*) What?

PHILIP: In the – I was in doorway, Miss. I was standing at thik door –

He indicates. His mind is racing.

OLD WOMAN: (*Frown*) Doing what?

Philip shifts a little on his feet.

PHILIP: I – uh – I came back, miss. A'ter school, miss. A'ter the bell.

OLD WOMAN: (*Sharply*) What for?

He looks at her. Beyond her, he can see the big map of Europe she had draped over the blackboard a few weeks ago. It is now on the wall, complete with brave Allied flags – and, for Philip, an inspiration –

PHILIP: To put another flag up, miss. In the big map, miss.

OLD WOMAN: To do what?

PHILIP: Berlin, miss.

OLD WOMAN: What do you mean, boy?

PHILIP: The Russians be there now, byun' um? Thoy be smashing through.

OLD WOMAN: Well – nearly there, but –

PHILIP: (*Cutting in*) And we ought to stick up their little flag on the map. Hammer and sickle. That's what I – any road, when I come back – there him was, wasna? I saw him. I saw Mark, miss. With my own eyes.

Mark, who cannot follow any of this, being the simplest child in the class, lets out another desperate cry.

MARK: Him couldn't have! No! Chunt true, miss!

But the old woman, for the time being, is concentrating all her attention on Philip.

OLD WOMAN: And what exactly did you see? What was he doing?

Again, Philip shifts from one foot to another.

PHILIP: Pooping, Miss.

A badly muffled explosion of unstoppable laughter from the class – instantly quelled.

OLD WOMAN: Quiet! All of you! (*Severely*) Philip. That is *not* the right word.

PHILIP: I – I mean – um – number two, miss. Him was doing his number two. On the table, miss.

The children are having great difficulty in not letting out another explosion. They have to hold their hands across their mouths, or chew on their knuckles.

MARK: (*Gasp*) Oh, I didunt – ! Oh, no, no, I didunt –

OLD WOMAN: Mark Binney.

MARK: (*Cry out*) Miss – No! No Miss No!

She lifts her hand and, so slowly it is almost like a slowed-motion scene, crooks her finger.

OLD WOMAN: Come out to the front. Come here, boy.

MARK: (*Choke*) Miss.

OLD WOMAN: Philip. You may go back to your desk. (*Threateningly*) For the while.

PHILIP: Yes, miss.

Philip passes Mark as the astounded and terrified boy drags
himself to the front. But he avoids looking at him.

MARK: Miss! No – No – Twarnt me, miss. Honest. Honest miss
    honest –

OLD WOMAN: We'll see about that, won't we, my boy? We are
    going to find out, aren't we? We're going to find out, even
    if it takes the rest of the day!

At the bandstand in the dance hall, emerging from the cover of
his umbrella with a heavy showy grin, Marlow's eyes
nevertheless flick about the floor as he sings of the old umbrella
man. The singer thinks he has glimpsed possible danger from
the balcony. The two mysterious men have moved from the bar
at the back of the balcony to come to the front, where they can
directly overlook the band stage and part of the dance floor.
They exchange creepy glances as they stare down at the 'singing'
Marlow, who is using his coloured umbrella as a prop for 'The
Umbrella Man' song.

FIRST MYSTERIOUS MAN: (*Hiss*) For God's sake!

SECOND MYSTERIOUS MAN: Wha– ?

FIRST MYSTERIOUS MAN: Face the other way! Watch the bar,
    you fool!

SECOND MYSTERIOUS MAN: And you watch your tongue.

FIRST MYSTERIOUS MAN: Face the other way, *please*. Watch
    the bar, *please*.

SECOND MYSTERIOUS MAN: Who'd be us, eh? Who in their
    right mind?

FIRST MYSTERIOUS MAN: (*Bitterly*) There you are.

The second mysterious man turns and watches the bar, his arms
folded. The barman, still cleaning glasses, thinks he is being
stared at. Marlow's attention ('gimlet-eyed' as his thrillers would
say) is now definitely concentrating on the distant figures at the
balcony, as he umbrella-twirls his way through the song.

MARLOW: (*Thinks, while singing*) *Those two – up there – One
    facing in, one facing out – What's going on? – That's standard
    Intelligence tactics – Watch yourself. Watch!*

The first mysterious man has his hand reaching inside his jacket
in a gunman's threatening, if over-stylized posture, eyes fiercely
clamped on the singing, umbrella-toting Marlow below. The

second mysterious man, getting very jumpy, is facing the other
way, arms folded. He squeaks urgently, side-of-the-mouth.

SECOND MYSTERIOUS MAN: Come on, come on, let him have
    it, will you? The barman is winking at me! He thinks I'm a
    – Come on! Do it!

His colleague picks up on a line in the song: a line in almost all
the songs.

FIRST MYSTERIOUS MAN: (*Side-of-mouth*) That's a good cue,
    eh? Break his bloody heart, eh?

And he takes out and levels the gun, but very
laboriously – Suddenly, in mid-note, Marlow dives low and
swings his umbrella up across himself – and a shot rings out at
almost the same moment – and then another – and on the third
splatt! –

The bullet holes are torn in the fabric of the umbrella in such
a way, such a pattern, that anyone behind it must be killed. But
Marlow is, almost magically, *not* behind the bullet-riddled
umbrella, but –

In direct line behind the umbrella, a clash on the drums as the
drummer stands with a look of total consternation, his fingers
clawing stiffly towards his neck – And, in tiny, gruesome delay,
the blood spurts and jerks from his throat. Screams from
dancers, terror from the dance band.

And almost immediately – Phut! Phut! Phut! –

Marlow, on his belly, where he has roll–roll–rolled, is the one
doing the firing, up at the balcony.

An alabaster-white little cupid on the lip of the balustrade
smashes apart as one of Marlow's bullets whips off it, with a singing
sound. The two mysterious men are hurtling at break-neck speed
for the exit. And the lugubrious barman, unfazed, continues
wiping the glasses. Trapped in an old tradition.

Reginald's eyes are popping, and his lips silently moving, as he
doggedly reads the battered paperback at the side of his hospital
bed.

REGINALD: (*Laboured*) His–fingers–cl-clawed – stiff–ly–
    towards–his–neck. In–a–tiny–de–lay–the–blood–j–jerked–
    and–spurt– (*Out loud, hiss*) Bloody hell.

The mortally wounded drummer, throat smashed to pieces, collapses over his drums in an almighty reverberating crash –

Outside the dance hall, the getaway car is screaming away from the pavement, hooting for passage, the rain still clattering down. Splish–splash! Marlow comes running onto the wet street – too late.

Reginald, reading, blows out his breath in disappointment.

Too late.

MR HALL: No, no. On time!

REGINALD: Wha– ?

MR HALL: Visitors, Reginald. Visiting time, my boy. You can put that book away now.

REGINALD: They shoot the wrong one –

MR HALL: What? Oh. In that bloody book.

REGINALD: Yeh.

MR HALL: Put it down. The hordes are upon us. Oh, you can smell the outside the world on their shoes, eh? Eh, my boy?

Through the double doors into the ward comes the flood of visitors for the official visiting hour. They pick out and then, so to speak, fall upon the appropriate beds, in a curiously vulpine manner. And then, a little after the first surge, comes Nicola.

Nicola looks across to Marlow's bed. He is half dozing, not at all interested in the idea of visitors. He is not aware of her scrutiny. Her expression, as she studies him unobserved, is maybe one of affectionate or even loving exasperation: but whatever it is, there is no trace of the villainous plotter and schemer of Marlow's alternate 'story'. But she sets her face into a smile, like someone determined to be brave, and walks forward, coming upon him as he seems to slip from his half-doze into a real sleep. He is propped against his pillowed back-rest. She looks at him. There is a sudden spurt of emotion on her, but she sensibly and Englishly puts it down.

NICOLA: Philip.

He opens his eyes at once. But it is like someone frightened. He stares at her.

Hello.

The brief, odd, flash of fear leaves him.

MARLOW: I was beginning a dream. I was drifting away, unanchored.

NICOLA: Where to?

MARLOW: School. Back to school.

NICOLA: God. One of those.

MARLOW: (*Heavily*) One of those.

NICOLA: I don't like those sort of dreams. I'm in the desk and they ask me what the capital of Iceland is or something and of course I never know –

MARLOW: Reykjavik.

NICOLA: Never know in the dreams, I mean.

They seem to examine each other.

MARLOW: What are you doing here?

NICOLA: (*Smile*) Oh. Punishing myself.

MARLOW: You look very – nice.

But the deliberation of the last word sounds like a put down or an accusation.

NICOLA: Don't say it like that!

But he keeps a near-or-actually-hostile stare on her.

> You are looking better. Your skin. (*Then, half-laugh*) Philip. Don't.

MARLOW: Don't?

NICOLA: Don't look at me like that.

MARLOW: Like what?

NICOLA: Like I'm your enemy, or – like something the cat brought in.

MARLOW: (*Suddenly*) It's not my imagination.

NICOLA: What isn't – ?

MARLOW: You are definitely up to something. I'm not making it up. You are *definitely* involved in some scheme or other.

She almost laughs, but not quite.

NICOLA: Good old Philip.

MARLOW: (*Nastily*) And it must be something to do with money.

Nicola tries to use a light tone: but it is obvious that she is not sure whether she should sit on the bedside chair or not. She is also half-distracted by the visitorless nod–nod–nod Noddy in the next bed, who is eyeing her with the nearest to lasciviousness his age and his condition allow.

NICOLA: Go on. This is fascinating.

MARLOW: *My* money.

She laughs – really laughs.

NICOLA: Oh, come on! You haven't got any!

Her amusement allows her to sit. Marlow looks at her, and comically tries to justify himself.

MARLOW: Not in cash, perhaps. Not in your actual old-fashioned, foldable, metal-strip portraits of Her Majesty. No. (*Sniff.*) Nor in coins, come to that. But – I have *assets*.

She considers the matter.

NICOLA: Your flat.

MARLOW: My flat.

NICOLA: A damp basement. That's very fashionable nowadays.

MARLOW: (*Stung*) And my work!

NICOLA: (*Quickly*) Yes. Of course.

MARLOW: My four detective stories.

NICOLA: Yes.

MARLOW: Three of which are out of print.

They look at each other. They start to laugh, but rather painfully so. She puts her hand across her mouth.

And the screenplay.

She stops laughing, takes her hand away.

NICOLA: What screenplay – ?

MARLOW: *Bingo!*

NICOLA: (*Puzzled*) Philip. What are you talking about, please?

MARLOW: The dot on every i, the crossbar on every t, the curl on each comma.

NICOLA: Come again?

MARLOW: With my own hands. With these buckled hands.

NICOLA: Philip –

MARLOW: Do you think I could *forget* a thing like that – ? Ten years ago. All right, it was ten years ago – I wrote that screenplay one holiday when I was feeling – when I had cantilevered heels.

NICOLA: Oh–well–I–wouldn't know, would I? That was long before you met me. What screenplay was this?

MARLOW: *The Singing Detective.*

NICOLA: (*Surprised*) Really?

MARLOW: And I put it away. I put it in a shoe-box. It's in a cupboard in the flat.

NICOLA: (*Light dawning*) Oh. That. Oh–h.

MARLOW: My God. Yes – that!

NICOLA: If it's the pages I *think* you mean, you threw them out. Ages ago.

Marlow repeats part of the phrase, with mock astonishment.

MARLOW: I threw them out.

NICOLA: If it's the one that – Yes. The one in the shoe-box.

MARLOW: (*Same mock incredulity*) The one in the shoe-box.

NICOLA: Philip. You know very well you did. What is this? What is all this?

They look at each other. He seems to change his attitude, all at once.

MARLOW: Oh, well, Easy come. Easy go.

NICOLA: (*Frown*) Was it the only copy?

MARLOW: (*Sigh*) Of course.

Pause. He is examining her, but with a detectable yearning. She is quick to pick up on it.

NICOLA: Never mind – eh?

MARLOW: Jesus.

NICOLA: What?

MARLOW: The way you sit. The way you – (*Stops.*) No. Those are the words of a song, almost.

NICOLA: You and your songs.

MARLOW: Yeh. Well. Banality with a beat.

Tentatively, she puts her long fingers and polished nails on the top of his hand as he rests on the turned-down sheet.

NICOLA: Will it hurt if I squeeze?

MARLOW: (*Hollow*) Yeh. Well.

NICOLA: Oh, you poor thing. But at least there's – you *are* improving.

MARLOW: In what, though?

NICOLA: Your skin. The way you – sort of move your head and arms. All that. I can see a big difference.

MARLOW: Except.

NICOLA: Except what?

MARLOW: I'm going mad.

NICOLA: Come on.

Then she falters, at the blazing ache in his eyes.

    What do you mean?

MARLOW: (*With precision*) I mean that I am going off my head.
    Round the bend. Bonkers. Losing my marbles. Cuckoo.
    Nuts. A candidate for the Funny Farm. That is what I
    mean. Bananas is what I mean. Got it?

NICOLA: (*Uneasy*) Do you want to talk about it? Or –

MARLOW: Sex!

NICOLA: What?

MARLOW: That's what it's about. Sex. Sex and lies.

She thinks she is about to come under attack, and shifts about a
bit.

NICOLA: You've been ill too long. You've been stuck with your
    own thoughts too long. That's all it is.

MARLOW: (*Suddenly*) I want to sleep with you again.

She blinks. Then –

NICOLA: Philip?

MARLOW: With a big mirror alongside.

NICOLA: Listen to me –

MARLOW: (*Cutting in*) So I can turn my head while I'm doing it
    and leer at myself. And so that when it starts shooting up in
    me and spurting out I can twist to one side coming off your
    hot and sticky loins and *spit* straight at my own face.

Silence. He is quivering. She takes her hand away, and looks
hard at him. Then –

NICOLA: My God. Philip.

His eyes blaze momentarily, then he subsides, sardonic again.

MARLOW: Well. It's an improvement, ennit?

NICOLA: What is?

MARLOW: Spitting at me. At my own reflection. Couple of
    weeks ago my idea of happiness would have been to spit
    into *your* face.

NICOLA: Christ Almighty.

MARLOW: Oh, yes, and him, too.

She is upset, agitated, unsure what to say or to do.

NICOLA: What are you doing about it? All this. These feelings.
    What can be done about them?

MARLOW: (*Gloomily sardonic*) Dunno. Write serious literature, I
    suppose. Or piss into the wind, like poets and priests do –

He stops, his expression changes.

Who are those two? *Who are they?*

She turns her head, startled, to follow the direction of his suddenly fearful gaze. Standing together in the middle of the ward – which is crowded now with visitors at almost every bed – are the two mysterious men.

They have the slightly worried air of men who think they might be at the wrong party. They are looking uneasily around the ward, but more particularly in the general direction of Marlow's and Noddy's beds. Their heads lean in to talk to each other, in a low-voiced, vaguely conspiratorial fashion.

NICOLA: I don't know. Are they anybody? Why do they bother you?

Marlow, staring at them, goes to say something, and then says something else.

MARLOW: Paranoia.

NICOLA: What – ?

MARLOW: (*Smile*) I am totally paranoid.

It is an unexpectedly sweet and defensive smile. She responds to it.

NICOLA: (*Smile*) You've got everything going for you, then. Haven't you?

They sort of laugh. Then his eyes flick away again to the two mysterious men, and he is worried. The two mysterious men have not moved from the middle of the ward. They are talking in low voices.

SECOND MYSTERIOUS MAN: (*Unhappy*) People are beginning to notice us. They are looking at us.

FIRST MYSTERIOUS MAN: Let 'em. They're all sick anyway, ent they?

But he looks less sure of himself, and less combative, than he sounds.

SECOND MYSTERIOUS MAN: You reckon that's him?

FIRST MYSTERIOUS MAN: The nurse said so.

SECOND MYSTERIOUS MAN: (*Worried*) We going to go up to him?

FIRST MYSTERIOUS MAN: What? When he's with *her*? Come on – you must be coco.

SECOND MYSTERIOUS MAN: Well, we can't stand here, can we?

FIRST MYSTERIOUS MAN: Why not? Why not? That's all we're
     ever given to do. That's all we're asked to do. Stand around
     like spare pricks.
SECOND MYSTERIOUS MAN: And we got to do something about
     it.
FIRST MYSTERIOUS MAN: Tell me what. You just tell
     me what.
Nurse Mills, coming into the ward, notices their awkwardness.
The way they are standing, not at any bed; their manner; the
oddly dated appearance of their clothes.
NURSE MILLS: Do you need any help – ?
They look at her like two men on the edge of fear.
SECOND MYSTERIOUS MAN: D–do we – ?
FIRST MYSTERIOUS MAN: Thank you, miss. No. We've seen all
     we wish to see. For the moment. (*To* SECOND
     MYSTERIOUS MAN) Let's go. We'd better – ah – *go*.
They turn on their heels, and walk away, too quickly, and
accelerating even more. Nurse Mills looks after them, puzzled.
Then she frowns, hesitates, and goes to the double doors to look
down the corridor. The two mysterious men are running at full
pelt down the long corridor, as though for their lives, almost
colliding with an approaching trolley. Nurse Mills turns from
the double doors, back into the ward, bewildered. She passes
down the ward, looking puzzled, towards Marlow and Noddy.
MARLOW: (*Calls*) Nurse.
NURSE MILLS: Yes, Mr Marlow?
MARLOW: Who were those two? Do you know?
NURSE MILLS: I've no idea – But they're very peculiar –
MARLOW: (*Intense*) In what way?
NURSE MILLS: They seemed – out of place, and – They ran
     away.
NICOLA: Ran – But why – ?
NURSE MILLS: I don't know. But you get some strange people
     lurking around the big hospitals nowadays. They're usually
     after the drugs. We have to be very careful.
She goes on her way, bringing Noddy a small beaker of
noxiously coloured liquid.
MARLOW: (*To* NICOLA) I knew there was something weird
     about those two – Did you notice the way they were

dressed? I'd like to know what the hell they were doing.
Why were they so interested in *me* –

NICOLA: But they weren't. Were they?

MARLOW: They were *staring* at me.

She looks at him. He realizes that he sounds odd, and makes a
tiny gesture of near-apology.

NICOLA: Well. Perhaps –

MARLOW: Don't humour me. Please. *Don't*.

NICOLA: No. All right.

A small silence. His troubled eyes swivel to look at the next bed.
Nurse Mills is having some difficulty in making Noddy drink
whatever it is he has to drink.

NURSE MILLS: *I'll* hold the beaker – No – *I'll* hold it – You just
drink it down – No! Don't! Don't spit it out. I shall only
have to bring you some more. No – *I'll* hold it. *I'll* hold the
– Come on, now. Be sensible – That's it. Just a drop more.
Come on. Only a little bit more –

Marlow's eyes turn back to Nicola.

MARLOW: (*Gloomily*) It's a thrill a minute in here. I can tell
you.

NICOLA: Can't we get you in somewhere else? Now you've got
some money coming in.

MARLOW: Money?

NICOLA: The option thing I was –

MARLOW: (*Cutting in*) Ah? The option?

She looks at him. Reassesses.

NICOLA: You were right of course. I knew more about it than I
– implied. I'm sorry.

MARLOW: Go on.

NICOLA: I thought I'd go and clean your flat. Well – you'd
been in hospital for such a long time. The plants were all
dead –

MARLOW: Good!

NICOLA: And there was mould on some of your – God, Philip.
The way you live.

MARLOW: You opened my letters. Right?

NICOLA: Most of them were from the *Reader's Digest* telling you
to open at once.

MARLOW: My prize numbers. Leave them alone. My *assets*.

NICOLA: And there – yes, there was this letter – I'm sorry –

MARLOW: About *The Singing Detective*.

NICOLA: Yes. From this film company. Production company.

MARLOW: Who are they?

NICOLA: New people, apparently. Featherwheel. I got my agent to check them out –

MARLOW: Who runs it?

NICOLA: A man called Finney.

MARLOW: Know him?

NICOLA: Never heard of him.

MARLOW: You don't sound so sure.

NICOLA: Of course I do! What do you mean?

MARLOW: In what context have you never heard of him?

NICOLA: A money context. My agent says he's one of those Angels. Theatre, *you* know. But obviously moving into films, or trying to. More fool him.

MARLOW: Where is this letter?

NICOLA: I've brought it with me.

MARLOW: And it checks out?

NICOLA: So it seems. For what it's worth.

MARLOW: I'll get some money? Straight away?

NICOLA: (*With some doubt*) So it *says*.

MARLOW: Who will do the screenplay?

NICOLA: (*Laugh*) Finney himself.

MARLOW: God! They all think they can write, don't they? Every little bleeder who can hold a ball-pen the right way up.

NICOLA: My advice is to take the money and run.

MARLOW: (*Gloomily*) Maybe you're right.

NICOLA: I *know* I am.

He looks at her, questioningly. She smiles.

MARLOW: I didn't expect to see you again.

NICOLA: I don't want to go away. No – I do, and I don't.

MARLOW: Fidelity is not exactly your strong suit, is it? (*Quickly*) I'm not trying to be nasty.

NICOLA: (*Smile*) I miss you. Sort of.

MARLOW: Wha–a–a–at?

NICOLA: No. I do. Much to my surprise. (*Leans in, sexily conspiratorial, with laughing eyes*) Can't we close the curtains?

MARLOW: What for?

NICOLA: Guess.

She shows him the tip of her tongue at her shiny lips, in what they both know to be a deliberate parody – and yet still remains provocative.

MARLOW: They wouldn't let us close the curtains.

NICOLA: Then get better! Quickly!

He keeps staring at her. He is mixture of contending hope and suspicion.

MARLOW: Are you – Nicola. What's going on?

NICOLA: What do you mean?

MARLOW: Why are you being so nice?

NICOLA: (*Laugh*) Change of policy.

MARLOW: Yes, but – why?

NICOLA: Now, don't start all that.

He considers the matter.

MARLOW: No. All right.

But his gaze is still clamped on her, in a bemused half-suspicious fashion. She suddenly bobs forward and kisses him, full on the lips.

Last seen running from the ward, the two mysterious men are still running, plunging heavily through the trees of the Forest. Out of breath, they have to stop, bending and gasping like beaten distance runners.

FIRST MYSTERIOUS MAN: (*Painful gasps*) We – we should not
    – We should not have run –

SECOND MYSTERIOUS MAN: (*Gasp*) Did we have a choice?

They look around, gloomily apprehensive, puzzled by the rank upon rank of trees.

FIRST MYSTERIOUS MAN: How have we – ? I mean, why *here*?
    What are we doing here? (*Pulling his gun*) What in God's
    name is this place?

They back up to each other, as they had in the dance hall. A jay suddenly screams from a near tree, scaring them.

SECOND MYSTERIOUS MAN: (*Nervous*) Perhaps we're – I
    mean, perhaps we –

But he stops, not knowing what to say.

FIRST MYSTERIOUS MAN: The question is – (*With difficulty*)
    The question *is* –

SECOND MYSTERIOUS MAN: Tell me.

FIRST MYSTERIOUS MAN: Are we going to be able to see the wood for the trees?

SECOND MYSTERIOUS MAN: (*Looks around.*) Here? I don't think so –

But the other suddenly clutches at him, urgently.

FIRST MYSTERIOUS MAN: Listen!

From way off, deep in the trees, unseen, Mr Marlow is heard, vainly calling for his son. Like a voice in a dream.

MR MARLOW: (*Cry*) Phil–ip! Where bist! Where be ya! Philip!

As the calls continue, the little sob in the first mysterious man's throat is one of despair.

FIRST MYSTERIOUS MAN: *Everybody* is looking for him! *Everywhere*. The bugger. Oh, the bugger.

At the hospital, Binney waits in the area by the lifts, in foot-jigging anxiety. Mr Marlow's calls can still be heard, as in a dream. A flood of departing visitors comes out of Marlow's ward, and Binney stands, anxiously, and then sees Nicola. His face relaxes as he sees her smile.

Back in the ward, Marlow, left alone, allows his hostility to break surface again in sour bubbles of bad 'writing' in which Nicola and Binney meet in the lobby.

BINNEY: You did it question mark.

NICOLA: I did it exclamation mark.

BINNEY: He signed question mark.

NICOLA: He signed exclamation mark.

BINNEY: Oh comma aren't you the clever one dash exclamation mark

He embraces her, searching out her mouth. They kiss, erotically. As they half break, she laughs.

NICOLA: Oh comma he's a morbid creature exclamation mark And he thinks I'm going back to him exclamation mark

They look at each other. They embrace, kiss, half break.

(*Laugh*) Oh, he's a morbid creature! And he thinks I'm going back to him!

Time passes, and the visitors have long gone. A trolley is being pushed into the ward, for the evening hot drink.

MR HALL: You see. They always turn *that* way first. Nine times out of ten. Is it fair? Do *you* think it's fair?

But Reginald has already resumed his reading. The trolley is at Marlow's bed.

STAFF NURSE WHITE: (*Briskly*) Gone deaf, have we?

Marlow focuses.

MARLOW: What? Oh. Sorry.

STAFF NURSE WHITE: Well. Which is it? Tea. Coffee. Ovaltine.

MARLOW: Coffee.

STAFF NURSE WHITE: Please.

MARLOW: Coffee. Please.

She gives him one of the few special spouted non-spill sort of beakers.

STAFF NURSE WHITE: You'll soon be able to manage an ordinary cup.

MARLOW: Will I?

STAFF NURSE WHITE: If you try a bit harder.

Her dislike is very evident. His eyes narrow.

MARLOW: Please.

STAFF NURSE WHITE: What?

MARLOW: Say 'please'.

But she just snorts and moves on to Noddy.

STAFF NURSE WHITE: Tea. Coffee. Ovaltine.

Nod–nod–nod. And a slack-mouthed half-gasp.

NODDY: Coffee.

STAFF NURSE WHITE: Please.

Nod–nod–nod. And a slacked-mouthed struggle.

NODDY: Ah – Ah – Ah –

STAFF NURSE WHITE: Oh, never mind.

She gives him a cup, moving on, gracelessly, as he continues to struggle to say something.

NODDY: Ah – Ah – Ah –

She has gone, with a squeak of the trolley, too late to receive the benediction of his suddenly successfully completed whole word.

– Ah – Ah – Arsehole!

Down the ward, Reginald suddenly emits a loud laugh as he reads. Mr Hall glares at him.

MR HALL: Amused, are we?

Reginald looks up.

REGINALD: 'S funny.

MR HALL: What is?

REGINALD: This bit.

And he returns to the page, reading avidly, but slowly, and moving his lips a little. Mr Hall glares at him, fiercely.

MR HALL: Thought it was supposed to be a thriller, that book of yours.

REGINALD: Yeh. It is.

MR HALL: Well, then.

REGINALD: That tart in the river.

MR HALL: Who?

REGINALD: In the book.

MR HALL: Yes? What about her?

REGINALD: It's not her at all!

And he laughs again, a not very pleasant sort of laugh.

MR HALL: Say no more. I've got the complete picture. It all makes sense.

The two policemen on the launch are slowly, gently, pulling in and up on to the launch the naked, drowned body of a young woman.

During which –

MARLOW: (*Voice over*) You think I fell for that? She thinks I fell, hook line and sinker. And look what'll happen! Look what I'll do. Rot her thieving, narrow, poisonous soul!

They get the body on to the launch, and cover it with a blanket. But, this time, as the blanket is about to cover her face – The dead girl is seen to be Nicola. Then the blanket goes over her face.

In his hospital bed, Marlow hisses out his breath, eyes hot with hatred. A moment. He composes himself. He smiles a secret smile. Then, out loud, but softly to himself –

'All shall be well, and all shall be well, and all manner of thing shall be well.'

Pause. His smile dies. He turns his head, to look at Noddy.

(*To* NODDY) You agree, don't you?

Blank-eyed, slack-mouthed, and his head nod–nod–nod–nodding, the old man can hardly be said to agree.

Even though a bouncy dance-band version of 'Ah! Sweet Mystery of Life' seeks to intrude.

6

Mr Marlow, grieving, with a black arm-band, waits in a dusky, wintry melancholy on the unroofed platform of the country railway station where a few months ago he had waved goodbye to his wife and son. A distant sheep baas.

Miles away a train huff-a-puffs along a single track through darkening, damp cold fields. The boy Philip sits stiff and pale by the window in what, oddly, appears to be the same carriage, full of the same soldiers, that had taken him (and Mrs Marlow) to London. But it is going the other way. It gradually becomes clear that this is a dream: a bad one.

As the adult Marlow's voice begins, find the empty seat opposite Philip: his mother is not with him.

MARLOW: (*Voice over*) I cannot now distinguish between the train that brought my mother and me to London and the one which took us back. Which took *me* back, I mean.

The soldiers are staring too fixedly at Philip, as though accusingly.

(*Voice over*) But I tell you – there was something odd about that journey – something not right – something I still dream about – dream about – dream –

Philip, during this, has been reacting uncomfortably to the implacable stares, whistling between his teeth, looking out of the window, fidgeting.

FIRST SOLDIER: Where is she? Eh? Where's your Mum, your lovely Mum?

PHILIP: In the ground.

FIRST SOLDIER: Oh, yes?

PHILIP: Yes.

FIRST SOLDIER: Covered in dirt?

SECOND SOLDIER: That was always on the cards.

FIRST SOLDIER: Covered in the old dirt. Her legs and all. Eh?

The soldiers laugh, nastily, as in a bad dream.

PHILIP: Yes. Covered over.

They stop laughing and stare accusingly at him.

FIRST SOLDIER: You done it. Didn't you? It's all your doing, Sonny Jim.

Rather than answer, Philip looks abruptly out of the window, and the train whistles – The whistle extends, unnaturally piercing, and the train is puffing and clattering out of sight. But the dream insists that there is a slow, creeping movement towards the scarecrow across the bumpy grass. The whistle gives way to an insistent, louder-than-natural, menacing caw–caw–caw of rooks.

Then a sudden chord of music as the scarecrow swivels and faces us, mouth opening into song, its face vaguely familiar. It 'sings' Al Jolson's version of 'After You've Gone' – a peculiarly threatening rendering in the manner of a knowing, ambiguously jocose leer.

The song clicks off, abruptly, on the stretching perspective of a dimly lit corridor. The one leading to Marlow's ward. As the music stops, there is the resonant, dream sound of heavy double doors opening and closing with a sudden flap–flap–flap.

Then, a figure in a nightmare, the scarecrow lurches into view, and resumes its menacing 'singing' as, arms stiffly outstretched, it tilts and teeters and clumps steadily and frighteningly towards the ward –

The lone, dream-like figure of Mrs Marlow stands on the Underground platform, staring down at the rails. The Jolson song continuing without interruption.

At the country station, Mr Marlow is waiting. The Jolson number continuing, binding together the bad dream.

Suddenly, Philip is running through the tunnels after being slapped by his mother, who, distressed, calls after him. She starts to run, too. But not so much like someone trying to catch up, as in a sudden, overwhelming panic: a snapping of all the nerves.

There is a sudden, slurred, half-jocose yet wholly menacing interjection on the original recording at this point from Al Jolson. This is delivered by the nightmare scarecrow, which has

208

reached Marlow's bed in the night-dark ward. It thrusts its
distorted and snarling face close in at a fear-struck Marlow.
Marlow swallows down a gasp of terror and stares back at the
scarecrow, eyeball to eyeball. There is no music.

MARLOW: (*Gasp*) No –

Very slowly – it seems – the scarecrow fades into the general,
obscure shapes of the darkened ward, among the snores and
grunts and sighs. Marlow knows now that he has awakened from
a bad dream. It takes him a moment to recover. Then, shaken,
he reaches for his cigarettes. His lighter click–click–clicks and
then suddenly flares.

> (*Voice over*) But I tell you, there was something odd about
> that journey – something not right – something I still dream
> about. I saw the scarecrow –

It is in Gibbon's room, the next day.

GIBBON: (*Too sharp*) Scarecrow?

MARLOW: (*Stares*) Scarecrow.

GIBBON: Sorry. Go on.

Marlow weighs up whether he is giving anything away, in view
of Gibbon's pounce on the word, then decides to continue. In
this full light he looks considerably better.

MARLOW: A scarecrow in a field by the railway. I – (*Suddenly*) I
    dreamt about that – thing last night. It had got out of the
    field.

GIBBON: Yes?

MARLOW: Even at the time – from the train, I mean – going to
    London and coming back again – looking out of the train
    window I had the very strong feeling that it was – alive.
    And – watching.

He stops. Gibbon waits. Then –

GIBBON: Watching?

MARLOW: Me. Watching me.

Marlow glares challengingly, like one expecting the word
'paranoia' to be lobbed at him.

GIBBON: So it has eyes.

MARLOW: What?

GIBBON: *Whose* eyes? Whose face?

MARLOW: Look, it's a scarecrow, not a –

GIBBON: (*Cutting in*) But if it is *watching* you – Mmm? Why? What for? What does it think you've done?

MARLOW: Look, this is a dream. Right?

GIBBON: Right.

They look at each other, almost as though squaring up for a fight.

MARLOW: I know the face. I know I know it. But I can't quite –

GIBBON: (*Cutting in*) Is it your mother?

MARLOW: (*Sharply*) What?

GIBBON: Your mother. Is it her face?

MARLOW: (*Savagely*) No!

GIBBON: (*Quietly*) How did she die?

MARLOW: She killed herself.

GIBBON: How?

MARLOW: (*Mumble*) River. In the river.

Pause. Gibbon frowns.

GIBBON: Are you – Is that really so?

MARLOW: (*Hostile*) What do you mean?

GIBBON: You have a young woman fished out of the river in your detective story.

MARLOW: So? (*Angrily*) So?

GIBBON: Well, I'm just a little surprised that – Well. I ask myself, is it very likely that you would so exactly duplicate such a traumatic event in your life in the pages of a –

MARLOW: The face! I know who it is!

The interruption is so powerful that Gibbon is momentarily thrown. He stares at Marlow, suspecting that it is deliberate, but not even sure what Marlow is talking about.

GIBBON: I'm sorry?

MARLOW: The scarecrow! It just came to me – all of a sudden –

GIBBON: Yes?

MARLOW: She used to frighten me. The bitch.

GIBBON: Your mother – ?

MARLOW: No! The teacher. The old woman in the village school. Pointing that finger. God rot her nasty old bones!

Marlow seems unduly excitable, and Gibbon, for a moment, cannot fathom him.

GIBBON: Aren't you being a little –

MARLOW: (*Interrupting*) You don't know writers. You just don't know. They'll use anything and anybody. They'll eat their own young.

GIBBON: So do rabbits when they are disturbed.

MARLOW: (*Quietly*) I didn't kill my Mum. It wasn't my doing.

Pause.

GIBBON: I can't imagine that anyone could ever have suggested it was.

Marlow's eyes flick away. He will not respond directly. Instead, with a sort of scorn, a sort of laugh –

MARLOW: Writers.

GIBBON: What about them?

MARLOW: Cannibals.

GIBBON: You think so?

Marlow glares at him. Then his expression, tone, changes.

MARLOW: Once. I did something bad – I mean, nasty – *really* disgusting – at school. At the primary school. And –

He stops. Gibbon waits. This time Marlow restarts himself.

I was nearly caught. I was in for it – and bad. But – I blamed somebody else. I pointed the finger elsewhere.

GIBBON: Long ago and far away.

MARLOW: I've never doubted since what people are really made of. We all have blood on our teeth.

In the village school – 'Long ago and far away' – a hand wavers up from the middle of the class. A girl with a blue ribbon in her hair, Barbara.

OLD WOMAN: Yes. Barbara.

BARBARA: Him was a-lurking by the big tree, miss –

OLD WOMAN: *He.* How many times!

BARBARA: He was, miss!

Mark, standing in front of the class, is blinking with incredulity.

MARK: But miss –

OLD WOMAN: (*Savagely*) Be quiet!

He swallows down his protest, with difficulty. Philip is watching and listening with a guilty intensity.

But did you *see* him go back into the school?

BARBARA: Yes, miss. And miss – Miss!

OLD WOMAN: Go on.

BARBARA: Him told – He told I –

OLD WOMAN: *Me.* How many times!

BARBARA: He *told* me, miss!

OLD WOMAN: Told you? Told you what?

BARBARA: That he – That he – Hooo!

OLD WOMAN: Barbara!

Barbara's face hardens out of its momentary spasm of doubt, and, with a jig of her body, a toss of her blue-ribboned hair, she kills –

BARBARA: Him said him was going to do his nasty on thy table, miss!

A sort of long sigh of awe, fear and pleasure rises up unquelled from the class.

MARK: (*Sob*) Oh, no – ! Chunt tru–u–ue – ! Oh, miss – !

He rubs his knuckles into his eyes in an attempt to stop the tears. Two or three more hands go up, urgently, excitedly.

CHILDREN: (*Variously*) Miss! Miss! And me – ! Him told I! Miss! I saw'n Miss! Me, and me, Miss!

Back in the present, Gibbon, for once, sits absolutely still as he listens to Marlow, who is, for once, talking in a quiet, matter-of-fact way.

MARLOW: I sat in my desk, perjurer, charlatan, and watched and listened and watched and listened as one after another they nailed that backward lad hands and feet to my story. I have not seriously doubted since that afternoon that any lie will receive almost instant corroboration and almost instant collaboration if the maintenance of it results in the public enjoyment of someone else's pain, someone else's humiliation.

A sudden change of voice, sudden intake of breath.

Oh, she beat him. Oh, she beat that poor boy, the vicious old bitch!

He regains calmness.

Interestingly – what is interesting – the boy was *himself* overwhelmed by the weight of the evidence. He was a backward child, though we didn't think in those terms at the time – among ourselves, I mean – I used to come across him sometimes in the woods. He'd be running. He was almost always running – 'What bist thou doing, Mark?' I'd

say. 'Trainin'' he'd answer. Just that. Training for what?
And – And this poor little sod came in the end to believe
that he *had* done it – 'Yes, miss.' Yes, miss!

He stops, working his face a bit.

GIBBON: (*Quietly*) That he had done what?

Marlow looks at him, haunted.

MARLOW: Shat on the teacher's table.

A little pause.

GIBBON: It has occurred to you, of course, that you were
yourself in extreme distress at the time?

Marlow ignores the point.

MARLOW: A few years ago I told something like the whole story to
a man who used to live in the same village – We were laughing
about it. Ho ho ho. 'I wonder', I said, 'I wonder what ever
became of Mark Binney?' That was my victim, Mark Binney.
'Don't you know?' and he was looking at me with an odd sort
of glint – nasty – you know, the way *you* do –

Gibbon acknowledges the side-hander with a nod and a smile.

Mark is in the loony bin, he said. Been there for years. A
complete nutter.

They seem to stare at each other.

GIBBON: Well –

MARLOW: (*Little boy voice*) 'Yes, miss.' (*Old woman voice,
nastily*) 'And you did, didn't you?' 'Yes, miss.' 'You came
back and you did this dirty thing – !' 'Yes, miss.' 'And you
are a filthy, wicked, horrible little – '

Marlow's brilliant but savage imitation suddenly ends in a choke
of distress. He starts to cry. Gibbon simply sits there and looks
at him. Marlow lifts his bent hands to his face, but is only able
to press the back of them to his eyes, weeping now openly,
brokenly. And Gibbon lets him cry. In a series of struggling, but
diminishing chokes in his throat, and a pathetic attempt to grin
or even to laugh in the middle of them, a now wet-faced Marlow
regains a form of self-control.

S–sorry.

GIBBON: Don't be. (*Then, unexpectedly sharply*) Stand up!

MARLOW: (*Gape*) What?

GIBBON: You can. You can do it.

Marlow stares at him, frightened. He has to moisten his lips before he can speak.

MARLOW: You think so – ?

GIBBON: Now or never!

Marlow stares. Swallows. Nods.

MARLOW: Yes.

He puts his buckled hands on the arms of the wheelchair and starts to strain –

GIBBON: Wait!

Gibbon rushes to the chair.

MARLOW: (*Gasp*) Now or never –

GIBBON: I just want to make sure the wheels are locked. Can't have you skeetering all over the floor. It would be rather untidy.

MARLOW: Yes. They are.

Gibbon folds his arms, looking down on him, and standing close.

GIBBON: Very well. Go ahead.

Marlow half grins at him, nervous.

MARLOW: Into each life some rain must fall.

GIBBON: Metaphysics.

MARLOW: Mu–sic.

And again he takes the strain, his face contorting as though taking part in a tug o' war. He manages to get almost half-way up, and holds the position, perilously. Then with a little yelp of pain, he thumps back too heavily into the wheelchair.

(*Quietly*) Ow. Ow. Ow. *Ow.*

Then he looks up, and a shift of sardonic humour in his mind shows in his eyes. A shift that throws up one of his precious tunes – the 1945 Inkspots/Ella Fitzgerald version of 'Into Each Life Some Rain Must Fall'. Marlow seems to cock his head to listen, then nod, twisting his mouth in a kind of smile, and conjuring up the conceit of Gibbon singing the opening verses.

During which, Marlow resumes the struggle to rise, his veins standing out, and sweat beginning to glisten. Then, yet more effort, up–up – and he is virtually standing, a triumph emphasized by taking over the song into his own mouth. At the piano-filled small pause in the vocal, they laugh at and with each other, in a shared victory.

Brought back into the ward by the porter, Marlow is almost comically, and certainly surprisingly for the recipients (who blink back, blankly), nodding and beaming to the left and to the right of him at each and everyone he can see. As Marlow reaches the bed, the porter clicks into life and automatically goes to help him out of the wheelchair. Marlow flaps a hand at him, and slowly, but with much less of a struggle than in Gibbon's room, again stands up.

PORTER: Ooo.

MARLOW: (*Proudly*) What you think?

PORTER: I think you been off the love apples, man.

Marlow laughs, but he cannot maintain his position, and falls across his bed.

Hey – come on – no hang-gliding –

MARLOW: Leave me. Leave me. I can do it! I can do it myself!

(*A long, whooping shout, still awkwardly sprawled*)

Whee–eee–oooooooh!

PORTER: (*Deadpan*) Geronimo.

And wheels the chair away. Marlow manages to pull himself more fully on to the bed, and, with a massive grunt, turn himself over so that he is lying on his back on top of the bed. He is glistening with sweat, and panting like someone at the end of a sprint. But he is laughing, quietly, to himself. Suddenly, though, he stops laughing. His eyes glint dangerously, narrowing in thought.

GIBBON: (*Voice over*) How did she die?

MARLOW: (*Voice over*) She killed herself.

GIBBON: (*Voice over*) How?

And Marlow speaks it out loud, to himself.

MARLOW: River. In the river.

Marlow creeps night-stealthy up the stairs of the house by the river, in his hospital garb. He hisses hatred at the 'Nicola portrait' on the wall.

GIBBON: (*Voice over*) You have a young woman fished out of the river in your detective story?

MARLOW: (*Hiss*) I do. I do. Yes. I do.

Beyond the stairs, Binney and Nicola, a little drunk, are dancing to 'Putting on the Ritz', from a compact disc player. She is only partly clothed, and in high heels. He is in some way rumpled, and not fully dressed. As they dance, in a desultory, sleepy fashion, they nibble at each other. The telephone rings. The mood, behaviour, changes instantly. They jerk apart.

BINNEY: This'll be it! Quick – Put the music off. This is it!

She scurries to the CD machine, and silences it. He picks up the telephone, tensing.

Featherwheel. Who's calling?

Now at the top of the stairs, Marlow, pressed flat against the wall, edges closer to the door of the living room, where he can better hear what he can discern –

(*Overheard, on phone*) Oh, I'm so – obviously, I am delighted – Yes. Yes. Thank you – Oh, no, that's no problem – Yes. I take the point –

Within the room, Nicola has the urgent air of someone who wants something in particular to be said, and is not hearing it said, as she looks at Binney on the phone.

(*On phone*) No. I can come out to Los Angeles at one day's notice, truly – Yes, very exciting indeed – Ah. Mmmm. You mean the scene in the dance hall – the bar and the balcony – Yes. I see. Yes, I think you have a point. Too enigmatic. Exactly. Too, too. Yes.

He looks at Nicola as he talks. She flashes urgent eyes, and points at herself, and slightly mouths a demanding 'Me! Me! What about Me!' He slightly turns away as he talks and listens, not pointedly, but enough to make her suddenly stiffen and frown.

(*On phone*) I can put that right, and patch and mend exactly where you – (*Listens.*) Oh, yes. I have all the chain of title documents. And now that I know you want to deal, I will Skypak them out to you first thing. Yes, my title to the option on the book, and to my screenplay, of course –

Nicola has moved around, beginning to glower now, so that she is in Binney's direct line again. She jabs a minatory finger inward at herself – Me! Me! Me!

(*On phone*) The other thing – The casting – You know who I – (*Listens.*) Yes? Yes?

Nicola's stance, expression, is tense with hopeful expectation.

(*On phone*) Well, you know who I – It should be Nicola Marlow, because she's – that's my understanding – (*A* sudden change.) *Who?* Oh – well now! – She's fabulous – fantastic – I mean, if we could get *her* – My God, that's wonderful –

He much more pointedly turns away from Nicola as he talks. Hopeful tension drains from her. Her face goes dead. Outside the room, Marlow is now right at the door, pressing close to listen, with a nasty delight.

(*Overheard, on phone*) Well, you have more experience of these things than I do, that's for sure. And after all it's basically *your* money, control-wise –

MARLOW: (*Soft*) You cheap little bastard.

Inside, Nicola is without hope. She does not know her next comment has already been delivered for her.

BINNEY: (*On phone*) – Fine. Fine! I'll see you very soon, then! And thank you. Thank you! Goodbye.

He puts the phone down, his back still to Nicola.

NICOLA: (*Flat*) You cheap little bastard.

BINNEY: Nicola. Listen. I have no power here. Listen –

NICOLA: No! You listen! *I* brought Philip's script to you. I conned him into signing away the rights for a tenth of what you're selling it for –

BINNEY: Oh, honey. You don't think I'm trying to cheat on you? I'll pay you what we agreed. You'll get your share –

NICOLA: It's not the money! It's not for the money. (*Almost a sob of despair*) It is *my* part. I play it. Me! We agreed. Mark, we agreed.

BINNEY: But you know damned well we can't get *control* over casting –

NICOLA: (*Yell*) No, I don't know!

BINNEY: 'Advice and consultation.' That's what we got. That's all anybody gets. You think I'm Spielberg? Advice and consultation.

NICOLA: (*Scream*) That wasn't our deal! It's *my* part. I play it. We agreed! It's my biggest chance!

He looks at her too evenly.

BINNEY: Aren't you a teeny bit too old now, Nicola?

Listening at the door, Marlow sucks in his breath in a mixture of malicious enjoyment of the question, and shock at the brutality of it.

But he is in reality lying on his back on top of his bed in the ward, brooding his way through the constructed Nicola–Binney scene.

MARLOW: (*Toneless*) Ding dong dell
     Pussy's in the well.

In the invented room, the invented Nicola takes the blow of Binney's last remark. Although overwrought and half drunk, she nevertheless begins with a simulated incredulity and an apparent (though bitter) calm.

NICOLA: Oh, perhaps. A teeny bit, yes. A teensy weensy millimetre or so nearer the garbage heap. Oh, yes. There are a few dinky lines here and there. See? On this dried-out parchment rather badly stretched over my crumbling bones. See? And my eyes, look. Bleared and bloodshot. My mouth – see? – look at the way it drools – !

BINNEY: Nicola – stop it – now, stop –

NICOLA: (*Not stopping*) The sag of it. The creak of it. The (*scream*) *used-up*ness of it –

Sensing danger, Binney half retreats, hands up in would-be rueful surrender.

BINNEY: OK! OK! OK! Enough! I'm sorry!

NICOLA: First you oh-so-casually throw away my one great chance –

BINNEY: (*Ineffectively*) No, no –

NICOLA: – and then you dig into my sense of my – of my – (*Anguished half-sob, half-scream, on the edge of hysteria*) You're a killer! My God, you're a killer! You smash up people's lives –

In the ward, the sickly inventing Marlow has the signs of a man who shows that he is suddenly not making *all* of it up. Nicola's words have been said somewhere, sometime, before – and they have been said to him.

(*Voice over*) – you're rotten with your own bile! You think you're smart but really you're very very sad, because you use your illness as a weapon against other people and as an excuse for not being properly human – ach! You disgust me! You sick little creep – You poisonous, malformed, cynical oaf! You –

Nurse Mills has arrived with a fresh tub of ointment, and sees his dark brooding.

NURSE MILLS: (*Ironic*) Having a good time are we?

MARLOW: Of course I am.

NURSE MILLS: You're not *in* the bed. How come?

The realization of what he has so recently achieved floods over him, transforming him.

MARLOW: (*Proudly*) I'm not *in* the bed because I stood up on my own two feet!

NURSE MILLS: You *did*?

MARLOW: I did.

NURSE MILLS: Oh, well done!

MARLOW: You watch me now! You see what happens! I'll be walking as far as those doors down there by the end of next week.

NURSE MILLS: But don't overdo it – Not all at once. That's how people get disappointed – But isn't that nice?

MARLOW: Nice? Nice is not the word! You should behave more like one of the disciples when they saw Our Lord walking on the water.

She laughs, and begins to close his curtains.

NURSE MILLS: Well – if you can stand up while I grease you, I might!

Marlow, crab-like gets himself into a sitting position on the bed, his feet on the floor. She watches, impressed.

MARLOW: (*Less exuberant*) I *think* I can stand up again, but I don't know for how long. My knees might –

NURSE MILLS: (*Interrupting*) Oh, I don't really expect you to. I'm just glad to see how much you're improving. It's marvellous.

He looks at her, a little surprised by the warmth of her voice.

MARLOW: You know – I think you are by far the nicest person I've met in a long time –

NURSE MILLS: (*Laugh*) Ah. But you haven't been anywhere in a long time.

MARLOW: As well as the most beautiful.

Her laugh dies. She looks at him. She is not smiling.

Your eyes.

NURSE MILLS: What about them?

MARLOW: Your mouth.

NURSE MILLS: Listen –

MARLOW: The way your head joins your neck. As though, as though – As though it is hesitating. No, as though –

NURSE MILLS: (*Interrupting*) I've brought you a fresh tub of – Stop it, please. Don't be silly.

He examines her, with what is only a half-bantering smile.

MARLOW: In fact, now that I look at you properly, I can see what you are.

NURSE MILLS: Oh. Can you indeed.

MARLOW: You are the girl in all those songs. Dee dum.

NURSE MILLS: What songs?

He suddenly turns his eyes away, and his voice shifts its tone.

MARLOW: The songs. The songs. The bloody, bloody songs.

She is not sure she likes this change.

NURSE MILLS: I wish I knew what you were talking about –

He turns his eyes back on her.

MARLOW: The songs you hear coming up the stair.

NURSE MILLS: Sorry?

MARLOW: When you're a child. When you are supposed to be asleep. Those songs.

Nod–nod–nodding Noddy, a mere foot or so away from one side of Marlow's closed curtains, still seems to be trying to communicate.

NODDY: S–su–Sssu–su –

He almost gives up, but then makes one more effort, which comes out almost as a shout –

S–ss–*Songs* – !

But there is no one to take any notice.

A record turns on the turntable of the wind-up gramophone in the front room of the small London terraced house, the needle biting and hissing along the deeply etched groove. The record is of the Ray Noble band playing the long, sweet introduction to 'The Very Thought of You', which eventually has a vocal by Al Bowlly.

The London Grandad sits alone in what had previously been seen only as a small, overcrowded room. He has a crate of stout on the floor beside him, upon which he rests his feet, and he seems to be listening with an unalloyed pleasure to the gramophone, glass in hand, drinking long draughts, and wiping his heavy moustache with the back of his hand.

The song, diminished only a little because of the narrow spaces and flimsy walls, flows up the tight, dingily lit, drab little stair. Where Philip lies under covers on a two-seater settee jammed close between a single bed and the wall, wide-awake, staring up at the ceiling, listening – expressionless. 'The Very Thought of You' drenches the air.

Downstairs, Grandad is pouring another bottle of stout. On the gramophone, Al Bowlly is singing. And, in a wider perspective than before, it can now be seen that the room contains a coffin. Then the door opens. Philip stands there in a shirt, only. It takes a moment for Grandad to register his presence, with a sudden, startled chink of beer bottle against his glass.

GRANDAD: Christ. You made me jump! Don't do that, boy –

Philip simply stands there, looking at him.

The scarecrow stands still and silent in the field. A song dies. The train passes, and Philip turns back from the window, where he has just looked out on the field, and his eyes suddenly glitter with an uprush of tears.

Mr Marlow is waiting in front of the milk churns on the small, unroofed platform, like a stone carving. But then he leans forward, intense. Puffs of smoke and chuff-a-huff sounds in the near-distance, and then the little train comes labouring into view, through the dusk. Philip is standing now at the carriage window, which is held open by its leather strap, leaning out as the train slows still more for its approach. Neither father nor son wave or smile as they see each other. The train expires in shush and hiss, and, before it properly stops, Philip has the door open. Father and son meet. Philip has a carrier bag, which Mr Marlow takes.

MR MARLOW: Hello, Philip.

PHILIP: Hello, Dad.

It is almost as though there is no feeling, as though nothing has happened. They look at each other. Then, without ceremony, they walk along the platform. As they do, Mr Marlow reaches out to hold the boy's hand. Philip fractionally hesitates, then clasps it. Mr Marlow and Philip trudge along a path through the wintry woods, in silence. Mr Marlow looks sidelong at his son from time to time, then –

MR MARLOW: Ant got enough for the bus, o'butty. Sorry. Pay
    day tomarra.
PHILIP: Don't mind walking.
MR MARLOW: 'Bout another five mile, I reckon.
PHILIP: Seven.
MR MARLOW: Aye. Seven.
Silence. They keep trudging. Then –
    (*Suddenly*) Did you *see* her?
PHILIP: Yes.
MR MARLOW: A'ter I meant. A'ter the – accident.
PHILIP: (*Quickly*) Yes.
They walk. Mr Marlow's distress is beginning to reach his voice,
though he tries to suppress it.
MR MARLOW: Lovely, was her?
PHILIP: Yes.
MR MARLOW: Peaceful, like?
PHILIP: Yes.
They walk on, and the trees stand closer as the path narrows,
and the light fades. Mr Marlow and Philip eventually come out
of the now dark trees in order to cross a sloping field. They walk
in silence for a while, as before.
MR MARLOW: Tired? Bist?
PHILIP: No.
MR MARLOW: (*Suddenly*) I love you, Philip. I love you, o'but.
    With all my heart.
PHILIP: Shhh!
MR MARLOW: What – ?
PHILIP: Somebody might hear us!
MR MARLOW: (*Puzzled*) What?
PHILIP: Some bugger might be listening, Dad. Kip tha' quiet!
Mr Marlow is as much worried as puzzled by the oddity of these
remarks.
MR MARLOW: Now, now – Philip – wos mean, my lad? There
    yunt nobody around, and even if there was –
PHILIP: (*Softly urgent*) Highsht!
He points sideways into the thickening gloom, using a local
word for 'listen with urgency'. About twenty or so yards away,
the scarecrow stands.
MR MARLOW: 'S only an old scarecrow, Philip. Him cont hurt tha'!

But the boy shakes his head, dumbly, unable to put something
dark and mysterious into words. They pass on, two figures
swallowed up in the ever encroaching darkness. The scarecrow
seems to watch the receding figures. It is the same one that
could be seen from the train. Their walk back from the station
to the village has clearly retraced part of the route taken by the
train. The scarecrow, in its battered old trilby, and long Army
greatcoat, its arm stiffly extended, looks near-human in a
menacing sort of way. Especially now, in the darkness. As we
come right up to it in the wintry gloom, Nicola's chanting,
crazed, little-girl-like voice can be heard.

NICOLA: (*Voice over*) Ding Dong Dell
    Pussy's in the well –

The nude portrait on the stairway wall at Binney's house is
splashed with vivid streaks of blood. Nicola's voice sounds.
    Who pushed him in?
    Who pushed him in?
There is an approaching ooh–ah of police car sirens. Distraught,
mad-eyed Nicola sits on the stairs rocking to and fro as she hugs
herself. She has blood on her hands and splashes of it on the rest
of her still only partly clothed body.
    (*Sing-song*) Ding Dong Dell
    Pussy's in the well.
    Who'll pull him out?
    Who'll pull him out?
She does not respond to the sudden, urgent knocking from the
front door, below. Beyond her, the living room is a bloody mess,
with scattered papers, overturned chair, broken
glasses.
    And Binney lies face up on the floor, clutching the phone, a
kitchen knife protruding from his throat. Knock–knock–knock
continuing, from down below. Amongst the scattered papers can
be seen the title page of the purloined screenplay, *The Singing
Detective*, randomly decorated with splashes of blood.
Knock–knock–knock.

Reginald, in the hospital ward, is reading as avidly as ever, still
moving his lips a little, silently, as he slowly drags his now

popping eyes along the line. He suddenly whistles long and low between his teeth, as though coming across something particularly shocking. Perpetually bored or isolated, Mr Hall bristles and glares at his neighbour, and shifts a little in his bed to get more comfortable.

MR HALL: You'll hurt yourself.

Reginald makes no response. But, a fraction later, he whistles softly again, and turns the page.

    (*Gratingly*) I say! You'll bloody hurt yourself.

REGINALD: What?

MR HALL: (*Snort*) Who invented the steam engine?

Reginald finally looks up.

REGINALD: Pass.

MR HALL: What?

REGINALD: Of course it was.

Mr Hall blinks, momentarily out-manoeuvred.

MR HALL: I *said* –

REGINALD: I know what you said.

MR HALL: I said you'll hurt yourself.

REGINALD: I heard.

MR HALL: All this activity.

REGINALD: What activity?

MR HALL: Whistling!

REGINALD: Yeh.

And he returns to the page.

MR HALL: Talk! Why don't you? Just a word. The odd nod now and again. You'll be discharged in a day or two –

REGINALD: Tomorrow.

MR HALL: Who said so?

REGINALD: Tomorrow. I'm going tomorrow.

MR HALL: (*Disappointed*) That's definite, is it?

REGINALD: Definite.

MR HALL: But who shall I talk to?

REGINALD: You can have this –

Holds up the paperback.

MR HALL: I prefer *human* intercourse, my boy.

REGINALD: You dirty old devil.

MR HALL: Reginald.

REGINALD: If you let me get on with it, I might finish, mightn't

I? Then you can have it.

MR HALL: 'I wandered lonely as a cloud – '

REGINALD: If you stop nattering.

MR HALL: Poetry. That's more my taste. I don't want corpses all over the place. Not in here. Not in *this* place, thanks very much.

Reginald looks around the ward with a sort of morbid satisfaction.

REGINALD: Wonder who'll go next.

MR HALL: (*Scared*) Out – do you mean?

REGINALD: Dead – I mean.

MR HALL: Don't. Oh, don't.

REGINALD: Old Noddy up the top end. Reckon he'll go next. Eh?

MR HALL: So long as it's not –

He doesn't finish.

REGINALD: That'll be three in a row in that bed.

MR HALL: (*Agitated*) Read your book. Go on. Get back to that book of yours.

REGINALD: (*With relish*) Yeh. He'll be the next. I can see it coming.

Down the ward, the poor old man nod–nod–nod–nods, mouth askew, eyes vacantly glazed. And yet, studying him, going behind his empty eyes, there are thoughts waiting to be released.

NODDY: (*Thinks*) I know what's going on. I know what they all think. I know. I know. Let me say it out loud. Let me *please* say it out loud, dear God. The story in – oh, *you* know . . . now, let me think – let me cast my mind back – *yes!* – oh, I've still got it! – The story in Judges chapter sixteen verses twenty-six to thirty. How about that for a memory?

Marlow, in the next bed, is at last trying to write with a pen again. He has it held in his hand by a kind of splint made by the hospital, like a pen-holder attached to his hand. A physiotherapist – a woman in a white coat – sits on the bed beside him, watching.

MARLOW: It's not very legible, and it hurts, but – I tell you one thing. For the first time in my life I shall have to really think about the *value* of each and every little word. That's dangerous, that is.

225

PHYSIOTHERAPIST: (*Smile*) Well, that rules out the
newspapers, then, doesn't it?

MARLOW: Except the *Sun*, and the *Star*. They don't have *words*
at all, do they? Perhaps I could work for Mr Murdoch.

PHYSIOTHERAPIST: Let me see.

Marlow lifts his club-like hand from the paper, which is on a
clipboard.

MARLOW: Can you read it?

She frowns at the clipboard.

PHYSIOTHERAPIST: (*Reads*) 'Upwards strokes and down – '
What's this? Ah. Yes. ' – and downward slopes and a
comma curls, making me hold – ' Yes. I can read it.
Making you hold what?

MARLOW: My breath.

She suspects some kind of obscure joke, and half laughs. But he
does not collude, and stares at her.

Words. Words make me hold my breath.

PHYSIOTHERAPIST: I see.

MARLOW: Who knows what you are going to say? Who knows
where they've been?

PHYSIOTHERAPIST: Well. Keep at it. You're doing very
well.

He can see that she has no idea what he is talking about.

MARLOW: Suppose they get together, and ganged up on us
when we weren't looking?

PHYSIOTHERAPIST: Who?

MARLOW: Words. The little devils. *Words*.

She looks at him, then looks at her watch.

PHYSIOTHERAPIST: Well – I'll pop in and see you some time
tomorrow afternoon –

MARLOW: Who made you say that?

PHYSIOTHERAPIST: What do you mean?

He stares at her, goes to say something, and changes it as he
speaks, with a slightly puzzled air.

MARLOW: If I wrote that down – 'Well dash I'll pop in and see
you sometime tomorrow afternoon', if I did, and I – No. It
doesn't matter. Doesn't matter.

She frowns a little, looking at him, then standing, giving him
back the clipboard.

PHYSIOTHERAPIST: Keep practising, that's the thing.
She gives him a nod, and walks away. He watches her go, with
the same puzzled air.
MARLOW: Yes. That's the thing. (*Thinks*) Keep practising
  comma that's the thing full stop
He begins to brood –
  (*Thinks*) When she gets out, supposing she were to walk off
  the page? Suppose – Supposing she disappears back into the
  alphabet? A collection of letters that has other uses –
  Suppose *I* am – a–a collection of . . .
But he visibly pulls himself back from a disturbing thought.
Noddy, in the next bed, is still quietly nod–nod–nodding, with
the hint of a drool from his twisted, slack mouth. Then –
NODDY: (*Thinks*) And Samson took hold of the two middle
  pillars upon which the house stood, and on which it was
  borne up – And Samson said, Let me die with the
  Philistines. And he bowed himself with all his might, and
  the house fell upon . . .
He makes a strange, wet-mouthed cackle. And noddingly looks
at Marlow. Marlow is resuming his efforts with his splinted
hand, very slowly, to write on the clipboarded page. As he lifts
his hand, the new word he has written is in a scrawl of capital
letters. BLOOD, it says.

Binney is lying in his own blood in the 1945 living room, in the
same position, with the same knife deep in his throat, clutching
the receiver of a 1945 telephone. But Marlow (in his Singing
Detective persona) is sitting in the same easy chair as he had
done before, with the whisky on the small table beside him. He
is sitting contemplating the dreadful scene. He sighs, then
strikes a match, blows out smoke.
MARLOW: (*Softly*) Well. I presume you made your call, Mr
  Binney. I *hope* you did. If it was long distance, don't worry
  about the bill.
He pulls the little string-pull which clicks off the light. The
room is turned into looming shapes and silhouettes. Marlow
sighs, just discernible. A chink of the glass, a gurgle of a
swallow, a suck in-and-out of cigarette smoke. Then –
  (*Softly*) So now we wait. We wait and we see.

Then the ceiling slides with light, as the headlights of a car flicker through the window, and switch off. Somewhere below, a car door slams. The silhouette of Marlow crosses the room. A cupboard door opens and closes. The sound of two pairs of footsteps coming up the stair. A moment, then the door into the room slowly creaks open. A residual light of some kind behind them shows the shapes of two men. It is the two mysterious men.

FIRST MYSTERIOUS MAN: (*Hoarse whisper*) Mr Binney? You here, sir? At home, are you?

Silence.

SECOND MYSTERIOUS MAN: (*Whisper*) Put on the light, why don't we?

Silence.

FIRST MYSTERIOUS MAN: (*Whisper*) Blood.

SECOND MYSTERIOUS MAN: What?

So startled, that he says it too loud.

FIRST MYSTERIOUS MAN: Shhhh!

SECOND MYSTERIOUS MAN: (*Gulp*) S–sorry –

They come more into the room. But, in doing so, the first mysterious man bumps his shin against a piece of sharp-edged furniture.

FIRST MYSTERIOUS MAN: (*Cry*) Ooof!

SECOND MYSTERIOUS MAN: Shhhh!

FIRST MYSTERIOUS MAN: Shhh your bloody self!

SECOND MYSTERIOUS MAN: All right, all right.

FIRST MYSTERIOUS MAN: Where's the switch?

SECOND MYSTERIOUS MAN: Well – it's usually on the wall, ain't it?

FIRST MYSTERIOUS MAN: Clever Dick.

SECOND MYSTERIOUS MAN: *You* find it then.

FIRST MYSTERIOUS MAN: God, the people I have to work with!

He gropes, finds a switch, illuminates the room.

SECOND MYSTERIOUS MAN: (*Offended*) I don't know why you say –

He stops, following the gasp and the stare of his companion. They look at the grisly sight. Then –

FIRST MYSTERIOUS MAN: Oh. The poor bugger.

SECOND MYSTERIOUS MAN: I thought his voice sounded funny –

FIRST MYSTERIOUS MAN: (*Sharply*) What?

SECOND MYSTERIOUS MAN: (*Defensively*) On the phone. When he rang. I mean – well –

FIRST MYSTERIOUS MAN: Of course his bloody voice sounded funny! Christ Almighty, what would *you* sound like with a knife stuck in your throat!

SECOND MYSTERIOUS MAN: All right. All right.

FIRST MYSTERIOUS MAN: What are all these papers?

SECOND MYSTERIOUS MAN: Perhaps it's –

FIRST MYSTERIOUS MAN: Yeh.

Silence. They contemplate the body.

We'd better not touch him.

SECOND MYSTERIOUS MAN: No.

They contemplate each other. The first mysterious man makes a helpless little gesture.

FIRST MYSTERIOUS MAN: I don't know what to do. I don't have the faintest idea.

SECOND MYSTERIOUS MAN: No. It's – No.

FIRST MYSTERIOUS MAN: I mean, who can we go to?

SECOND MYSTERIOUS MAN: The top.

FIRST MYSTERIOUS MAN: What?

SECOND MYSTERIOUS MAN: Go straight to the top. Whitehall, it'll have to be.

The first mysterious man seems worried by this, sucking in his breath, then scratching his head.

FIRST MYSTERIOUS MAN: We're *supposed* to be in Intelligence, aren't we?

SECOND MYSTERIOUS MAN: Yes, but –

FIRST MYSTERIOUS MAN: Well, then. That's what we're *supposed* to use. (*Taps his skull.*) This up here. The old grey mare.

SECOND MYSTERIOUS MAN: What do the papers say? All these bits of paper.

FIRST MYSTERIOUS MAN: Yeh. That's a point, ennit?

He kneels down beside the body, and picks up one of the sheets of paper. He reads, but slowly, moving his lips silently, almost exactly like Reginald does.

SECOND MYSTERIOUS MAN: (*Eventually*) What's it say?

The first mysterious man ignores the question, continuing to read, to frown, to move his lips. The second mysterious man sighs, looks around the room, sees Marlow's glass on the table, ambles over to it, sniffs it cautiously, then drinks the whisky in it, down in one gulp.

FIRST MYSTERIOUS MAN: God Almighty.

The second mysterious man wipes the back of his hand across his mouth.

SECOND MYSTERIOUS MAN: What's the matter? What is it?

FIRST MYSTERIOUS MAN: It'd take a more cleverer man than me to make any sense of it –

SECOND MYSTERIOUS MAN: *And* one with a better grasp of grammar.

FIRST MYSTERIOUS MAN: What?

SECOND MYSTERIOUS MAN: A more better grasp, *you* would say.

FIRST MYSTERIOUS MAN: Now look here –

SECOND MYSTERIOUS MAN: Sorry.

FIRST MYSTERIOUS MAN: You smart arse. You little shit.

SECOND MYSTERIOUS MAN: (*Smirk*) I plead guilty, your honour.

FIRST MYSTERIOUS MAN: I mean, a time like this – Nit-picking at a time like this. In the middle of this bloody peril.

SECOND MYSTERIOUS MAN: Let's forget it. I spoke out of turn.

FIRST MYSTERIOUS MAN: I probably went to a better school than you did, for a start.

The second mysterious man appears not to like this.

SECOND MYSTERIOUS MAN: Oh? Where was that then?

They look at each other.

FIRST MYSTERIOUS MAN: That's it, ennit? That's the point. You put your finger right on it.

The second mysterious man runs his tongue over his lips, nervously.

SECOND MYSTERIOUS MAN: Have I? H–How – How do you mean – ?

FIRST MYSTERIOUS MAN: We don't know a bloody thing about our – who or what or why or – I mean, it's all blank, ennit?

SECOND MYSTERIOUS MAN: Not filled in, do you mean?

FIRST MYSTERIOUS MAN: Padding.

SECOND MYSTERIOUS MAN: Still –

FIRST MYSTERIOUS MAN: No 'still' about it. It's a fact. A hard and fast fact. And you can't argue about it! We're padding. Like a couple of bleed'n sofas.

SECOND MYSTERIOUS MAN: You never use my name, do you?

FIRST MYSTERIOUS MAN: Do you ever use mine?

They look at each other.

SECOND MYSTERIOUS MAN: (*Quietly*) Oh, God. You're right. You're completely –

They keep looking at each other. Then –

FIRST MYSTERIOUS MAN: There's blood on this paper. All over it.

SECOND MYSTERIOUS MAN: Yes. But what does it say? The paper, I mean.

The first mysterious man frowns down at it again. Like one reluctant to expose himself.

FIRST MYSTERIOUS MAN: It says – oh, I don't know – it says 'Who killed Roger Ackroyd?'

SECOND MYSTERIOUS MAN: (*Worried*) Who?

FIRST MYSTERIOUS MAN: (*Worried*) Christ knows. He ain't a foreigner, is he?

SECOND MYSTERIOUS MAN: But do we know him? Have we come across him? It sounds – Is it on our list? – Well, it's vaguely sort of – familiar. Has a sort of *ring* to it.

FIRST MYSTERIOUS MAN: *I* don't know the name.

SECOND MYSTERIOUS MAN: Roger whatsit.

FIRST MYSTERIOUS MAN: *I* don't know him from Adam.

SECOND MYSTERIOUS MAN: (*Sadly*) No.

They look at each other. The first mysterious man has a sudden new gleam in his eye.

FIRST MYSTERIOUS MAN: But it's a clue. Everything – all things mean something. All things *point*. Weren't we taught that at the Depot? *Absorb*. Ponder. *Act*. One, Two, Three.

SECOND MYSTERIOUS MAN: Yes, but –

FIRST MYSTERIOUS MAN: That singer. Perhaps *he* done it. The crooner.

SECOND MYSTERIOUS MAN: I wouldn't be totally surprised.

FIRST MYSTERIOUS MAN: We lost him. Didn't we. The bugger.

SECOND MYSTERIOUS MAN: We lost *him*, but has he found *us*?

The thought bothers them. They look around, cautiously. Then
– pulling his gun –
FIRST MYSTERIOUS MAN: (*Whisper*) Search the place. Every
    room.
SECOND MYSTERIOUS MAN: (*Whisper*) Every cupboard.
FIRST MYSTERIOUS MAN: (*Whisper*) Every nook. Every cranny.
    If he's here, we'll find the bugger.

In the line upon line of bare trees and melancholy depths of
black and brown of the woods at dusk, coming along the path
between the wintry trees, Mr Marlow is calling –
MR MARLOW: Where be ya! Philip! Philip! Where bist! Philip!
He stops, utterly puzzled and frustrated, surrounded by dead
bracken.
    (*To himself*) Him was here a minute ago – (*Calls again*)
    Philip! Come on, o'butty! Where bist!
Philip has rediscovered his gnarled old oak and is once again
perched in the topmost cleft. He can clearly hear his father, and
even see him through the bare branches, way below. But he
holds himself very still, and very expressionless.
    (*Below*) Philip! Why doosn't thou answer! Philip! What's
    the matter, o'but? Where bist! Philip!
Then the calls from below cease. Philip waits. And watches. He
sees his father move away, back on to the path. The boy's face is
expressionless. His adult voice is heard, speaking for him.
MARLOW: (*Voice over, urgently*) Don't trust anybody again!
    Don't give your love. Hide in yourself. Or else they'll die.
    They'll die. And they'll hurt you! Hide! Hide!
Mr Marlow walks slowly away, a dejected man, his shoulders
drooping. He is staring at the ground a few yards in front of
him, almost as though looking for something he has lost on the
path. Philip begins the slow and difficult climb down from the
special tree, hand over hand, foot searching for hold on the
branches below.
NICOLA: (*Voice over, enraged*) – you're rotten with your own
    bile! You think you're smart but really you're very very
    sad, because you use your illness as a weapon against other
    people and as an excuse for not being properly human –
Mr Marlow walking slowly, in the same dejected manner, eyes

cast down. And then Philip catches him up. But the boy is not on the path. He keeps alongside, or a little behind, but careful not to be seen. It is clear that Mr Marlow is unaware that he is being observed, but Philip, as he quietly keeps pace, is avidly studying the sad and self-absorbed man. Then Mr Marlow suddenly stops walking. He stands dead-still. A long, strange moment, in which both he and his watcher remain absolutely motionless. Then, suddenly, Mr Marlow – imagining himself to be alone and unobserved – throws back his head and lets out one long and strange and almost animal-like cry of absolute grief and despair. Philip, in cover, watches this terrible release of anguish with wide eyes, and yet no obvious expression. He remains completely still.

And in his hospital bed, Marlow, too, is as still and tense as the boy he once was. Then –

MARLOW: (*Whisper*) Dad – ?

Mr Marlow stands still and silent on the woodland path. He sighs, then suddenly walks on, but with the same gait as before. And then Philip breaks cover, runs after him, and falls into step beside him.

MR MARLOW: Oh. There thou bist.

PHILIP: Ay. Here I be.

They walk on. Almost slyly, certainly shyly, Philip reaches for and then curls his hand into his father's hand, as they walk.

Night-time in the hospital ward, and in the small pool of light from his bed lamp, Marlow practises writing on his clipboard, his splint in place and the edge of his tongue out with concentration and effort. He stops. He thinks. The sounds of the sleepers become more evident, or even obtrusive. The clock moves on.

Later still, and dark, and full of snores and whistles and grunts. Marlow's bed lamp is off. He, too, sleeps. The boy's voice seems to sound in his head.

(*Voice over*) Doosn't trust anybody again! Doosn't give thy love. Hide in theeself. Or else they'll die. They'll die. And they'll hurt you! Hide! Hide!

As in a dream, Mrs Marlow runs through the tunnel after her son, soundlessly calling his name. Dream-like, too, the Police launch bob–bobs on the water, and the Policemen grapple with the body of a drowned young woman.

Flap–ap–ap! go the double doors, and clump–thump–thump go heavy feet on the floor of the ward. But Marlow, apparently reawakened, and once more in the small private pool of light from his bed lamp, seems too preoccupied by his clipboard writing practice to be aware of the dream-like clump–thump of heavy feet, coming to his bedside.

Standing by the bed is a Policeman, in uniform, his helmet on. He looks like an apparition, at first, in the half-light of the night ward.

MARLOW: What's the loveliest word in the English language, officer? In its sound, I mean. The sound it makes in your mouth, and the shape it makes on the page. Mmm? What do you think?

The Policeman seriously considers. Then –

POLICEMAN: Fit up?

MARLOW: Come, come. That's two words. And forget your hobbies for a moment. Think about the English language. The loveliest word.

POLICEMAN: That's not my bag, sir. Now is it?

MARLOW: Well. I'll tell you. Ee–el–bee–o–double u. Elbow.

POLICEMAN: Very useful. An elbow.

MARLOW: What?

POLICEMAN: In my line of work.

MARLOW: (*Staring at him*) All right. What have I done?

POLICEMAN: No, no.

MARLOW: Then what have I not done?

POLICEMAN: I'm sorry, sir. But I have some bad news.

MARLOW: Riot shields to be banned? Is that it?

The Policeman looks at him. Silence.

POLICEMAN: Your wife.

MARLOW: (*Quickly*) I'm not married.

POLICEMAN: Oh, but I thought –

MARLOW: (*Suddenly*) What's happened to her? What's she done?

POLICEMAN: I am referring to Mrs Nicola Marlow.

MARLOW: My ex-wife. Yes.

POLICEMAN: Oh, but –

MARLOW: All right! All right! My wife! Get on with it, man!

POLICEMAN: I don't know how much you know – *knew* – about her present, I should say *most recent* circumstances, sir –

MARLOW: What are you getting at?

POLICEMAN: I don't know whether you – She has been living with – Our inquiries so far indicate, sir, that she has been living with a Mr Mark Finney –

MARLOW: (*Agitated*) Binney. Mark Binney, did you –

POLICEMAN: Finney, sir. F for Freddie. A film producer, it seems.

MARLOW: (*Staring*) Go on.

POLICEMAN: Early this morning the Hammersmith Station received a distraught call from – from Mrs Marlow. She said she had – well, sir, I'm sorry – she'd stuck a knife in the throat of this Mr Finney –

MARLOW: Not *Binney*. You're sure?

POLICEMAN: Finney. F for Freddie. Excuse me, sir, but –

MARLOW: No, no. Please. Continue.

POLICEMAN: And that this Mr Finney, F for Freddie, was dead.

MARLOW: Dead.

POLICEMAN: Dead.

Marlow stares at him.

MARLOW: With a D.

POLICEMAN: What?

MARLOW: (*Gritting his teeth*) Go on. Go on.

POLICEMAN: We sent a patrol car. Straight away. When the officers eventually gained access to the premises in question – with some difficulty, sir . . .

MARLOW: (*Sharply*) Where is this?

POLICEMAN: The Mall by the bridge, sir. Hammersmith.

Marlow expels his breath in a hiss. The Policeman frowns, decides to continue.

Mrs Marlow was sitting on the stairs, sir. In a state of what we call extreme distress, sir. She had blood all over her. And in the room upstairs – well – it was as she had described, sir. Stabbed, with a large kitchen knife. A Habitat knife, sir.

Marlow is too shaken not to repeat the ridiculous detail.

MARLOW: Habitat?

POLICEMAN: Tottenham Court Road.

MARLOW: Where?

POLICEMAN: Tottenham Court – Oh. Yes. In the throat, sir. In his throat. Sticking out of his – yes.

MARLOW: (*Very shaken*) Jesus – but – but –

POLICEMAN: Naturally, we read your wife her rights, sir. She was, well, of course, she was taken into custody. And – ah – Well, she was described as docile and co-operative, sir. The arresting officers had no reason to – But when she was being taken to the patrol car – Well – she suddenly made a run for it. Taking the arresting officers very much by what you might call surprise, sir. Especially as she was in a condition of near-undress sir.

MARLOW: (*Trembling*) What do you – What are you saying?

POLICEMAN: Half-naked.

Marlow openly begins to weep, and the Policeman is soon embarrassed by Marlow's unrestrained crying.

MARLOW: (*Sob*) I've got to – got to – I've got to wake up –

POLICEMAN: (*Harsher*) She managed to get on to the bridge itself –

MARLOW: (*Sob*) Yes.

POLICEMAN: Whereupon she threw herself into the bleed'n river. Maximum embarrassment all round.

MARLOW: (*Choke*) Yes.

POLICEMAN: Wake up.

MARLOW: (*Sob*) What?

POLICEMAN: Wake your bloody self up.

MARLOW: (*Weep*) Yes.

Suddenly a brighter beam flickers on to his face. The night nurse flashes her torch on him. The Policeman is not there.

NIGHT NURSE: What's the matter? What's all this noise for?

MARLOW: S–sorry –

NIGHT NURSE: You go to sleep.

Marlow, fully awakening to his grief and isolation, swallows back his sobs, and nods and nods.

MARLOW: Yes. Yes. I'm – Yes.

NIGHT NURSE: Go back to sleep.

Indifferent, she moves away. Marlow shudders, looks around the darkened ward, at its shapes, and listens to the sounds of sleeping male patients. He reaches for his inevitable cigarette, and his eye falls on Noddy in the darkened, adjoining bed. Noddy, too, is awake. Nod–nod–nod–nod. Marlow stares. Then –

MARLOW: (*Whisper*) You all right, Pop?

Noddy's eyes are fixed on Marlow, in so far as the nod–nod–nod of his head allows. But there is no answer. And the clock moves on.

Day bright, day busy. Diligent, determined Marlow is still practising writing on his clipboard, splint in place, tongue out with effort.

What's the loveliest word in the English language, nurse? In its sound, I mean. The sound it makes in your mouth, and the shape it makes on the page. Mmm? What do you think? Or – (*Slight frown*) – have I asked you this before?

Nurse Mills has come with his drug, in a little egg-cup-sized container, and a spoon. She puts water into his glass.

NURSE MILLS: The loveliest? Rose. No – *Primrose.*

MARLOW: No, no.

NURSE MILLS: Opey.

He takes the drug, speaks with it in his mouth, almost incomprehensibly.

MARLOW: (*Mouth full*) Ee–el–bee–o–double u –

NURSE MILLS: (*Severely*) Drink! Come on.

He swallows the water she gives him, then nearly chokes.

What's the –

She follows the direction of his suddenly wild and fearful eyes – Standing by the doors, looking very uncertain, his helmet politely under his arm, is what seems to be the same Policeman.

MARLOW: (*Gulp*) No.

Nurse Mills gives him a curious look, and goes quickly over to the obviously uncertain Policeman. Marlow watches with a sick horror. Nurse Mills and the Policeman talk, but they are too far away for Marlow to hear.

(*To himself*) Please. I didn't – No. I didn't mean it – !

The Policeman nods and smiles and Nurse Mills laughs. The
Policeman turns to go, looking absently down the ward, away
from Marlow, then suddenly stops, says something. She nods,
turns back to Marlow, and the Policeman rather stiffly walks
down towards the other end of the ward.

NURSE MILLS: (*Returning*) I always thought they knew their
    way around –

MARLOW: (*Croak*) Wha–what did he want?

NURSE MILLS: (*Laugh*) The women's ward.

MARLOW: What?

NURSE MILLS: Yes. His mother was taken in yesterday –

MARLOW: But – but –

NURSE MILLS: But it was a lucky accident, his wandering in
    here. He recognized a friend.

Marlow blows out air, supreme relief.

    What's the matter?

MARLOW: Nothing!

Down the ward, the Policeman contemplates Reginald – who is,
of course, reading and moving his lips. And then, with a nasty
little smile, he leans in, and puts the crook of his finger over the
top of Reginald's paperback, pulling it down a little.

REGINALD: (*Startled*) 'Ere!

And then his face changes.

POLICEMAN: Well, well, well.

REGINALD: (*Uneasy*) Oh. Hello.

POLICEMAN: Hello, officer.

REGINALD: (*Uneasy*) Yeh. Well.

POLICEMAN: I hadn't got you down as a *reading* man, Reginald.

REGINALD: Yeh. Well.

His eyes are darting about, as though instinctively looking for
a means of escape. Unceremoniously, the Policeman plucks
the book out of Reginald's hands, and looks at it.

POLICEMAN: What's this, then? A Janet and John book – ?

REGINALD: What? Ooo?

POLICEMAN: (*Reads*) 'He did not think the human body was so
    crimsonly liquid. The blood had gushed out of the severed
    vein as though it had been longing to escape the – ' Gawd!

REGINALD: (*Nervously*) No – 'S good – straight up –

The Policeman can see that ultra-respectable-looking Mr Hall,

238

in the adjoining bed, is extremely interested.

POLICEMAN: They say this sort of stuff doesn't corrupt.

MR HALL: (*Pleased*) Well, there you are. What is there to say? There you are, officer.

REGINALD: It's *good* –

POLICEMAN: (*To* MR HALL) See what I mean? He reads this and he goes out and pinches a video-cassette machine.

REGINALD: (*Indignant*) Who does?

POLICEMAN: *You* does.

REGINALD: (*In formal tones*) I've paid my debt to society.

POLICEMAN: Oh, have you? What *you* think and what *I* think are not the same, my lad. Keep your nose clean. Or I'll snip it off for you.

REGINALD: God Almighty.

POLICEMAN: What you in for?

REGINALD: Heart.

The Policeman laughs, unpleasantly.

POLICEMAN: You got no bleed'n heart.

REGINALD: Oh, now –

POLICEMAN: I'll be watching out for you (*A departing little snigger*) We can fit you up with a pacemaker, Reggie.

Reginald pretends to smile at him as he goes, but as soon as the Policeman has his back to him, the smile fixes into a scowl.

REGINALD: The berk.

MR HALL: (*Appalled*) Who have I been next to all this time? What sort of person – ?

REGINALD: A *human* person.

MR HALL: But what have you done? Why are the Police interested in you, my boy?

REGINALD: Mind your own, Mr Hall. Keep your long nose out of it –

MR HALL: Good heavens. Is that the way to speak to me? Good heavens above. Reginald, Reginald.

But disgruntled Reginald pointedly finds his place in his book again, leaving Mr Hall to his splutters. Reginald's lips once again begin silently to form the words, with difficulty.

REGINALD: (*Voice over*) Inch–by–inch–they–went–through– the–room. There–was–only–one–place–left–now–

In the half-dark of Binney's house the two mysterious men place themselves, stealthily, on either side of the big cupboard doors where Marlow the Singing Detective had hidden himself. They are like huntsmen half thrilled half frightened by the dangerous nature of their prey. Behind them, Binney lies on the bloodied carpet, the knife in his throat.

FIRST MYSTERIOUS MAN: (*Whisper*) You open it. I got to keep my hands free.

SECOND MYSTERIOUS MAN: (*Whisper*) Why not shoot straight through the door?

FIRST MYSTERIOUS MAN: (*Whisper*) Open it!

The second mysterious man, very nervous, swings open the door and moves rapidly out of the possible line of fire. The first mysterious man is aiming the gun, holding it out in a two-hand clutch, lethally. His tensely expectant expression changes. He sighs. He lowers the gun.

SECOND MYSTERIOUS MAN: (*Whisper*) Empty?

FIRST MYSTERIOUS MAN: (*Very loudly*) As Mother Hubbard's.

So loud, after the whispering, that it all but makes the other jump. They look at each other, almost accusingly.

SECOND MYSTERIOUS MAN: He's one step in front of us all the time. We got to accept that.

The first mysterious man snaps on the lights again, angrily, illuminating the shambles.

FIRST MYSTERIOUS MAN: I don't accept nothing. We'll root him out. We'll find the sod.

SECOND MYSTERIOUS MAN: But where do we look? Up a gum-tree?

The first mysterious man is staring down, in distaste, at the bloodied corpse of Binney.

FIRST MYSTERIOUS MAN: I tell you this – there's no such thing as a perfect hiding place, whatever kind of tree it is.

SECOND MYSTERIOUS MAN: Oh, no?

FIRST MYSTERIOUS MAN: No! Sooner or later – somewhere or other – he's bound to give himself away.

In the ward – the real hiding place – Nurse Mills sticks a thermometer in Marlow's mouth, and then takes his wrist to count his pulse. Her expression changes, and she looks at him.

His now almost lesion-clear face is nevertheless glistening with sweat.

NURSE MILLS: Gosh. You're hot, Mr Marlow. Now don't you go and get any complications or anything silly like that. You're doing so well. Drink plenty of water. You hear?

Thermometer in mouth, he nods, but too much like one distracted, too hot and too bothered. Nurse Mills drops his wrist, takes out the thermometer.

Let's see what's going on here.

She reads the thermometer, and frowns.

I think you've been overdoing it again, my lad. (*At his non-response*) Hey. Where are you?

Music grows, from a fevered hinterland. The Henry Hall Dance Band Version of 'The Teddy Bears' Picnic'. The Singing Detective's side-of-the-mouth persona comes on the wings of the music –

(*Voice over*) Too many people were getting to ask the same question. And it wasn't because they wanted to polish my shoes for me. No, sir –

The Dance Hall forms a proper arena for the dance music, and Marlow steps forward to bounce into the lyric of 'The Teddy Bears' Picnic'. And, lo, Mr Hall is on the xylophone, ding–donging away, and Reginald strum–strums on the bass. They half covertly glance across at each other as Marlow warbles. The song continues through the dissolve, without interruption.

The continuing music now helps to reveal the dell, with Mrs Marlow on her back, her heels digging into the soft ground, her legs apart, her skirt up, her blouse open, and Raymond on top of her, his trousers down around his ankles. 'The Teddy Bears' Picnic'. Philip, wriggling forward on his elbows, parts the ferns and foxgloves, in order to see what is going on.

On the Underground platform, in a tunnel of dank gloom, Mrs Marlow stands alone. The song continues its coy syncopations.

In the woods, Mr Marlow and Philip are walking home, hand in hand, to the same tune.

Each patient at each bed is 'playing' one of the instruments in the dance band. Mr Hall is still at the xylophone, on his bed trolley, and Reginald still thrums the bass. Then, when the vocal picks up the verse again, it is Marlow who 'sings' in his bed. But as he 'sings' he slowly, awkwardly, realistically, gets out of his bed, and, as a real patient in his condition would when walking for the first time in half a year, moves slowly, totteringly, but determinedly to the centre of the ward. Standing, he sucks in his breath as the music abruptly ends, an intake of air before the release of an unrestrained and exultant shout.

MARLOW: Look! Look at me! I did it! I walked! I can walk! Look! Look at me!

The ward is completely back to normal, with no trace of the previous musical activity. And Marlow lifts his arms in exultation. The other patients look at him, some with more interest than others.

MR HALL: He's bellowing again. Listen to him.

REGINALD: (*Mildly*) Well, it's nice to be able to walk, Mr Hall.

MR HALL: Yes, but you don't have to make a song and dance about it, do you?

Exultant Marlow lowers his arms, swivels unsteadily, and slowly, with tremendous effort, and always on the point of falling, begins to walk back to his bed. Nicola appears in the open double doorway, with a hold-all. She is so startled to see him on his feet that she is rooted for a moment, incredulous. Then she drops the bag and rushes forward –

NICOLA: Philip – What are you doing! What do you think you're –

MARLOW: (*Smirk*) Walking.

But his face rivulets sweat.

NICOLA: For heaven's sake – supposing you fall over – Philip. Hold on to me. You're not ready for this!

MARLOW: (*Sweat*) Hold on to *you*?

She looks at him, wryly, well understanding the other resonances of the question.

NICOLA: There aren't too many others around any more, Philip.

They seem to study each other. His face is still wet.

MARLOW: Be bop a loo bop.

NICOLA: Yes. But isn't it about time you climbed down out of your tree?

Marlow and Nicola stand as before, examining each other, but in the middle of a now totally empty ward. A place in the mind.

MARLOW: Well – one thing's for sure – I'm going to – (*Gasp*) – I'm going to walk right out of here. I'm not staying in this place!

NICOLA: But are you going to stay in this condition?

MARLOW: (*Passionately*) No!

NICOLA: I don't just mean your skin and your joints.

MARLOW: (*Subdued*) No.

NICOLA: (*Gently*) You nasty old sod.

The real ward reasserts itself. Nurse Mills, appearing in the doorway, is startled to see Marlow (alone) where he is, and rushes forward to take his arm.

NURSE MILLS: What are you doing! What do you think you're –

MARLOW: (*Smirk*) Walking.

NURSE MILLS: But what if you fell – You can't do this on your own. Not yet. You must take it in stages.

MARLOW: (*Gasp*) No.

NURSE MILLS: Now, steady –

MARLOW: (*Grunt of effort*) By tomorrow I –

He nearly falls. She grabs him tightly, with both arms.

NURSE MILLS: Stand still.

MARLOW: I shall – I shall – *Ooch*! I shall walk right–out–of–here. With *my things*.

NURSE MILLS: Oh, will you indeed?

MARLOW: (*Delighted*) Nicola isn't in the river!

NURSE MILLS: What?

So surprised, she steps back, and lets him go momentarily. Himself so surprised by the removal of her arm, and on the wrong foot in his painfully slow progress, he goes down like a felled tree. Thump! Arms and legs all over the place.

MARLOW: Ow! Ow! Ow! Ow! Ow!
Nurse Mills quickly stoops over him, to try to pull him up.
NURSE MILLS: I told you – oh, I told you – I – (*To the ward*)
    Can I have some help?
MARLOW: Ooo. Ooo. Christ –
NURSE MILLS: You're too heavy for – (*Loudly*) Can I have some
    help!
There seems to be no response. Then, running up, almost out of
nowhere, come the two mysterious men.
FIRST MYSTERIOUS MAN: All right, nurse. All right.
SECOND MYSTERIOUS MAN: He's too heavy for you, nurse.
NURSE MILLS: Gently –
MARLOW: Sorry – sorry – oooh –
The two mysterious men lift him up. He stands between them,
his face once again oozing with sweat.
NURSE MILLS: Back to his bed. That one, over there.
FIRST MYSTERIOUS MAN: Gently does it, sunshine.
SECOND MYSTERIOUS MAN: A small step for a man, but a giant
    leap for a cripple.
And they start to snigger, nastily, childishly.
NURSE MILLS: This is not the time for – here. Sit him on his
    bed. *Gently*! That's it . . .
MARLOW: (*Gasp*) Thank you.
NURSE MILLS: Yes. Thank you very much.
FIRST MYSTERIOUS MAN: Good job we came, eh?
SECOND MYSTERIOUS MAN: You're telling me!
FIRST MYSTERIOUS MAN: And this is the one we came to see.
SECOND MYSTERIOUS MAN: You're telling me.
Marlow, recovering from the pain of his fall, looks up at them
from his position, sitting on the bed. They are looming above
him.
NURSE MILLS: These are not visiting hours, you know.
FIRST MYSTERIOUS MAN: Well, they are *now*, sweetie. Bugger
    the rules.
SECOND MYSTERIOUS MAN: And bugger the regulations.
She is looking at them suspiciously, recognizing them now as the
two men who had behaved strangely on an earlier occasion.
NURSE MILLS: Who are you? What do you want here?
FIRST MYSTERIOUS MAN: Those are *exactly* the right questions.

SECOND MYSTERIOUS MAN: On the nail. Or is it, on the nose they say nowadays?

FIRST MYSTERIOUS MAN: Whenever *that* is.

Marlow is staring at them in increasing alarm.

MARLOW: Am I hot? Is it because I am hot or – ? (*Suddenly*) I don't know you. I have no idea who you are or what you want.

FIRST MYSTERIOUS MAN: Ho, I see. Disowning us now, are you?

SECOND MYSTERIOUS MAN: Bloody orphans, are we?

NURSE MILLS: I'm sorry. I'm grateful for your help – but I must ask you to leave.

FIRST MYSTERIOUS MAN: Leave?

SECOND MYSTERIOUS MAN: Leave?

FIRST MYSTERIOUS MAN: We're fed up, lady. Up to here! We get all the shit.

SECOND MYSTERIOUS MAN: And one shooter between us.

MARLOW: What? What – ?

FIRST MYSTERIOUS MAN: Bang! Bang! And why?

SECOND MYSTERIOUS MAN: And what for?

FIRST MYSTERIOUS MAN: We're never told.

SECOND MYSTERIOUS MAN: Our roles are unclear.

FIRST MYSTERIOUS MAN: No *names*, even. No bloody handles.

MARLOW: (*Croak*) Nurse? Nurse – !

But Nurse Mills is not there. Worse still, Marlow's bed is the only bed, islanded in an otherwise empty ward, in which the light is oddly different, unsettlingly tinged. There is just Marlow and the two mysterious men, and no help in sight. A nightmare. Marlow tries to struggle up off the bed.

FIRST MYSTERIOUS MAN: (*Reasonable tone*) Where are you going?

MARLOW: Home.

SECOND MYSTERIOUS MAN: But that's off the page, ennit?

The first mysterious man uses the flat of his hand on Marlow's chest, pushing him back down.

FIRST MYSTERIOUS MAN: You're going nowhere, sunshine. Not until we settle this.

Marlow looks around for help, and can see none. He moistens his lips.

MARLOW: S–settle what – ?

FIRST MYSTERIOUS MAN: Who we are. What we are.

SECOND MYSTERIOUS MAN: That's right. That's absolutely right.

Suddenly, they grab hard at Marlow's arms. He cries out.

MARLOW: No–o– !

FIRST MYSTERIOUS MAN: Tell us! Come on!

They are twisting and twisting Marlow's arms, painfully.

SECOND MYSTERIOUS MAN: Own up! Own up!

MARLOW: Ow! Ow! Ow! Ow – !

FIRST MYSTERIOUS MAN: We'll break you apart!

SECOND MYSTERIOUS MAN: Limb from limb!

MARLOW: Aaaaaaaagh!

The first mysterious man cuffs him hard across the head.

FIRST MYSTERIOUS MAN: Hold your noise!

SECOND MYSTERIOUS MAN: Speak English!

They start systematically to hit him.

MARLOW: (*Scream*) Help – ! Help! He–e–lp – !

Marlow's pathetic and terror-filled cries and screams reverberate along the empty, stretching, similarly dream-like corridor. The terrible sound dips under for a side-of-the-mouth style, Singing Detective voice over –

> (*Voice over*) Personally, I don't want to walk down no mean streets, not me. But there's no money in picking bluebells – Am I right? Or am I right?

And suddenly he is there, walking up the corridor towards the double doors of the ward where the sick Marlow is screaming for help. He stops, pushes back his trilby, looks at us with a sardonic twist to his mouth.

> Will you listen to that? Can you hear the guy? Anyone'd think somebody was twisting his arm. What I say is – when you're dealing with the Devil, then praise the Lord and pass the ammunition. There's no point in making a song and dance about your troubles. I am not wrong. Neither am I wrong.

He reaches inside his jacket, pulls out his gun, blows on the barrel, and then suddenly runs, shoulders bunching, and crashes through the double doors – which go *wap–waap–wap–wap!* – into the nightmare ward. A wretched, flat-out Marlow is being

246

brutally maltreated by the two mysterious men. They spin
round at the noise of the doors –
FIRST MYSTERIOUS MAN: Christ! The warbler!
MARLOW: Help – !
SECOND MYSTERIOUS MAN: Use the shooter! Quick!
Redundant advice. The first mysterious man is already diving to
the floor, gun coming out at the same time. And the second
mysterious man rolls out of range – Marlow the Singing
Detective fires and is fired at. But Marlow in the bed is wet with
sweat, eyes goggling in shock and terror, as the bullets whine
and splatt!
MARLOW: (*In bed, yell*) Nicola! Nicola – ! Quickly! Quickly – !
The gunfight continues in what is now a properly peopled ward,
all the beds in place, complete with their normal inhabitants.
The Singing Detective crouches behind first one bed and then
another, firing. The second mysterious man cowers under a bed,
hands to his ears. Explosions and bullets and – peevish Mr Hall,
perpetually reading Reginald, nod–nodding Noddy each get a
bullet-hole in the middle of the forehead. Crouching Marlow,
the Singing Detective, finally gets in the one shot that matters,
across the length of the bloodied ward – The first mysterious
man crashes back–back–back, shot in the chest, and falls,
spreadeagling. The second mysterious man, quivering, rises
from cover, hands raised in surrender.
SECOND MYSTERIOUS MAN: (*Sob*) Please – oh, please –
The Singing Detective stands, his eyes cold, and slowly,
carefully, holding his gun in both hands, takes aim, mercilessly.
   (*Cry*) No! Please don't! Oh please please don't! Please!
The bedbound and sweating Marlow is extremely agitated.
MARLOW: (*Shout*) Wait! Wait – !
But his other persona, the Singing Detective, is carefully,
coldly, double-handedly aiming the gun.
   (*Shout*) No! Wait! That's murder!
The Singing Detective's eyes flicker, registering the call. Then
he looks at us –
   Will you listen to that? Murder, he says. I call it *pruning*.
   Only one of us is going to walk out of here. Sweeter than
   the roses.
And he suddenly fires – phut! phut! – In the bed, Marlow jerks

violently, as a bullet hole is drilled into his forehead. And lies still.

> (*Voice over, side-of-mouth*) I suppose you could say we'd been partners, him and me. Like Laurel and Hardy or Fortnum and Mason. But, hell, this was one sick fellow, from way back when. And I reckon I'm man enough to tie my own shoe-laces now.

But now the ward is back to normal, and busy, with all the patients in place, and Staff Nurse White and Nurse Mills at the lower end, with the drug trolley.

NURSE MILLS: (*To* REGINALD) Ope–y.

She interrupts his reading to give him tablets on a spoon.

STAFF NURSE WHITE: Haven't you finished that silly old book yet?

Reginald swallows his tablets, holds up the book, proudly.

REGINALD: Last page, ennit?

MR HALL: (*Sarcastic*) Good heavens above. I think that calls for some sort of celebration, my boy.

Nurse Mills laughs. 'Peg o' My Heart' on harmonicas slowly swells, then the curtains around Marlow's bed are opened from inside, by Marlow himself. He has dressed himself. He walks slowly, unsteadily, away from his bed, 'Peg o' My Heart' reaching full pitch.

Nicola arrives in the double doorway with the hold-all. She goes to rush to help Marlow, then checks herself. Marlow looks at her, and then around the ward. 'Peg o' My Heart' fades away.

MARLOW: (*To himself*) I think I've cracked this case, folks.

> (*Then, out loud*) Nicola. Have you brought my hat?

There is a sudden glitter of tears in her eyes, and she laughs, nods, opens up the hold-all as she comes to him, pulling at the Singing Detective's old trilby hat. Marlow winks at her, veritably the Singing Detective, and puts the hat on, jauntily.

> (*Loudly*) Goodbye, everybody! Good luck! Keep your noses clean!

ASSORTED VOICES: Goodbye. Good luck. Take care.

But Reginald cannot bear to drag his eyes away from the page. His lips move a little as he clambers along the last line.

REGINALD: (*Laboriously*) And–her–soft–red–lips–clam–clamp–*clamped*–themselves–on–his. The–End –

248

He lowers the book.

Lucky devil!

Nicola and Marlow leave the ward and make their way along the corridor towards the outside world. He leans heavily upon her for support. Their slow progress is accompanied by the sound of Vera Lynn sweetly promising 'We'll Meet Again'.

The song, in turn, yields up fleeting images from Marlow's real story – the train, his father waiting at the small railway station, the torments in the classroom, the Forest cottage, London house, the gilded bridge and the slow river, and so on. And then, across a green sea of trees, as 'We'll Meet Again' reaches towards its end, Philip perches in the treetop, staring out, intense, accusing.

Abruptly, the song ends. Birdsong swells. The boy stares, stares, as a breeze stirs the trees, shush–a–shush–ashoosh. Then –

PHILIP: When I grow up, I be going to be a detective.

And then, unexpectedly, he grins. All the while, along the corridor to freedom, Marlow struggles on, leaning on Nicola. They disappear from view. The empty corridor is resonant with the birdsong and the sound of the wind in the leaves.

Dennis Potter was born in 1935 and graduated from Oxford University in 1959. His many television plays and screenplays—*Dreamchild, Pennies from Heaven, The Singing Detective*—have won him outstanding critical acclaim. His script for the movie *Pennies from Heaven* was nominated for an Academy Award. His novel *Blackeyes* is also available from Vintage Books.